The RTI Approach to Evaluating Learning Disabilities

The Guilford Practical Intervention in the Schools Series

Kenneth W. Merrell, Founding Editor
T. Chris Riley-Tillman, Series Editor

www.guilford.com/practical

This series presents the most reader-friendly resources available in key areas of evidence-based practice in school settings. Practitioners will find trustworthy guides on effective behavioral, mental health, and academic interventions, and assessment and measurement approaches. Covering all aspects of planning, implementing, and evaluating high-quality services for students, books in the series are carefully crafted for everyday utility. Features include ready-to-use reproducibles, lay-flat binding to facilitate photocopying, appealing visual elements, and an oversized format. Recent titles have companion Web pages where purchasers can download and print the reproducible materials.

RECENT VOLUMES

The RTI Approach to Evaluating Learning Disabilities

Joseph F. Kovaleski
Amanda M. VanDerHeyden
Edward S. Shapiro

THE GUILFORD PRESS
New York   London

© 2013 The Guilford Press
A Division of Guilford Publications, Inc.
370 Seventh Avenue, Suite 1200, New York, NY 10001
www.guilford.com

Printed in Canada

This book is printed on acid-free paper.

Last digit is print number: 9   8   7   6   5   4   3

The authors have checked with sources believed to be reliable in their efforts to provide
information that is complete and generally in accord with the standards of practice that are
accepted at the time of publication. However, in view of the possibility of human error or changes
in behavioral, mental health, or medical sciences, neither the authors, nor the editors and publisher,
nor any other party who has been involved in the preparation or publication of this work warrants
that the information contained herein is in every respect accurate or complete, and they are not
responsible for any errors or omissions or the results obtained from the use of such information.
Readers are encouraged to confirm the information contained in this book with other sources.

Library of Congress Cataloging-in-Publication Data

Kovaleski, Joseph.
  The RTI approach to evaluating learning disabilities / Joseph Kovaleski, Amanda M.
VanDerHeyden, Edward S. Shapiro.
      pages cm. — (The Guilford practical intervention in the schools series)
  Includes bibliographical references and index.
  ISBN 978-1-4625-1154-9 (pbk.)
    1. Learning disabled children—Education—United States.   2. Response to intervention
(Learning disabled children)—United States.   3. School improvement programs—United
States.   I. Title.
  LC4705.K68 2013
  371.90973—dc23
                                                                                    2013004105

To Susan, the love of my life,
and to Mary and Kevin, my pride and joy
—J. F. K.

For my dad, who believed in curiosity, learning,
and the unlimited potential of all children
—A. M. V.

To Dr. George Davis,
who made the miracle of my first grandson,
Milo Thomas Shapiro, possible
—E. S. S.

About the Authors

Joseph F. Kovaleski, DEd, is Professor of Educational and School Psychology and Director of the Doctoral Program in School Psychology at the Indiana University of Pennsylvania. He serves on the Advisory Board of the RTI Action Network at the National Center for Learning Disabilities (NCLD) and on the Editorial Board of *School Psychology Review*. In 2005, Dr. Kovaleski, with Edward S. Shapiro, initiated RTI in Pennsylvania through the Pennsylvania Training and Technical Assistance Network. He has published articles, book chapters, and Web-based content on RTI and other topics related to school reform and school psychology.

Amanda M. VanDerHeyden, PhD, is a private consultant, researcher, and national trainer who has worked in a number of school districts and is President of Education Research and Consulting, Inc., in Fairhope, Alabama. She serves on the Advisory Board of the RTI Action Network at the NCLD and is also a member of the NCLD's Education Programs Committee and a panelist at the Institute of Education Sciences, U.S. Department of Education. Dr. VanDerHeyden received the Lightner Witmer Early Career Contributions Award from Division 16 (School Psychology) of the American Psychological Association (APA). She is Associate Editor of *School Psychology Review* and has published numerous articles and books related to RTI.

Edward S. Shapiro, PhD, is Professor of School Psychology and Director of the Center for Promoting Research to Practice in the College of Education at Lehigh University. A recipient of the Senior Scientist Award from APA Division 16, he is the author or coauthor of a number of books. Dr. Shapiro is best known for his work in curriculum-based assessment and nonstandardized methods of assessing academic skills problems. He is currently collaborating with the Pennsylvania Department of Education in developing and facilitating the implementation of RTI in the state.

Preface

The passage of the Individuals with Disabilities Education Improvement Act (IDEIA) in 2004 introduced the public in general and school personnel in particular to the concept of response to intervention (RTI). This law and its accompanying regulations in 2006 gave school districts (i.e., local education agencies) the option of using an assessment of a student's RTI as an alternative to the traditional ability–achievement discrepancy approach for determining eligibility for special education under the designation of specific learning disabilities (SLD). Although the term itself was fairly new at the time, RTI had developed as a construct since the original enactment of the Education for the Handicapped Act (EHA; Public Law 94-142) in 1975. Because the assessment of a student's RTI requires the provision of effective interventions, much of the attention both before and after IDEIA 2004 has been appropriately focused on RTI as an overall construct for school reform. Indeed, numerous books, articles, and professional workshops and conferences for school personnel have focused exclusively on the infrastructure of curriculum, instruction, and interventions that are widely seen as essential features of RTI as a model for school reform. With the exception of policy guidelines developed by state departments of education, little has been written about the exact procedures for using RTI as part of a comprehensive evaluation of students thought to have SLD and to need special education.

This book is intended to fill that void. We provide guidance for school psychologists and other members of multidisciplinary evaluation teams who are attempting to utilize RTI for SLD evaluations. Our task is to provide a set of practical procedures and examples of how RTI can be assessed as well as how other aspects of the definitional requirements for evaluating students thought to have SLD can be orchestrated to produce a comprehensive evaluation of the student. Because so much has been written on the components of implementing RTI as an instructional system, we will not present detailed information about this aspect of RTI, although some coverage of the infrastructure needed to implement RTI will be presented (see Chapter 2) to orient the reader as well as to provide a basis for the analysis of the instructional environment that is required in the law. Rather, we present a dissection of the existing federal SLD regulations and those assessment procedures that we consider best practices based on research as well as our collective experience with implementing RTI in schools.

Our explication of RTI as an assessment system begins in Chapter 1 with a historical review of how RTI came to be institutionalized in federal law as well as details about the legal requirements for determining SLD. It is important to understand not only the extensive concerns that led policymakers away from traditional approaches to assessing students with SLD (namely, the ability–achievement discrepancy) in terms of how individual students were assessed, but also how those assessment approaches resulted in unintended negative consequences on schooling in general that needed to be addressed. In this chapter, we also explain how RTI became favored as a viable alternative to traditional approaches because of its potential to drive school reform in conjunction with parallel provisions of the No Child Left Behind (NCLB) Act of 2001. We present in this chapter the rationale for RTI as part of a comprehensive evaluation drawn largely from student data that are gathered during the course of interventions, and explain why other extensive psychological testing is often unnecessary.

The focus of the majority of the book is the specific requirements of the IDEA Regulations (2006) for the identification of SLD, presented in sequential order as they appear in the regulations.[1] We start, however, in Chapter 2 by describing the infrastructure of assessment, instruction, and intervention that must be in place for assessment teams to use RTI as part of the comprehensive evaluation for SLD. Based on a three-tier model of support, we describe how schools can be structured to deliver core instruction and supplemental interventions that ensure that the "I" in RTI is implemented with fidelity.

Chapter 3 addresses the first component of the SLD requirements, the assessment of the student's academic performance in relation to age or state standards. School psychologists and other assessment specialists have a long history of evaluating a student's school performance, typically through the use of norm-referenced measures of academic achievement. Although these measures are not excluded from consideration in an RTI system, the focus of this chapter is on assessment procedures that are more closely aligned with the process of teaching and learning, including curriculum-based measurement (CBM), curriculum-based assessment (CBA), and curriculum-based evaluation (CBE). In addition, the use of other data, including statewide tests and computer-based assessments, is detailed. Specific procedures for operationalizing the gap between the performance of a student with a possible SLD and that of typical peers are provided.

In Chapter 4, we describe specific procedures for calculating the student's rate of improvement (ROI) in response to robust, research-based interventions, with ample examples from practice. Techniques for progress monitoring, analyzing graphed data, and quantifying a student's ROI are provided and explained. We further suggest parameters for determining the extent of deficiency regarding a student's assessed RTI.

Chapter 5 is the first of two chapters describing how assessment teams can rule out whether a student's academic performance is a result of causal factors other than SLD. In Chapter 5, the requirements to rule out conditions such as visual impairment, hearing impairment, motor problems, intellectual disability, and emotional disturbance, as well as factors such as culture, environmental or economic disadvantage, and limited English proficiency, are analyzed, and we suggest assessment procedures for documenting these conditions. In Chapter 6 we describe procedures for ruling out "lack of instruction" as the reason for a student's school problems. This

---

[1]The 2004 law was titled "The Individuals with Disabilities Education Improvement Act" (IDEIA). However, because of the long association of the acronym IDEA with this law, we use IDEA to refer to the current law and regulations.

provision of the IDEA Regulations is perhaps the most challenging aspect of this iteration of federal law and pertains to all evaluations of students thought to be eligible for special education, whether a system chooses to use RTI or not. The concept that school teams must assess and document the sufficiency of core instruction and individualized interventions, as well as conduct repeated assessments of students' academic performance and report the results to parents, is a direct reflection of the nexus between NCLB and IDEA. This component of the IDEA Regulations represents the most substantial change from past versions of IDEA and reflects the aspiration to directly address the unintended consequences of past iterations as detailed in Chapter 1. In Chapter 6, we provide detailed procedures for ruling out lack of adequate instruction.

The IDEA Regulations for the assessment of students thought to have SLD have historically included the requirement that the student be observed in a regular education setting. In Chapter 7, we consider best practices for conducting these observations because we believe that this essential aspect of a comprehensive evaluation is often conducted in a perfunctory manner. We also present procedures for linking more formal observations with other academic assessment data in understanding the student's academic performance.

Chapter 8 addresses how assessment teams can most effectively involve parents in the assessment process, which has been a historic provision in IDEA. Included in this chapter are field-based ideas regarding communicating assessment results to parents, involving parents on intervention teams, enlisting parental support for and involvement in interventions, and protecting a child's and family's legal rights throughout the evaluation process.

In Chapter 9, we describe how the data collected during the comprehensive evaluation of the student are analyzed to determine eligibility for special education. Judgmental criteria about which students are eligible for special education when RTI is used as part of the comprehensive evaluation are described. In addition, we present how the data collected during the evaluation process are integrated into a comprehensive evaluation report. Two case studies are provided to exemplify the RTI approach: one for a student found eligible for special education (as SLD) and one for a student found not to be eligible.

An important feature of IDEA since its inception has been the idea that the evaluation team would not only provide a determination of eligibility for special education but also design a robust program of specially designed instruction for the student who qualifies for special education. Chapter 10 provides details about how data collected during the process of implementing RTI can be harvested to create effective individualized education plans (IEPs) that can set the stage for improving students' academic performance.

In Chapter 11, we address a number of legal and practical applications of using RTI in determining a student's entitlement for special education, using a "frequently asked questions" format. Specific attention is given to legal ramifications as well as to how school assessment teams and school administrators can best manage the change from traditional approaches for eligibility determination to RTI.

Throughout this book, we predominantly use examples from elementary schools (K–5) because most students with SLD are identified during these grades. However, we believe that the assessment procedures and decsion-making guidelines presented in this book have application for all students and schools on a K–12 basis. In addition, our coverage of the assessment of RTI largely uses examples of student difficulties in the areas of reading and mathematics because assessment practices in those areas have been most thoroughly investigated at this time.

Acknowledgments

We would like to acknowledge the contributions of those who assisted us on this project. We are grateful to the support and guidance of our editor at The Guilford Press, Natalie Graham, and to Chris Riley-Tillman, who provided an insightful review of our original manuscript. We extend our gratitude to colleagues who provided material for the various case examples, including Dick Hall and Matt Gormley. Finally, we would also like to thank a team of graduate students in school psychology at the Indiana University of Pennsylvania—which was led by Michael J. Boneshefski and included Stephanie Kello, Courtney Kuncelman, and Evangelia Maragouthakis—who assisted us with a wide range of production details.

Contents

CHAPTER 1

Historical and Legal Background for Response to Intervention

In this chapter we present the history of how specific learning disabilities (SLD) have been operationalized in law and regulation since the passage of the Education of the Handicapped Act (EHA; Public Law 94-142) in 1975, along with the controversies and unintended consequences that followed. We trace how the concept of an ability–achievement discrepancy that formed the basis of SLD identification for more than 30 years fell into disrepute, and how an assessment of the student's response to intervention (RTI) emerged as a federally approved alternative. Following this history, we examine the current iteration of the Individuals with Disabilities Education Act (IDEA) and its requirements for identifying SLD, with special emphasis on RTI.

HISTORICAL BACKGROUND

The EHA

The enactment of the EHA in 1975 was a landmark event in American public education. The act guaranteed a free and appropriate public education (FAPE) for all school-age children who had an identified disability and were in need of special education. It further required school districts to conduct "child find" activities to identify all students who qualified for these programs and services and articulated a list of disabling conditions that governed which students were eligible. Implementation of the new law began in 1977 after the publication of the first EHA regulations. Both the act and the regulations included SLD in the list of disabilities. The term had been coined a decade earlier by Samuel Kirk (1962). The basic definition of an SLD in the act was as follows:

> A disorder in one or more of the basic psychological processes involved in understanding or in using language, spoken or written, which disorder may manifest itself in the imperfect ability to listen, think, speak, read, write, spell, or do mathematical calculations. Such disorders include

such conditions as perceptual handicaps, brain injury, minimal brain dysfunction, dyslexia, and developmental aphasia. Such term does not include children who have learning problems which are primarily the result of visual, hearing, or motor handicaps, of mental retardation, of emotional disturbance, or environmental, cultural, or economic disadvantage. (§620[b] [4] [A])

The 1977 regulations operationalized the definition with these now well-known provisions:

A team may determine that a child has a specific learning disability if: (1) The child does not achieve commensurate with his or her age and ability levels in one or more of the areas listed in paragraph (a)(2) of this section, when provided with learning experiences appropriate for the child's age and ability levels; and (2) The team finds the child has a severe discrepancy between achievement and ability in one or more of the following areas: (i) Oral expression; (ii) Listening comprehension; (iii) Written expression; (iv) Basic reading skill; (v) Reading comprehension; (vi) Mathematics calculation; (vii) Mathematics reasoning. (U.S. Department of Education [USDOE], 1977, p. 65083)

Notable in this language is the concept that students identified with SLD would demonstrate a level of academic performance that would be unexpected based on their assessed ability. In neither the law nor the regulations was the term "intelligence" used; however, the term "ability level" was translated by practitioners into intellectual functioning, serving as a proxy for ability. Thus students who were failing in academic areas but had subaverage IQs would not be deemed eligible because their academic skills would be expected to be well below average. Only students who displayed an ability–achievement discrepancy would qualify as having SLD. How this ability–achievement discrepancy would be quantified was left to the states, which generally transferred this responsibility to local education agencies (LEAs). As a result, SLD was introduced with little guidance as to how it would be implemented across school districts and states.

The Aftermath of the EHA

The operationalization of SLD was almost immediately challenged, particularly in a series of studies conducted at the federally funded Institute for Research on Learning Disabilities at the University of Minnesota (one of several such national institutes funded to research SLD). In an article summarizing 5 years of their research at the Institute, Ysseldyke and colleagues (1983) reported the following, using the term learning disabilities (LD):

- "The special education team decision-making process . . . is at best inconsistent. . . . [T]eam efforts usually were directed toward . . . a 'search for pathology'" (p. 77).
- "Placement decisions made by teams . . . have very little to do with the data collected on students" (p. 78).
- "There currently is no defensible system for declaring students eligible for LD services" (p. 79).
- "When we applied several commonly used definitions of LD to low-achieving students in regular classes, over three fourths could be classified as LD by at least one defini-

tion. . . . [M]any school-identified LD students were not classified as LD by at least one criterion" (p. 79).

- "There are no reliable psychometric differences between students diagnosed with LD and those simply considered to be low achieving" (p. 80).

Given the lack of coherence in the approaches used to identify students with SLD, it could well have been predicted that the numbers of students so identified would skyrocket. Indeed, between 1977 and 1990, the percentage of the school-age population identified as SLD grew from 1.8% to 5.2% (USDOE, 2010; see Figure 1.1). This dramatic increase in the number of students diagnosed with SLD was fueled by a number of unintended consequences of the EHA, and the SLD construct in particular. Very little attention was paid to the fact that the typical symptoms of SLD that might signal an evaluation process were neither unique nor specific markers for the presence of SLD. That is, one of the most common "symptoms," poor reading performance, might occur for a variety of reasons that had nothing to do with a child having a disability. Diagnosing SLD, then, became a process of ruling out other causes of poor academic performance like inadequate instruction, and systems did not have very strong procedures in place to make such rule-out judgments. (We discuss these diagnostic challenges and recommend procedures in Chapter 6.) There was also perhaps undue optimism that diagnosing a child with SLD would lead to specialized instruction and supports that would consistently and positively improve student learning once the diagnosis was made. Finally, there was a potential bias or conflict in the sense that the people making the diagnostic judgments often were the same people who had been trying to instruct the very students who were not performing at the expected level. Essentially well-meaning adults believed that diagnosis would improve learning, felt that they had done what they could to improve the student's learning in the general education classroom, and had a diagnostic construct that favored overdiagnosis by design.

Teachers received training at the preservice and in-service levels to become sensitized to "hidden disabilities," which purportedly required special teaching techniques beyond what could be provided in the general education classroom. Teachers who had always faced large numbers of students who were not proficient in basic skills came to believe that they were incapable of effectively instructing any student who required careful teaching. In contrast to today's universally accepted hallmarks of providing robust evidence-based instruction in ways that are adapted to suit the needs of the students (i.e., differentiated instruction), teachers during this time came to believe that students were best helped by referring them for testing that would lead to placement in special education, so that the students could "get the help that they need." Many educators further believed that there were unique aptitude-by-treatment interactions (ATIs) that could be identified through testing and would lead to unique instructional practices in special education (Reschly, 2008). For example, if students with reading deficiencies performed poorly on tests of visual–motor integration (e.g., the Bender Visual–Motor Gestalt Test; Koppitz, 1963), it was presumed that the visual–motor (processing) problem was the cause of the reading difficulty. The theory was that improving the student's deficient processing would result in immediate gains in reading skills because, in essence, the obstacle preventing reading performance was being removed. Students, particularly those in special education, would receive noncontextualized visual–motor training in an effort to improve their reading skills (e.g., Frostig & Horne, 1964). Unfortunately for the countless students who spent their educa-

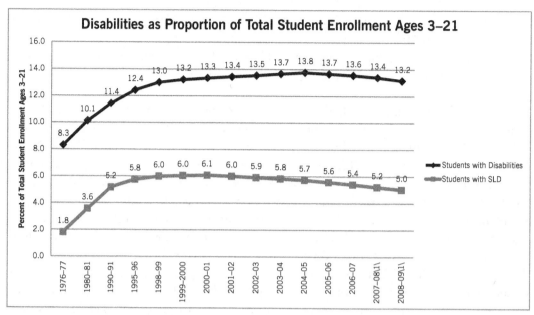

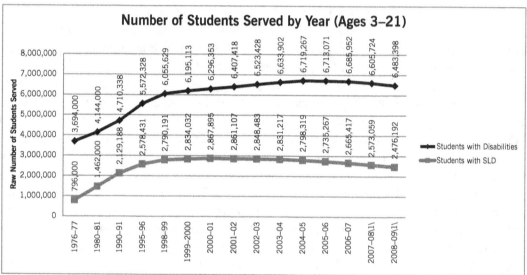

FIGURE 1.1. Growth in the prevalence of students identified with SLD since the passage of the EHA. From U.S. Department of Education, Office of Special Education Programs, Annual Report to Congress on the Implementation of the Individuals with Disabilities Education Act, selected years, 1979 through 2006; and Individuals with Disabilities Education Act (IDEA) database, retrieved September 13, 2010, from *www.ideadata.org/PartBdata.asp*. National Center for Education Statistics, Statistics of Public Elementary and Secondary School Systems, 1977 and 1980; Common Core of Data (CCD), "State Nonfiscal Survey of Public Elementary/Secondary Education," 1990–1991 through 2008–2009 (table prepared September 2010).

tional careers engaged in such activities, empirical research consistently failed to support such approaches (Kavale & Mattson, 1983; Myers & Hammill, 1976).

By the late 1980s, a number of researchers and policy experts began to speculate that the rampant growth of students with SLD reflected an overidentification of students with disabilities rather than an excellent job of child find. Rosenfield (1987) hypothesized that many students who qualified for special education as students with SLD were actually "curriculum casualties" (p. 27), with the implication that their deficits could be prevented or remediated through more effective teaching in general education.

In a seminal article, Madeline Will (1986) captured a prevailing sense that many of the students being identified with SLD could be adequately served in the general education classroom without special education identification if teachers could be assisted to use effective instructional practices with all students. This proposed "regular education initiative (REI)" included a number of supports including building-based educational programming driven by students' needs, early identification and intervention, and the use of evidence-based instructional practices. As a result of the REI, a number of now-familiar programs and procedures were initiated, including the use of the problem-solving model in various teaming structures (e.g., instructional support teams, instructional consultation teams), team teaching in special education, and increased inclusion of students with disabilities in general education. Many of these initiatives were intended to decrease the numbers of students in special education (particularly those identified with SLD) by creating an improved general education environment that would address students' academic deficiencies prior to and in lieu of special education consideration.

Although many of these programs produced the desired outcomes (Hartman & Fay, 1996; Kovaleski & Black, 2010), the number of students with SLD continued to grow throughout the 1990s from 5.2% in 1990 to an all-time high of 6.1% in 2000 (see Figure 1.1). It seems clear that the issues that Ysseldyke and colleagues (1983) had identified regarding the assessment process fueling overidentification remained, as the ability–achievement discrepancy continued to be the only procedure identified in federal regulations for the identification of SLD.

IDEA 1997

By 1997, concerns about overidentification were so pervasive that a provision was added to IDEA to prohibit school districts from identifying students as having disabilities if the reason for their academic difficulties was a result of "lack of instruction in reading or mathematics" (IDEA 1997, §614[b][5]). This provision reflected not merely the situation in which students fail to attend school (e.g., because of homelessness or transience), but was also aimed more particularly at students failing to learn because of ineffective instruction. The Report of the Committee on IDEA Amendments to the U.S. Senate explains the thinking of the Congress at the time:

> There are substantial numbers of children who are likely to be identified as disabled because they have not previously received proper academic support. Such a child often is identified as learning disabled, because the child has not been taught, in an appropriate or effective manner for the child, the core skill of reading. . . . Therefore, in making the determination of a child's eligibility, the bill states that a child shall not be determined to be a child with a disability if the determinant factor for such a determination is lack of instruction in reading or math or limited English proficiency. The Committee believes this provision will lead to fewer children being

improperly included in special education programs where their actual educational difficulties stem from another cause and that this will lead schools to focus greater attention on these subjects in the early grades. (S. Rep. No. 105-17, 1997, p. 19)

Clearly the intent of Congress was twofold: (1) to limit the number of students incorrectly identified as having SLD, and (2) to do so by requiring multidisciplinary evaluation teams to rule out situations in which effective instruction was not provided. It is interesting to note here that concerns about misidentification were reflected in the original definition of SLD in the EHA in 1975, wherein the regulations stipulated that a child considered to have SLD must have been "provided with learning experiences appropriate for the child's age and ability levels"(§121a.541[a][1]) in addition to other exclusionary factors. That is, even the original law recognized that there were causes other than disability that could lead to academic deficits, and that appropriate and effective general education teaching needed to be in place before a disability could be determined. However, that concept was largely ignored by practitioners, leading to the enhanced language about ruling out a lack of instruction in IDEA 1997. Nonetheless, how the rule-out for lack of instruction was to be accomplished was not operationalized, and the provision was again ignored in practice. In addition, IDEA 1997 maintained the ability–achievement discrepancy as the only option for identifying students with SLD, so the problems continued.

Concerns about Overall Student Proficiency

During this period, concerns about overidentification were matched by a national preoccupation with the overall lack of proficiency of American students in acquiring basic academic skills. The publication of *A Nation at Risk* (National Commission on Excellence in Education, 1983) is often cited as the seminal bellwether in this regard as it focused attention on the failure of America's students in maintaining pace with those in other developed countries. Lower standards, reduced expectations, and ineffective teaching were cited in this report as direct causes of the decline in American student performance. Much of this concern centered on reading, which was seen as a foundational basic skill, yet had been the subject of the so-called "reading wars" in which theorists argued about which instructional procedures were most effective in producing proficient readers. Two important commissioned reports were published in 2000 and 2001. First, a National Reading Panel was commissioned by the U.S. Department of Education. The National Reading Panel report was published in 2000 and specified the "five big ideas" in reading. It attempted to put an end to philosophy-based arguments about reading instruction and initiated a national focus on the identification and use of research-based instruction. The National Reading Panel report was important as much for its content as it was for its role in helping to change the tenor of the discussion to focus on using reading instruction that was shown to work in research and preventing (as opposed to simply responding to) reading failure for students. In 2002 a second commissioned report appeared, authored by the President's Commission on Excellence in Special Education. This report raised alarms about the extent to which schools were unnecessarily placing children into special education, particularly students of minority ethnicity, and emphasized the need to use research-based instruction as part of the eligibility decision. The President's Commission on Excellence in Special Education specifically called for the use of RTI procedures. We describe these findings in greater detail below, but first let us continue with the keystone policy and legislative events that set the stage for RTI.

These events culminated in the revision of the Elementary and Secondary Education Act (ESEA), which was famously relabeled the No Child Left Behind (NCLB) Act in 2001. NCLB required that schools use scientifically based instructional procedures. The term "scientifically based" appeared more than 100 times in the act (Sweet, 2004). In fact, one section of the law defined effective instruction in reading as incorporating the five big ideas specified by the National Reading Panel (§1208[3]). The law also set a target date of 2013–2014 for schools to bring 100% of their students to proficiency, along with interim targets defined as adequate yearly progress (AYP). The sense of Congress that core instruction needed to improve as reflected in the Senate Report of 1997 was at this point fully actualized in law, and the impetus was placed squarely on general education. It was clear that Congress understood that this message needed to be conveyed in both major national educational laws (NCLB and IDEA).

Concerns about the Ability–Achievement Discrepancy Approach

Meanwhile, on the special education side, two notable events happened in the early years of the new century that were related directly to the ongoing ferment about SLD. In 2001 an "LD Summit" gathered a number of researchers and policy experts to address the current state of SLD identification and to make recommendations for changes in law and practice. As summarized by Bradley, Danielson, and Hallahan (2002), the summiteers criticized the ability–achievement discrepancy approach, characterizing it as a "wait-to-fail" model because students who displayed academic difficulties in the early grades were often not identified with SLD until their discrepancies increased to a significant level, at which point these students were older, had experienced a prolonged period (years) of failure, and it was improbable that students could catch up. It should be noted here that the authors were not advocating for increased identification of students with SLD in the primary grades, but rather were calling for early and robust intervening during these formative years, with the expectation that early intervention could bring the students to proficiency and prevent the need to identify them with SLD.

The summit participants also criticized the actual assessment practices that were commonly used and sometimes still are used in determining an ability–achievement discrepancy, noting that these tests frequently did not assess the critical instructional outcomes that forecast long-term learning success (e.g., phonemic awareness, numeracy). Instead, assessment often centered on IQ estimation, and these assessments could not be demonstrated to lead to useful instructional recommendations for the target students.

> **IQ tests frequently did not assess the critical instructional outcomes that forecast long-term learning success (e.g., phonemic awareness, numeracy).**

These concerns about the use of "IQ testing" were based on a number of landmark studies conducted during the 1990s that indicated that students with ability–achievement discrepancies could not be differentiated from students with low achievement who did not show an ability–achievement discrepancy (so-called slow learners) on a number of variables related to learning (e.g., Torgesen et al., 1999; Vellutino, Scanlon, & Lyon, 2000). In particular, IQ was shown not to be a good predictor of which students were likely to acquire age-appropriate reading skills. In reviewing this research for the LD Summit, Fletcher and colleagues (2002) concluded that students with LD could be distinguished from other students (including those with attention-deficit/hyperactivity disorder [ADHD]), but not on the basis of an IQ–achievement discrepancy. What is particularly notable about this research is the finding that students with low IQs and commensurate achievement could indeed acquire age-appropriate reading skills when provided with robust interventions. However, in a system based on delivering special education services only to those who displayed an ability–achievement discrepancy, low-achieving (i.e., at-risk) students who did not show a discrepancy were systematically denied special education services. This situation is seen by many as unfair and illogical, as it is based on a reified concept that has never had an appropriate level of empirical support. Stanovich (1999), reflecting on positions taken by Kelman and Lester (1997), addressed this issue with a particularly troubling comment, "It is rare for the advocates of discrepancy-based definitions to articulate the theory of social justice that dictates that society has a special obligation to bring up the achievement of individuals whose achievements fall short of their IQs, rather than simply to bring up the skills of those with low skills, period" (p. 353). The question here is not whether some students have SLD, as there appear to be clearly identifiable markers to differentiate such students; it is whether the concept of expected underachievement has validity. Consensus was emerging among policymakers, researchers, and practitioners that school districts have an obligation to bring all students to proficiency and effective interventions should be available to any student who needs support to attain important learning objectives.

Response to Intervention

To address the issue of delivering robust interventions to students failing to acquire basic skills, participants of the LD Summit recommended the use of RTI as an alternative procedure for assessing students for possible SLD. This concept, which is the focal point of this book, had as its basic premise the notion that a student's response to robust interventions is the best evidence for the existence of SLD rather than the student's performance on a group of norm-referenced tests. That is, students who demonstrate a need for intervention support and then fail to improve their performance in the face of effective instruction delivered with a high degree of fidelity would be deemed to be those who were most in need of special education services.

The conclusions of the LD Summit, and particularly the advocacy for the use of RTI, were reiterated by the President's Commission on Excellence in Special Education, which was impaneled in 2001 to advise Congress on the scheduled reauthorization of IDEA. The commission heard extensive testimony about the state of special education and made a number of far-reaching recommendations. In their 2002 report, the commission stated that the current special education system valued process and compliance over results (i.e., student learning) and called for the use of rigorous research-based practices to improve the results of special education. The commission also criticized the extant procedures used to identify students with disabilities, especially the use of intelligence tests in the identification of students with SLD:

> The Commission fully supports expert recommendations made repeatedly in testimony and the scientific literature that the current methods of assessing the presence of SLD be changed. The Commission recommends that appropriate steps be taken to amend current federal regulations to indicate that IQ achievement discrepancies (and therefore IQ tests) are not neces-

sary for the identification of children as having a learning disability. . . . Eliminating IQ tests from the identification process would help shift the emphasis in special education away from the current focus, which is on determining whether students are eligible for services, towards providing students the interventions they need to successfully learn. There is little justification for the ubiquitous use of IQ tests for children with high-incidence disabilities, except when mild mental retardation is a consideration, especially given their cost and the lack of evidence indicating that IQ test results are related meaningfully to intervention outcomes. (p. 25)

Like the LD Summit Report, the commission's report pointed to the use of RTI as a preferred assessment procedure in the determination of SLD:

The Commission recommends that the identification process for children with high-incidence disabilities be simplified. Assessments that reflect learning and behavior in the classroom are encouraged, with less reliance on the assessments of IQ and achievement that are now predominant. A key component of the identification process, especially to establish education need and make this decision less subjective, should be a careful evaluation of the child's response to instruction. (p. 26)

Although the use of the term RTI was introduced to the field in the reports of the LD Summit and the President's Commission on Excellence in Special Education, the concept that more functional, classroom-based assessments could and should be used in identifying students for special education eligibility had a history that ran parallel to the implementation of EHA/ IDEA. Efforts to systematize a direct assessment of academic skills began in the 1970s through the development of data-based program modification (Deno & Mirkin, 1977), curriculum-based assessment (Gickling & Havertape, 1981), and curriculum-based measurement (CBM; Deno, Marston, & Tindal, 1986). In fact, by 1983, Ysseldyke and colleagues, in the aforementioned work at the LD Institute, had concluded that curriculum-based measures were technically adequate for use in both informing instruction and making more critical eligibility decisions. It is regrettable that these procedures did not become the default assessment practices for SLD identification rather than the ability–achievement discrepancy approach during the early years of the EHA. Nonetheless, these direct assessment procedures continued to develop during the past three decades with continued support cited for their technical adequacy in published research (Fuchs, Fuchs, Hosp, & Jenkins, 2001; Good & Jefferson, 1998; Marston, Fuchs & Deno, 1986; Tindal, 1993; Tindal & Marston, 1996)

> A key component of the identification process, especially to establish education need and make this decision less subjective, should be a careful evaluation of the child's response to instruction.

IDEA 2004/2006

The culmination of this national ferment about SLD and how it is identified was reached with the reauthorization of IDEA in 2004. In the run-up to reauthorization of the law in 2004, the issues described above were clearly on the minds of legislators. As indicated in the Senate Report on IDEA (S. Rep. No. 108-185, 2003), senators expressed the opinion that issues regarding the identification of students with SLD were inextricably tied to the overall failure of America's schoolchildren in acquiring basic skills, and displayed an awareness of research that indicated the efficacy of scientifically based reading instruction in bringing at-risk students to appropriate levels of proficiency:

> The committee is greatly concerned that too many children are being identified as needing special education and related services, and has sought approaches to help prevent students from being inappropriately identified for services under IDEA. Research shows that with appropriate, early regular education interventions, many children can learn to perform effectively in the regular education environment without the need for special education services. These procedures also have the promise of reducing the amount or intensity of services needed for children who ultimately do get appropriately referred for special education. (S. Rep. No. 108-185, 2003, p. 23)

The House Committee Report on IDEA (H. Rep. No. 108-77, 2003) further articulated the idea that students who were capable of being adequately educated in general education were being incorrectly identified as having SLD:

> A child cannot be determined to be a child with a disability solely because the child did not receive scientifically based instruction in reading. With the combination of programs authorized under the Elementary and Secondary Education Act, particularly Reading First and Early Reading First, and the prereferral services concept . . . the Committee hopes that local educational agencies will improve their reading and literacy instruction to enable all children to read at grade level by the third grade. The Committee believes that these changes will help reduce the number of children being inappropriately referred to, and identified under, special education and should encourage schools to improve their programs on these subjects in early grades. (H. Rep. No. 108-77, 2003, p. 106)

The conceptual connectedness of this language to that of NCLB, which was passed in 2002, is quite apparent, and reflects an understanding of the need for schools to situate issues regarding students with SLD within a general educational framework. Thus NCLB and IDEA were introduced within 3 years of each other as companion acts or mutually referential legislation. Together, they envisioned a seamless system of supports based on the use of scientifically based instruction in both general and special education, with an overall mission of bringing all students to proficiency in basic skills.

> **NCLB and IDEA envisioned a seamless system of supports based on the use of scientifically based instruction in both general and special education, with an overall mission of bringing all students to proficiency in basic skills.**

Furthermore, the Senate Report embraced the findings of the President's Commission on Excellence in Special Education regarding problems with IQ tests:

> The committee believes that the IQ–achievement discrepancy formula, which considers whether a child has a severe discrepancy between achievement and intellectual ability, should not be a requirement for determining eligibility under the IDEA. There is no evidence that the IQ–achievement discrepancy formula can be applied in a consistent and educationally meaningful (i.e., reliable and valid) manner. In addition, this approach has been found to be particularly problematic for students living in poverty or culturally and linguistically different backgrounds, who may be erroneously viewed as having intrinsic intellectual limitations when

their difficulties on such tests really reflect lack of experience or educational opportunity. (S. Rep. No. 108-185, 2003, p. 27)

Finally, the legislators expressed approval for allowing districts to use alternative methods of identifying students with SLD, using RTI:

> The bill allows local educational agencies to make an eligibility determination through . . . a process based upon a child's response to scientific, research-based intervention. The [President's] Commission recommended that the identification process . . . be simplified and that assessments that reflect learning and behavior in the classroom be encouraged, with less reliance on the assessments of IQ and achievement. (S. Rep. No. 108-185, 2003, p. 27)

The language used in the House Committee's report is important historically because it represents the most explicit legislative language to this point recognizing that the process of diagnosing students with SLD may include very high error rates and may actually do more harm than good for the children receiving the diagnosis. The early warning signs of this eventual conclusion had been raised almost immediately after the passage of the EHA in 1975 with findings from the LD Institute and replicated by a number of independent research teams. Because the very diagnostic construct of SLD had been one promoted primarily through advocacy rather than well-controlled diagnostic accuracy studies, it is not surprising that the diagnostic construct itself has invited diagnostic error (VanDerHeyden, 2011). If a child was enrolled in a school where many or most students were low performing and that child was somehow referred for eligibility consideration, there was a good chance that a diagnosis of SLD could and would be made. Sarason and Doris (1979) characterized this process as a "search for pathology," and many research teams documented that, once a child was referred for evaluation, diagnosis and eligibility were almost certain outcomes (Algozzine, Ysseldyke, & Christenson, 1983; Ysseldyke, Vanderwood, & Shriner, 1997), whether the child met the local diagnostic criteria or not (Macmillan, Gresham, & Bocian, 1998; Macmillan & Speece, 1999). The overdiagnosis of children with SLD perhaps would not have mattered if the advocates' intentions had been fulfilled. That is, if eligibility systematically led to stronger learning trajectories and higher rates of learning and adaptive outcomes for those students made eligible for SLD, then overdiagnosis might not be considered such a problem. However, the research data are not clear on this point. Based on the evidence, we seem to know a great deal about how to accelerate learning trajectories for struggling students, but the eligibility and subsequent placement decision may have little to do with ensuring that the right (i.e., effective) instructional strategies are consistently delivered to the students who need them. Because special education services have not been found to consistently raise the achievement and reduce the risk for students with SLD (Kavale & Forness, 1999), then all professionals who care about student learning outcomes must question the validity of the diagnostic construct. Messick (1995) expanded the definition of construct validity to include the intended and unintended consequences of using an assessment, and coined the term "consequential validity." In education, consequential validity for the diagnosis of SLD assessment has been questioned based on research data showing that students are often misdiagnosed and that their diagnosis does not predictably lead to appreciably positive changes in their long-term academic success (Cortiella, 2011).

The repeated use of the term "scientifically based" in the NCLB legislation underscores a recognition on the part of decision makers that evidence is the best basis for selecting action in the helping professions. Evidence-based practice began in medicine but resonated with a similar movement in education called "data-based decision making." Data-based decision making grew out of the work of applied behavior analysis, precision teaching, curriculum-based assessment, and positive behavior supports. Each of these areas of research and practice shared a commitment to the notion of consequential validity and viewed student learning data as the most important arbiter (selector) for instructional actions and, more broadly, system resource-allocation decisions in schools including referral to special education. This framework was consonant with evidence-based practice in that it recognized research evidence as the best basis for selecting treatments but extended the logic by showing how ongoing student assessment data could (and should) be used to evaluate potentially promising assessments and treatments and make adjustments accordingly to ensure optimal learning outcomes. This framework is now referred to as RTI and represents a major step forward for helping professionals committed to consequential validity.

Early efforts to diagnose SLD have been fraught with technical problems and obfuscated by procedural debates that have distracted us from what parents may consider to be the heart of the matter. Can we reliably identify children who need intervention, and can we demonstrate that the interventions provided are indeed helpful to those children? This opportunity for clarity around the central questions of SLD diagnosis makes new challenges apparent in diagnostic decision making. First, how will we define SLD? In other words, what constitutes a "true positive" diagnostic finding? Second, what diagnostic rule-out criteria can be usefully applied to identify children in need of special education services under the category of SLD? Third, what diagnostic rule-in criteria can usefully be applied to diagnose causes of poor academic performance and lead directly to interventions of demonstrated benefit? Fourth, how will we evaluate whether these service decisions are made accurately and efficiently and create better outcomes for students given the SLD diagnosis than those students would have had if not diagnosed?

In her book *Overtreated: How Too Much Medicine Is Making Us Sicker and Poorer*, Brownlee (2007) criticizes the medical field for providing too much treatment, details the substantial tangible and intangible costs associated with providing too much treatment, and suggests that decision makers in medicine typically ignore the costs associated with overtreatment for a variety of reasons. One of the most well-known debates on overtreatment in medicine has centered on the routine screening for prostate cancer. When one considers (1) the accuracy of the screening device, (2) the consequences of failing to detect a prostate cancer or the probability of death from an undetected prostate cancer, and (3) the consequences of unnecessary treatment when a false positive screening error is made, the data are fairly clear that annual prostate screening does more harm than good. In 2012 a medical panel convened and recommended that routine screening for prostate cancer be abandoned, and this led to some amount of protest from the public who embrace the "more is better" logic in medicine and view any efforts to constrain medical assessment and intervention as tantamount to rationed health care that will be bad (not better) for Americans.

Education is guilty of similar logic errors. Too often our efforts and decisions are guided by illogical premises and do not seek to specify the ingredients or procedures that can be demonstrated to do the most good and the least harm in the most efficient way. For many years, advocates promoted identification of students with SLD, demonstrating a belief that making the diagnosis would be useful to the students and their families. Whereas some students and their families have realized benefits from being diagnosed with SLD, the diagnostic reality in many schools has been that the diagnosis did not lead to an appreciable reduction in the risk of negative outcomes and an appreciable increase in the probability of positive outcomes for those students who were diagnosed. Practitioners commonly state that data must be "triangulated," which is another way of saying that when multiple sources of evidence all point to the same conclusion, then the conclusion has a higher probability of being true.

We fully support the need for reliable and valid assessment (American Educational Research Association [AERA], American Psychological Association [APA], & National Council on Measurement in Education [NCME], 1995); however, we will argue for what we consider to be "smarter" diagnostic decision making that seeks to obtain the needed information at the lowest cost to make the most accurate decision that carries the highest yield for students. As Macmann and Barnett (1999) have shown, more assessment data do not necessarily lead to more reliable or accurate decisions. Overassessment and overtreatment have been persistent problems in education as evidenced by the tremendous number of students diagnosed with SLD and the questionable consequential validity of their diagnosis. At the same time, there is little doubt that many students require support to attain basic proficiencies.

> **Overassessment and overtreatment have been persistent problems in education as evidenced by the tremendous number of students diagnosed with SLD and the questionable consequential validity of their diagnosis.**

RTI offers an opportunity to select assessment and intervention procedures that produce the greatest benefits to students in need of intervention to attain expected learning outcomes. In this book, we detail diagnostic procedures that pay attention to the accuracy and efficiency of assessment *and* intervention procedures. We also detail procedures that can be used with sufficient specificity to identify causes of poor academic performance and to develop interventions that can work to improve learning when properly used. Most important, we describe how the use of RTI in diagnosing SLD gives us an opportunity to quantify the value of SLD diagnosis and drive assessment and intervention efforts in schools to improve learning, reduce risk of failure, and generally ensure the consequential validity of SLD.

PROVISIONS FOR RTI IN IDEA LAW AND REGULATIONS

In this section we explore the statutory and regulatory provisions of IDEA that authorize the use of RTI as part of a comprehensive evaluation of students suspected of having SLD. In most cases, the actual language of the regulations will be referenced because the regulations provide the operationalization of the statute. In reviewing these provisions, it is best to start with those that pertain to the definition of who is eligible for special education and what constitutes a comprehensive evaluation.

Comprehensive Evaluation

The IDEA regulations define a "child with a disability" as one who has one or more listed disabling conditions (e.g., SLD) and "who, by reason thereof, needs special education and related services" (§300.8). An evaluation of a student suspected as being eligible for special educa-tion must determine whether the child has one of the designated disabilities as well as the "educational needs of the child" (§300.301[c][2]). The regulations indicate that the evaluation must "use a variety of assessment tools and strategies to gather relevant functional, develop-mental, and academic information about the child, including information provided by the par-ent" (§300.304[b][1]) not only to determine the existence of a disability, but also to identify the specially designed instructional procedures needed to make progress in the general education curriculum. These regulations also indicate that the evaluation team may not rely on a single measure to determine disability, must use instruments that are psychometrically sound and not racially or culturally discriminatory, are provided in the child's native language, are adminis-tered by trained personnel, are not compromised by a child's physical impairment, and must include an assessment of all areas of suspected disability. In a provision that will have an impor-tant implication for the use of RTI, the regulations articulate that as a first step in planning a comprehensive evaluation of a student, the team should review data that already exist regard-ing the student, including "evaluations and information provided by the parents of the child; [c]urrent classroom-based, local, or State assessments, and classroom-based observations; and [o]bservations by teachers and related services providers" (§300.305[a][1]). The evaluation team then plans additional assessments that may be needed to determine eligibility; however, as we describe later, the team is expected to use the existing data in its evaluation and is not required to provide further assessments if existing data are sufficient to address various aspects of the referral questions.

Lack of Instruction

The IDEA regulations of 2006 also featured enhanced language regarding the special provision for ruling out a lack of instruction as the cause of the student's school difficulties. While the 1999 regulations simply indicated that a child could not be determined to have a disability if the determining factor was a lack of instruction in reading or math, the 2006 regulations required a rule-out of a "lack of appropriate instruction in reading, including the essential components of reading instruction (as defined in § 1208[3] of the ESEA)" as well as a "lack of appropriate instruction in math; or Limited English proficiency" (§300.306[b]). The language regarding reading instruction is particularly telling and reflects an awareness of the research that had been done in the area of reading since the 1999 reauthorization of IDEA, particularly as sum-marized by the National Reading Panel in 2000. The aforementioned big ideas in reading that had been articulated by the National Reading Panel had been enumerated in §1208 of NCLB:

> The term "essential components of reading instruction" means explicit and systematic instruc-tion in phonemic awareness; phonics; vocabulary development; reading fluency, including oral reading skills; and reading comprehension strategies.

In essence, what Congress established was a general education law (NCLB) that required explicit scientifically based instruction in reading and mathematics, and then reinforced this provision in IDEA by articulating that students who had not received this instruction could not be identified as having a disability if that lack of instruction was the determining factor. These mutually referential provisions provide the linchpin in creating a system in which RTI, or more specifically, the provision of a multi-tier system of service delivery, is the essential feature for both general and special education.

RTI as a Component of an Evaluation for SLD

In introducing RTI as an alternative method for use in the determination of SLD, Congress first established in law its concerns about IQ testing and the ability–achievement discrepancy: "a local education agency

> **Congress established a general education law (NCLB) that required explicit scientifically based instruction in reading and mathematics, and reinforced this provision in IDEA by articulating that students who had not received this instruction could not be identified as having a disability if that lack of instruction was the determining factor.**

shall not be required to take into consideration whether the child has a severe discrepancy between achievement and intellectual ability in oral expression, listening comprehension, written expression, basic reading skills, reading comprehension, mathematical calculation, or mathematical reasoning" (§614 [b][6][A]). The regulations reinforced this provision by indicating that "the State must not require the use of a severe discrepancy between intellectual ability and achievement for determining whether a child has a specific learning disability" (§300.307[a][1]). Interestingly, these provisions put the decision about using the ability–achievement discrepancy in the hands of local school districts (local education agencies), and indicate that the state may not interfere with this decision.

The regulations follow with a landmark provision that "the State…*[m]ust* permit the use of a process based on the child's response to scientific, research-based interventions, and *[m]ay* permit the use of other alternative research-based procedures for determining whether a child has a specific learning disability" (§300.307[a][2–3]; italics added). These provisions thus allowed local school districts to opt for RTI by requiring that states give them that option. This provision also allowed states to require RTI. It also allowed states to consider other alternative procedures but does not require them to do so, nor do the regulations articulate what these procedures might be.

The Four Criteria for SLD

The regulations embedded the RTI option in its four-part criteria for the identification of SLD, which are schematically depicted in Figure 1.2. The first two criteria are inclusionary; that is, students must display these characteristics to be identified. The second two criteria are exclusionary; that is, these factors must be ruled out prior to identification of the student as having SLD. Given the structure of this provision, which we describe below, it is clear that the four criteria are additive, in that a student must display the requisite evidence of SLD according to each of the four criteria, and may be disqualified from identification as SLD if one of the criteria is not met. Criterion 1 requires that "the child does not achieve adequately for the child's age or to meet State-approved grade-level standards in one or more of the following areas, when provided with learning experiences and instruction appropriate for the child's age or state-approved grade-level standards: oral expression, listening comprehension, written expression, basic reading skill, reading fluency skills, reading comprehension, mathematics calculation, mathematics problem-solving" (§300.309[a][1]). It is critical to note that this language is new to IDEA 2006, in that it represents the first time that the regulations regarding SLD contextualize

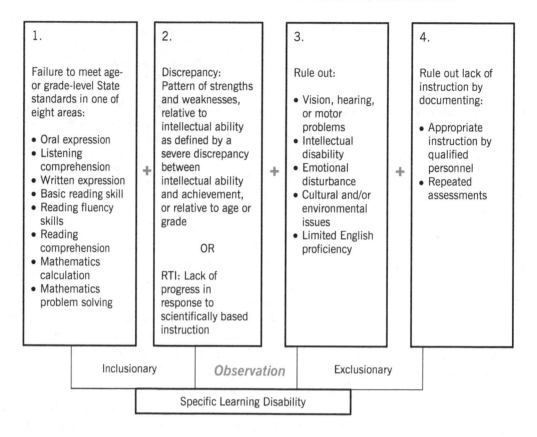

FIGURE 1.2. Schematic diagram of IDEA regulations regarding the criteria for determining SLD.

the student's deficiencies in relation to age or grade level standards rather than to the student's ability (i.e., IQ). Two interesting ramifications emerge from this new provision. First, students with above-average IQs who have average academic achievement would not qualify as having SLD, even if there was a significant discrepancy between IQ and achievement. This situation applies regardless of whether the school district uses RTI or the ability–achievement discrepancy approach (see Criterion 2 below). Second, students who have deficient academic skills in relation to age or grade-level standards, but who have subaverage IQs above the level of an intellectual disability, may be identified as having SLD if the school district uses RTI (in Criterion 2). Generally, these students would be excluded from identification as SLD if the district continued to use an ability–achievement discrepancy approach. We present operational procedures for qualifying students under this criterion in detail in Chapter 3.

Criterion 2 stipulates that a child may be identified as qualifying for SLD under this criterion in one of two ways, based on the decision made by the local school district regarding RTI. The first option is to use RTI: "the child does not make sufficient progress to meet age or State-approved grade-level standards . . . when using a process based on the child's response to scientific, research-based intervention"(§300.309[a][2][i]). Specific procedures for operationalizing and quantifying a student's RTI are covered in Chapter 4. Alternatively, school districts may choose to determine eligibility under this criterion if "the child exhibits a pattern of strengths and weaknesses in performance, achievement, or both relative to age, state-approved grade-level standards, or intellectual development, that is determined by the group to be relevant to the identification of a specific learning disability, using appropriate instruments" (§300.309[a][2][ii]). Using this option, school districts would be able to continue using an ability–achievement discrepancy, as indicated by the inclusion of "intellectual development" in this definition. This language also provides some structure for states to approve alternative procedures, as described earlier. Implementation of an ability–achievement discrepancy approach or alternative procedures will not be addressed in this text because the ability–achievement discrepancy approach has no empirical support for its validity and the alternative procedures have not been specified and thus could include presumably any set of processes with equally weak empirical support.

Criterion 3 is similar to that used in previous iterations of IDEA in which the evaluation team determines that students' academic deficiencies are not the result of "visual, hearing, or motor disabilities; mental retardation; emotional disturbance; cultural factors; environmental or economic disadvantage; or Limited English proficiency" (§300.309[a][3]). Procedures for ruling out these factors are presented in detail in Chapter 5.

Criterion 4 is another groundbreaking provision in IDEA 2004/2006 in that, for the first time, it operationalizes how a school district must document its determination that the student's deficiencies are not the result of the lack of instruction. In these provisions, the evaluation team is required to collect "data that demonstrate that prior to, or as part of, the referral process, the child was provided appropriate instruction in regular education settings, delivered by qualified personnel; and [d]ata-based documentation of repeated assessments of achievement and reasonable intervals, reflecting formal assessment of student progress during instruction, which was provided to the child's parents" (§300.309[b][1-2]). Although the essence of this language sounds remarkably like the infrastructure needed for delivery of RTI (see Chapter 2), it is notable that this criterion applies to all evaluations, even if the school district chooses to use the ability–achievement discrepancy instead of RTI. If the school district does use RTI under Criterion 2, it has the added responsibility under Criterion 4 to document "the instructional strategies used and student-centered data collected" (§300.311[a][7][i]), as well as the "strategies [used] for increasing the child's rate of learning" (§300.311[a][7][ii][B]). Clearly, the authors of these regulations wanted to ensure that parents were informed about the quality of their child's basic instructional program as well as the effects of targeted interventions to improve performance prior to and as part of the evaluation process. The intent here seems not only to encourage school districts to improve their academic programs for children at risk of school failure, but also to enhance the communication process between schools and parents, which if not handled well often leads to acrimony and legal action. We describe specific procedures for operationalizing these provisions in detail in Chapter 6.

The Observation Requirement

In the IDEA 2006 regulations, SLD remains the only disability for which a classroom observation is required, even though formal behavioral observations have long been considered a best practice assessing students with other difficulties, especially those involving behavior and emotionality. The IDEA provisions require evaluation teams to "use information from an observation in routine classroom instruction and monitoring of the child's performance" (§300.310[b][1]). This provision makes salient the importance of conducting observations in the general education classroom during typical instructional periods. As we describe further in Chapter 7, it is logical to conduct such observations during instruction in the areas in which the child is having difficulty (e.g., reading class). One might further conclude from this language that observation in the classroom is important not only to appraise the student's performance but also to ascertain the nature of the teacher–student instructional interaction. It is also notable that the observation provision involves gathering information regarding the monitoring of the child's performance, which implies that observation of the student is not a "one-shot" affair, but should occur with some regularity. Finally, this provision allows for the classroom observations to be conducted either before or after the student is formally referred for an evaluation for the determination of eligibility for special education. We present more about using data gathered prior to receiving permission for evaluation next.

Planning the Comprehensive Evaluation

As indicated previously, IDEA and its regulations include the concept that the comprehensive evaluation will be planned on an individual basis for each student who is thought to be eligible for special education. Rather than relying on a standard battery of tests, the evaluation team is charged with reviewing all of the existing data about the student that may pertain to the decision regarding eligibility as well as the eventual design of an instructional program that will meet the student's needs. As a first step in this process, evaluation teams should review data collected from many sources as part of regular classroom assessment and instruction. Schools routinely administer state tests, conduct universal screening of all students in a number of academic areas, and even conduct individual assessments such as those required for Title I services. In conceptualizing classroom assessment in general education for students experiencing difficulties as part of an overall problem-solving process, the Heartland Area Education Agency (2006) created the RIOT/ICEL assessment matrix in which the instruction (I), curriculum (C), environment (E), and the learner (L) are assessed through review (R), interview (I), observation (O), and testing (T). Clearly, data are being collected on a regular basis on all students, particularly those who are experiencing academic or behavioral difficulties.

Procedurally, all of these assessments are understood as screening for the purpose of improving the student's instructional program and for identifying those students who require further general education interventions. As such, written parental permission for conducting these assessments is not required when these assessments are conducted for these purposes (see IDEA §300.302). However, because these data may be useful in terms of special education decision making, it is important for the evaluation team to extensively review and consider this extant information when a referral is made. In essence, what the evaluation team does is request parental permission to review the existing data for a new purpose, that is, the determination of eligibility for special education and the planning of the eventual special education instructional program. The evaluation team also evaluates these data in terms of their sufficiency in addressing the two important eligibility questions. The concept here is that evaluation teams plan for new assessments only when they are needed to address referral questions that cannot be answered from data that have already been collected. For students being considered for

> **Evaluation teams plan for new assessments only when they are needed to address referral questions that cannot be answered from data that have already been collected.**

determination of SLD, the referral questions include all four criteria described above, including:

- Are the student's academic skills significantly deficient in relation to age and state standards?
- Is the student's RTI significantly deficient from other students (when the school district selects RTI as its designated procedure for eligibility decision making)?
- Have other conditions been ruled out as the source of student's academic difficulties?
- Are the student's academic difficulties a result of a lack of instruction?

As we present in detail in the following chapters, assessment data that are collected routinely through the process of providing RTI to improve students' performance in regular education need to be harvested to address these questions as part of a comprehensive evaluation. If the data are insufficient to answer these questions, additional assessments are appropriate.

An important part of planning a comprehensive evaluation is the thorough involvement of the student's parents. The IDEA regulations include numerous provisions to ensure that parents are apprised of the instructional program that has been provided for the student in general education, the nature of the specialized interventions that were provided in response to the student's academic deficiencies, and all data that were collected as part of universal screening or monitoring of the student's progress during intervention. With this information, parents can contribute meaningfully to the planning of any subsequent assessment procedures needed for a comprehensive evaluation and ultimately participate more fully in developing an individualized educational program (IEP) if the student is found to be eligible for special education.

Establishing Local Evaluation Criteria

The IDEA 2006 regulations continue to provide protections for parents who desire to request a comprehensive evaluation for their child or who disagree with a school district's determination of eligibility and want to request an independent educational evaluation (§300.502). To understand how school districts that are implementing RTI as part of their eligibility decision making for SLD may appropriately respond to these requests, it is important to first note that the regulations expect that the district has developed "agency criteria" that are used when it initiates a comprehensive evaluation for eligibility for special education (§300.502 [e]). For school districts using RTI as its chosen method (for Criterion 2), it is prudent for the school district to articulate its assessment procedures as part of an approved policy, including a full description of how RTI is assessed. In doing so, the school district not only establishes operating procedures for conducting its own evaluations, but also creates parameters for how parent-initiated evaluations in the private sector will be conducted and how independent educational evaluations may be approved for eligibility decision making.

An interesting ramification of these provisions is that determination of a student's ability–achievement discrepancy may not be evidentiary for SLD in a district that has chosen to use RTI in lieu of the ability–achievement discrepancy approach. Because the regulations stipulate that "a local education agency shall not be required to take into consideration whether the child has a severe discrepancy between achievement and intellectual ability" (§614 [b][6][A]), it seems reasonable to conclude that a parental request for evaluation of a child suspected as having SLD would include an assessment of the student's RTI, and specifically not include an assessment of an IQ–achievement discrepancy, if the school district's agency criteria indicate its choice of RTI. Similarly, an independent evaluation conducted at public expense should conform to the school district's agency criteria, such that the independent evaluation should include an assessment of the student's RTI rather than an assessment of an IQ–achievement discrepancy. Furthermore, if an ability–achievement discrepancy is assessed, the evaluation must include direct assessment of the delivery of effective instruction delivered by qualified personnel and monitored via repeated assessment to rule out lack of instruction as a cause of poor achievement. This requirement pertains even if the evaluation is conducted outside the school setting and even if the school does not have a well-planned and well-implemented RTI system in place.

Current Status of the Use of RTI in the Comprehensive Evaluation Process

Since the promulgation of the 2006 IDEA regulations, states and local school districts have responded to the opportunity to use RTI as its required or recommended procedure for implementing Criterion 2 of a comprehensive evaluation of a student thought to have SLD with a high degree of variability. Zirkel and Thomas (2010), in a national survey of states' implementation of RTI found that 12 states had required the use of RTI in SLD evaluations. Of these, five states also prohibited the use of the ability–achievement discrepancy approach, while four states allowed for some combination of RTI and discrepancy approaches (which appears to be contradictory to the language in the regulations that indicates that local education agencies use one approach *or* the other). Three other states had partially recommended RTI to its constituent school districts. The authors further reported that in other states, departments of education had established guidelines or recommendations about the use of RTI rather than requiring it per se. Pennsylvania has taken a particularly interesting approach to the issue—school districts must apply to the Commonwealth's Department of Education to use RTI in lieu of the ability–achievement discrepancy approach, and are approved if they can demonstrate a strong implementation of a multi-tier system of supports and have defendable practices for gathering RTI data. The upshot of this state-level variability, especially with the majority of states not making clear policy decisions, is that local school districts are again in the position of deciding their local policy about the use of RTI. Many at this point seem to be taking a "wait-and-see" posture. Many others are working on developing an effective multi-tier infrastructure before moving to the use of RTI in eligibility decision making.

CHAPTER 2

Implementing RTI as School Reform

Instructional Prerequisites for Using RTI for Eligibility Decision Making

The use of RTI as part of a comprehensive evaluation of students thought to be eligible for special education presupposes that interventions have been chosen based on the student's needs as reflected in assessment data and in consideration of the intervention's scientific research base and that these interventions have been implemented with a high degree of fidelity. One of the initial concerns about using RTI for eligibility decision making has been historic problems with delivering high-quality interventions to students who are not succeeding in school. For example, research with problem-solving teams indicated frequent lack of follow-through from team recommendations to actual teacher implementation (Flugum & Reschly, 1994; Telzrow, McNamara, & Hollinger, 2000). In essence, a legitimate question can be raised as to whether it is appropriate to assess a student's RTI when the intervention is either not reasonably expected to produce improvement or is not delivered with adequate fidelity. Consequently, it is critical to articulate those curricular and instructional features that need to be in place to ensure that the "I" in RTI has been effectively implemented.

> A legitimate question can be raised as to whether it is appropriate to assess a student's RTI when the intervention is either not reasonably expected to produce improvement or is not delivered with adequate fidelity.

Diagnostic errors occur when interventions are installed into settings that are not "adequate host environments." What do we mean by an adequate host environment? Consider, for example, a classroom where much of the allotted instructional time is devoted to noninstructional activities like transitions, where students are not engaged, and where students are lacking the prerequisite skills needed to benefit from the instructional content that is being provided. One might reasonably predict that students in this setting would perform poorly on a grade-level measure. An individual intervention deployed in this context will not likely produce useful decision-making data. For one thing, it would be difficult to know which student required intervention if most students performed below benchmark on the screening measure. Second, in this class and others like it, the "need" for intervention would likely outpace the capacity of the system to manage the interventions well. Third, a highly targeted intervention might show that the student could learn when instructed on content that is well aligned with the child's skill level and the intervention involved features like explicit instruction, frequent corrective feedback, and daily reinforcement for improved performance. However, the student's probability of academic failure may be unchanged because the remainder of the instruction in the classroom is not optimized. Addressing core instructional problems is a matter of efficiency (it is more efficient to treat a classwide problem as a classwide problem rather than 25 individual learning problems), efficacy (learning outcomes are improved to a greater extent when instructional errors and deficits are addressed), and accuracy (diagnostic decisions are more accurate when scores are normally distributed in a classroom and most children demonstrate that they have learned the skills that have been taught). This chapter articulates features of the general education infrastructure that are essential to implementing RTI.

The idea that RTI may be understood more broadly than an option for evaluating students who are thought to have SLD is reflected in most published definitions of the term. For example, in the seminal monograph produced by the National Association of State Directors of Special Education (NASDSE; Batsche et al., 2005), RTI is defined as "the practice of (1) providing high-quality instruction/intervention matched to student needs and (2) using the learning rate over time and level of performance to (3) make important educational decisions" (p. 5). Similarly, Torgesen (2007) described RTI as having two meanings, one as an instructional system for providing increasingly intense interventions, and second as an assessment system used to make instructional decisions, including the determination of eligibility for special education. To date, the great majority of publications about RTI have focused on the instructional aspect of these definitions and have in many cases expanded the meaning of RTI to include overall efforts to reform general education practices (Brown-Chidsey & Steege, 2005; Burns & Gibbons, 2012; McDougal, Graney, Wright, & Ardoin, 2010). It is notable that a number of states (e.g., California, Florida, and Pennsylvania) have actually expanded the term to "response to *instruction* and intervention" (RTII) to emphasize the provision of effective core instruction for all students as well as robust intervention for those fewer students who need instructional support. We predict that these terms will eventually be replaced by multi-tier service delivery system, which better reflects the essence of this systems change.

In this regard, RTI is conceptualized as emanating not only from IDEA but also from NCLB, in that these national laws are mutually referential and share common conceptual and procedural underpinnings, including:

- Scientifically based curriculum, instruction, and interventions.
- Early identification of learning problems.
- Ongoing monitoring of student progress to determine the effect of curriculum and instruction.
- Design and implementation of remedial and individualized interventions for students who do not experience learning success with general education instruction alone.
- Inclusion of all students in a single accountability system.
- Documentation of student outcomes (e.g., through the assessment of annual yearly progress).

It is not the purpose of this text to provide an exhaustive treatment of RTI as a program of school improvement; however, we will articulate with sufficient detail those programmatic features that should be in place if practitioners aspire to use RTI for eligibility decision making. It is important to address these infrastructure minimums with some specificity because much of the information that is culled in a comprehensive evaluation using RTI is actually developed during instruction and intervention in the general education program. Failing to put these features in place compromises the validity of an assessment of a student's RTI.

KEY FEATURES OF THE RTI INFRASTRUCTURE

In the decade or so since the term RTI was introduced, there has been a fair amount of consistency regarding those features that define an RTI or MTSS "system." The framework provided in the NASDSE monograph (Batsche et al., 2005) articulates three fundamental components of RTI: multiple tiers of intervention, use of the problem-solving method to make instructional decisions, and integrated data collection to inform decision making. In a 2008 memorandum, the Department of Education's Office of Special Education and Rehabilitative Services (OSERS) identified four features that were common to most RTI models: "(1) high-quality, evidence-based instruction in general education settings; (2) screening of all students for academic and behavioral problems; (3) two or more levels (sometimes referred to as 'tiers') of instruction that are progressively more intense and based on the student's response to instruction; and (4) continuous monitoring of student performance" (p. 6). In a survey of states regarding their implementation of RTI, Zirkel and Thomas (2010) posited a fifth feature, the assessment of treatment fidelity of the instruction and interventions.

For our purposes in this text, we define RTI as a system of assessment, curriculum, and instruction that includes the following components:

- Multiple tiers of increasingly intense, evidence-based interventions.
- Standards-aligned core curricula.
- Research-based, differentiated instructional strategies in general education.
- Universal screening of students' academic skills.
- Team-based analysis of student data using the problem-solving method.
- Continuous monitoring of student performance.
- Monitoring of treatment integrity for instruction and intervention.

Each of these features will be described as they are implemented in a multi-tier model. This discussion starts with a description of a three-tier model that has become synonymous with RTI.

THE THREE-TIER MODEL

The concept of RTI as a framework for providing effective instruction and intervention has been almost universally associated with a multi-tier model, as depicted in a triangular form. Although the number of tiers varies to some degree depending on the source, a three-tier format is most commonly used (cf. Office of Special Education and Rehabilitative Services, 2007b). As indicated in Figure 2.1, the use of a triangle to explain RTI is based on the idea that, as one moves conceptually through the tiers, the number of students decreases and the intensity of intervention increases.

Tier 1 (the base of the triangle) involves all students in general education and focuses on the provision of effective instruction with appropriate differentiation for the needs of individ-

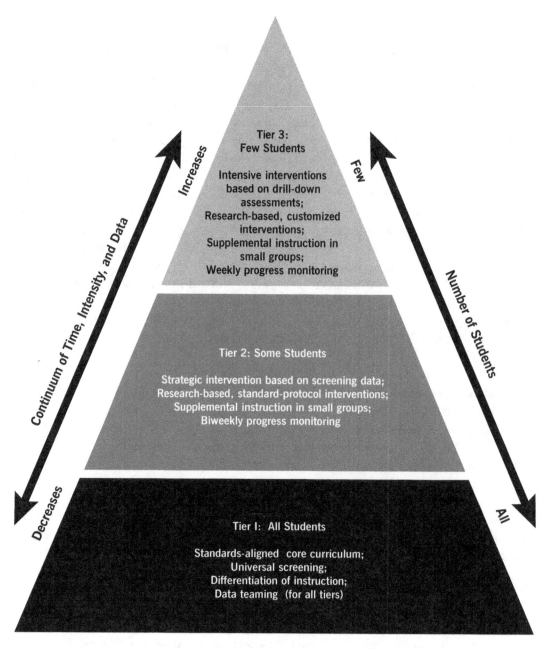

FIGURE 2.1. Graphic depiction of a three-tier model of instruction and support.

ual students. At this stage, benchmark assessments are conducted with all students to gauge the overall performance of students at a particular grade level and to identify those students who need further supports in Tiers 2 and 3. A critical issue in Tier 1 is the extent to which the general education program of curriculum and instruction is effective in bringing a high percentage of students to proficiency. Borrowing conceptually from mental health models, NASDSE (Batsche et al., 2005) proposed that 80% of students should be successful at this tier. The focus for problem-solving teams at this tier is the overall performance of students as a group and the discussion of instructional strategies is aimed at moving all students to proficiency in basic skills.

The data collected through universal screening in Tier 1 are also used to identify those students whose performance level is deficient enough to warrant further intervention. In the early days of RTI, there was a short-lived debate (Fuchs, Mock, Morgan, & Young, 2003) about whether interventions at Tier 2 should be individually customized by a problem-solving team, as had been practiced in precursor models such as those in Iowa (Tilly, 2003) and Pennsylvania (Kovaleski, Tucker, & Stevens, 1996), or should be based on a standard protocol approach (Vaughn & Fuchs, 2003). In the problem-solving model, team members use assessment data to identify the problem, set a goal, and develop an intervention for a particular student. In a standard protocol approach, students with common instructional targets based on assessment data are grouped to provide highly robust interventions targeted to those needs. For example, as a result of universal screening, students displaying phonemic awareness difficulties would receive a phonics-based intervention while students with comprehension deficits would receive a comprehension-based intervention. The emerging consensus, and the position taken in this text, is that the standard protocol approach is best suited for Tier 2, and the problem-solving approach most useful at Tier 3. As we describe later, the teaming approach that is used at Tier 2 to identify the instructional groups and to match the standard protocol interventions continues to use a problem-solving format in its deliberations.

In our model, Tier 3 is reserved for intensive problem-solving for individual students who failed to make progress in Tier 2 or those found upon initial assessment to be at such high risk of failure that intensive interventions are immediately required. At Tier 3, students receive customized interventions based on a more extensive analysis of their academic skills. Unlike some models, Tier 3 in this conceptualization does not include special education. Rather, frequent monitoring of the student's RTI during the course of this intensive intervention serves as the basis on which to make a decision about potential referral for determination of eligibility for special education. Special education in this model becomes a system of intensive supports in which programs and services articulated on the student's IEP are delivered in the least restrictive environment according to the student's needs. As such, students receiving special education services may participate in tiered intervention to the extent needed to ensure they meet their learning goals.

> **Special education in this model becomes a system of intensive supports in which programs and services articulated on the student's IEP are delivered in the least restrictive environment according to the student's needs.**

Essential features of each tier of instruction and assessment are summarized in Table 2.1 and described below.

TABLE 2.1. Essential Components of Multi-Tier Systems of Support

Tier 1

- Instructional program is aligned to state standards.
- Instructional program differentiates instruction to meet individual needs of students.
- Universal screening is conducted effectively.
  - Screening measures are related to important educational attainments.
  - Screening measures predict future performance.
  - Screening measures yield reliable scores.
  - Screening measures are brief and efficiently administered.
  - Screening measures can reflect small increments of change in student performance.
- Data teams consume student performance data to plan and evaluate instruction.

Tier 2

- Intervention is provided in small groups.
- Standard protocol interventions are used.
- Intensity is greater than what is provided at Tier 1 (i.e., more explicit instruction, greater opportunities to respond, more frequent corrective feedback).
- Progress is monitored each week or every other week for all students to adjust participation in small-group instruction and determine need for Tier 3.
- Time is allocated on the master calendar for Tier 2 instruction.

Tier 3

- Assessment is conducted with the individual student to identify an intervention that can be expected to improve performance if correctly used.
- Interventions are more intensive than what is provided at Tier 2 (i.e., instruction may have to drop back several levels to establish missing skills, individualized corrective feedback is necessary to establish and maintain correct student responding).
- Data teams evaluate the data.
- Progress is monitored each week and the school examines the percentage of students served at Tier 3 who remain in the risk group at subsequent screenings.

Tier 1

Tier 1 of a three-tier model includes programmatic features of high-quality instruction in general education. It is notable that many of the models and procedures on which RTI is based (e.g., problem-solving teams, instructional support teams) did not actually address instruction in general education, but focused on students who were potential referrals for special education (Kovaleski & Black, 2010). These precursor models consisted primarily of Tier 2 or Tier 3 activities. However, since the development of these models in the 1980s and 1990s, national attention has focused less on addressing referrals to special education and more on the overall proficiency of all students. As indicated earlier, this focus has been based on widespread concern about the failure of many students to acquire basic skills, as indicated by performance on both state assessments and on national measures such as the National Assessment of Educational Progress (NAEP). For example, Lyon (1998) cited data that indicated that, although 5% of children learn to read effortlessly, and 20 to 30% acquire reading skills readily when instructed, a full 60% of students can be expected to face significant challenges in learning to read. In fact, for 20 to 30% of children, learning to read is one of the most difficult skills that they need to master during their development, and 5% of children continue to struggle with reading even after explicit systematic instruction is provided. The need to assess and adjust instruction at Tier 1 is based on the notion that effective instruction of basic skills cannot be assumed, but must be facilitated and supported.

Troubling data such as these were a fundamental rationale for convening the National Reading Panel in 1997. In identifying its "big ideas in reading," the panel challenged schools to provide explicit instruction in phonological awareness, phonics, vocabulary, fluency, and comprehension for all students (National Reading Panel, 2000). As described in Chapter 1, these big ideas were actually institutionalized in law in No Child Left Behind (NCLB). Similarly, the National Mathematics Panel issued its report in 2008, again with the intention of guiding practitioners in the fundamentals of teaching mathematics. Readers interested in additional articles regarding evidence-based practices at multiple tiers of instruction in reading and mathematics should see Gersten and colleagues (2008, 2009); Haager, Klingner, and Vaughn (2007); Jimerson, Burns, and VanDerHeyden (2007); McGraner, VanDerHeyden, and Holdheide (2011); and VanDerHeyden (2009).

Tier 1 of a three-tier model includes four key features: robust, standards-aligned core curricula; evidence-based instructional practices; universal screening of basic academic skills; and grade-level teaming to analyze data, set system targets for improvement, adjust core instruction, and make screening decisions.

Standards-Aligned Curricula

Teachers need good tools to teach effectively and realize desired outcomes for their students. *Curriculum* is a general term that refers to the "what" in what should be taught and learned in school, including the goals and objectives of the field of study, along with their scope and sequence, and importantly, the materials used to teach these intended targets. For example, in reading and language arts, a school district's curriculum is its plan about what and how to teach the aforementioned big ideas. Usually, this plan is operationalized to a large degree by the materials purchased by the district to be used by its teachers (i.e., the reading and math series).

To guide school districts in their development of reading and language arts curricula, most states provide a set of standards that should be based on scientific research (e.g., the National Reading Panel). To the extent that states have provided districts with robust standards, a district's reading curriculum can be evaluated according to the extent to which it aligns with the state standards. In lieu of national standards, which have yet to be developed and institutionalized, some organizations (e.g., the Florida Center for Reading Research) have attempted to provide guidance to practitioners in this regard by disseminating analyses of published reading series in terms of their coverage of the five big ideas. However, given the difficulty with maintaining current reviews in the face of frequent iterations of published reading series, current reviews are not available. Similarly, reviews of curriculum materials in mathematics are not readily available. Consequently, local practitioners need to establish their own criteria by which curriculum materials are evaluated prior to acquisition by the local school entity.

Currently, an effort for states to adopt the same curriculum standards has emerged. Known as the Common Core State Standards (*www.corestandards.org*), the initiative was begun by the Council of Chief State School Officers, the chief school administrators for the state departments of education across the nation. In addition, the development of the Common Core State Standards was endorsed by the National Governor's Association. As of September 1, 2012, 45 states and three territories have adopted the Common Core State Standards. These standards define the knowledge and skills students should have within their K–12 education careers so that they will graduate high school able to succeed in entry-level, credit-bearing academic college courses and in workforce training programs.

In developing and evaluating curricula aimed at teaching basic skills, school districts should consider the following factors:

- The curriculum should be aligned with state standards.
- The curriculum should provide coordinated instructional sequences.
- The curriculum should facilitate explicit teaching of the big ideas in the domain.
- The curriculum should allow for large- and small-group instruction and should lead to large amounts of practice opportunities to maximize student engaged time.
- Clear opportunity should exist for differentiation of instruction, including scaffolding during the initial skill acquisition as well as opportunities to generalize or transfer skills.
- There is evidence that curriculum materials have produced strong outcomes when implemented with integrity (e.g., 80% success).

How these factors can be ascertained is described in Table 2.2.

Research-Based Instruction

If the curriculum is the "what" to teach, instruction is the "how" to teach. Instruction consists of the planned actions that teachers use to facilitate learning. Over the past 20 years, there has been a gradual shift from using intuitive or theoretical approaches to classroom teaching to the identification of instructional strategies based on empirical research. Although not universally embraced, many educators have recognized the folly of educational fads (Ellis, 2001) and have taken a more rigorous approach to their discipline. Not coincidentally, it has been frequently noted (e.g., Sweet, 2004) that NCLB uses the term "scientifically based instruction" more than 100 times.

Guidance for practitioners in regards to research-based instructional practices has been based on independent research and increasingly on meta-analyses of large numbers of relevant research studies. Both the National Reading Panel (2000) and the National Mathematics Advisory Panel (2008) provided syntheses of research on instructional practices. The University of Oregon's Center for Teaching and Learning (Thomas Beck, 2006, pp. 5–6) identified nine general features of instruction, including:

- Instructor models instructional tasks when appropriate.
- Instructor provides explicit instruction.
- Instructor engages students in meaningful interactions with language.
- Instructor provides multiple opportunities for students to practice.

TABLE 2.2. Key Factors Related to Standards-Aligned Curricula and Evidence That Factors Are in Place

Curriculum factor	Evidence
Curriculum is aligned with state standards.	• There is substantial overlap between skills and content taught in each subject and the specific items described in the state content standards at each grade level.
Curriculum provides coordinated instructional sequences.	• There is a logical flow from basic to more advanced skills in a sequence that corresponds to research literature (e.g., sequence of letter sounds to be taught; sequence of math computational skills to be presented). • An instructional calendar specifies time points by which certain skills ought to be mastered by all students. • Student assessment data are available to know whether most students are meeting benchmarks.
Curriculum facilitates explicit teaching.	• Explicit teaching techniques that address the skills and content for that subject and grade are described in the curriculum materials. • Teaching techniques include specific procedures for teacher instruction, including teaching scripts and routines. • Skills to be taught are not merely embedded in more generic teaching guides, but are explicitly stated and connected to particular lessons designed to establish those skills for students.
Grouping practices maximize student engaged time.	• Strategies for creating flexible instructional groups during core instruction that match instruction to student skills are described. • Clear focus is given to instructing students at their instructional levels.
Instruction moves from initial scaffolding to transfer and generalization.	• The curriculum includes ample strategies for providing instructional supports (scaffolding) during skill acquisition as well as specific strategies for application of skills in real-life contexts that allow for generalization and transfer of learning. • Adequate instructional time is provided for fluency building to ensure students reach mastery for essential skills. • Strategies are provided to promote retention of learned skills. • Strategies are provided to support students who do not master skills at expected time points.
Implementation with high integrity leads to positive outcomes for students.	• Procedures for assessing the integrity of curriculum delivery are part of the curriculum and are used on a regular basis (e.g., peer coaching, administrative observation). • There is evidence that the core curriculum produces proficiency for at least 80% of students.

- Instructor provides corrective feedback after initial student responses.
- Instructor encourages student effort.
- Students are engaged in the lesson during teacher-led instruction.
- Students are engaged in the lesson during independent work.
- Students are successfully completing activities to high criterion levels of performance.

Hattie (2009) synthesized a number of meta-analyses for a wide range of instructional strategies, often producing some surprising results. In general, Hattie concluded that active and guided instruction (e.g., direct instruction) is more effective than instructional approaches that aim to passively facilitate a student's learning (e.g., discovery learning). Similarly, the active use of learning strategies by students themselves has been shown to produce improved outcomes, autonomy, and self-regulation. Hattie envisions schools in which administrators and staff conduct internal appraisals of the effects of their instructional efforts and work in collaborative peer arrangements in which research-supported instructional practices are discussed, implemented, and evaluated.

> **Active and guided instruction (e.g., direct instruction) is more effective than instructional approaches that aim to passively facilitate a student's learning.**

Differentiated Instruction

It is well understood that every teacher confronts groups of students who vary widely in skill levels. Of all of the ways in which students can be diverse (e.g., culture, "learning styles"), it may be that differences in prerequisite skills associated with various instructional domains may be the most challenging aspect of teaching. For example, a typical kindergarten teacher is responsible for a group of 5-year-olds, some of whom can read fluently in connected text, while others do not have knowledge of letter names or sounds. Yet the expectation is that all of these students will achieve kindergarten-level accomplishments by year's end. Clearly, teachers need to actively differentiate their instruction to meet the needs of all of their students.

The first step in differentiating instruction to accommodate students' varying skill levels is to have a clear understanding of what those skill levels are. Every classroom teacher needs to use both summative and formative assessment in planned and strategic ways to specify students' performance in the sequence of skills to be taught. Many reading and math series have embedded assessments, and teachers have historically used informal techniques (e.g., analysis of seat work and homework, random calling) to continually appraise student learning (Stiggins, 1988). Teachers also have access to summative assessments such as state-provided examinations and/or commercially available tests provided by their school districts. Year-end summative assessments are less useful because they are only updated annually at best and do not reflect the progress that occurs (or does not occur) as instruction is provided. As a result, schools are using universal screening to assess students' performance on benchmark tasks that are closely related to instructional objectives. Additional details about these assessments are included in the next section.

Once teachers have a thorough understanding of the various instructional levels of their students, they can then meaningfully plan for instructional arrangements (e.g., whole-group instruction, small-group instruction, cooperative learning groups, student pairs) to strategically use available instructional time. As Hattie (2009) has described, instructional arrangements do not lead directly to academic attainments unless the time available is used productively for active teaching and learning. Within each instructional arrangement, teachers need to scaffold instruction so that they are teaching each student within the appropriate zone of proximal development (Vygotsky, 1978). The importance of teaching at each student's instructional level has been a well-established educational maxim (Gickling & Armstrong, 1978). In less technical language, this means making sure each child has mastered the prerequisite skills to be successful in the current lesson. If students have not mastered the prerequisite skills, the teacher must back up and provide instruction at a level where the child can respond accurately and fluently with instructor support until independent mastery is demonstrated.

How each teacher manages the daunting task of individualizing instruction for each student is perhaps the true essence of the "art" of teaching. Increasingly in multi-tier models, differentiation is supported by having specialists, coaches, instructional assistants, and other personnel "push in" during core instruction time. In addition, supplemental instruction in Tiers 2 and 3 provides for extended opportunity for individualization. Instructional technology has already been shown to be an important tool in differentiating instruction and will likely be pervasive in the future.

Universal Screening

The concept that students' level of proficiency on key academic skills should be periodically assessed has taken hold in thousands of schools throughout the country. There are three major purposes of universal screening assessments: (1) to assist teachers in planning for differentiated instruction, as described above; (2) to screen for those students who displayed deficiencies in the acquisition of basic skills so that appropriate intervention can be delivered; and (3) to assess the overall level of proficiency for groups of students to evaluate the effectiveness of the educational program. To meet these goals, screening instruments must have the following characteristics:

- *Screening measures must be related to important academic attainments.* Screening instruments need to assess directly those skills that are key to school success. These constructs include the terminal objectives themselves (e.g., reading comprehension, mathematical problem solving) as well as "marker variables" (e.g., phonemic awareness, mathematical computation) that serve as critical attainments in developing the target skill and forecast future success. It is only in recent years that educators have focused on these types of direct assessments. Historically, assessments such as kindergarten screening included tasks that differentiated among students of various developmental levels (e.g., block building, design copying), but were not related to functional academic skills.

- *Screening measures must be predictive of future performance.* Universal screening instruments are most helpful when they are strongly predictive of performance on the terminal objectives, which in most cases is related to state standards of learning. Because attainment of standards is assessed by students' performance on statewide tests, assessments should be highly correlated with those test results in the relevant domains. The ability to identify useful cut points that maximize efficiency in targeting students in need of intervention (e.g., through Receiver Operating Characteristics [ROC] curves and other classification analyses) is a related dimension of the choice of screening instruments.

• *Screening measures must yield reliable scores.* To be useful, assessments must be reliable so that the decision made on one occasion based on the score is consistent with the decision on another occasion or with another child. Stated another way, results need to be a function of the student's relative proficiency on the skill assessed rather than who is doing the assessment (interrater reliability), which form of the test is being used (alternate form reliability), or variability across administrations (test–retest reliability). Thus, the same psychometric characteristics that are necessary with more traditional tests also pertain to universal screening devices (AERA/APA/NCME, 1999).

• *Screening measures must be brief and efficiently administered.* Schools are in a constant struggle to balance the amount of time students are actively engaged in instruction, which is highly correlated with student outcomes, with the time required to periodically assess students' academic attainments. Consequently, an important feature of the selection of universal screening instruments is the relative ease and efficiency of their administration. The most useful instruments should be brief, require modest levels of training of administrators, and allow for rapid and accurate scoring. For this reason, curriculum-based measurement (CBM), which features 1- to 3-minute probes delivered individually by teams of teachers and specialists, has been frequently utilized for universal screening. Similarly, the emergence of computer-based assessments has been welcomed in many schools because, unlike CBM, they can be used to assess whole classes of students at the same time. Instruments that require extended administration time (e.g., 45 minutes per pupil) may have great benefits for conducting the in-depth skills analyses for students who displayed significant deficiencies in Tiers 2 and 3, but are poorly suited for universal screening. In regards to the frequency of universal screening, we have found that assessment three times per year (fall, winter, spring) provides timely information while maintaining maximum time for instruction. Efficient administration of screening measures for most schools means taking inventory of existing measures and ensuring that redundant tools are removed from the assessment lineup. It is an unfortunate reality that in many schools students are overassessed, and this overassessment comes at a direct cost to available instructional time. When schools make the mistake of collecting too much assessment data, there is a tendency for those schools to fail to consume the data for decision making and instructional action, perhaps because they are so busy collecting the data or are simply overwhelmed by the volume. An assessment inventory, in which decision makers specify what assessments are currently used to make what decisions and then a take a critical approach to eliminate any assessments that are not useful (i.e., do not advance student learning outcomes with their use), is a vital element to effective screening.

• *Screening measures must be sensitive to small increments of change.* Finally, universal screening instruments need to provide a fine-grained analysis of student performance across administrations, so that changes in student performance can be accurately analyzed. As we describe in the following section, teachers need to monitor students' performance on these measures to plan instruction, to identify students needing intervention, and to evaluate the effectiveness of their curriculum and instructional strategies.

Additional information about the logistics of conducting universal screening, along with its uses in assessing the lack of instruction provision, will be presented in Chapter 6.

Data-Analysis Teaming

The process of having teachers and other school specialists meet to address the needs of students and plan instructional changes has been a staple of school improvement efforts for more than three decades. From its earliest conceptualizations, these staff collaborations have emphasized tactics of group problem-solving process as the operating procedure of these meetings (Chalfant, Pysh, & Moultrie, 1979; Ikeda, Tilly, Stumme, Volmer, & Allison, 1996; Rosenfield & Gravois, 1996). Alternatively identified as the problem-solving model (Marston, Lau, & Muyskens, 2007) instructional support teams (Kovaleski et al., 1996), instructional assistance teams (Graden, Casey, & Christensen, 1985), instructional consultation teams (Rosenfield & Gravois, 1996), and other titles, these teams share a process by which members identify the problem, set a goal, identify solutions, plan implementation, intervene, monitor student response, and evaluate outcomes. These problem-solving procedures have typically been used to address instructional and behavioral challenges with individual students and would, in current RTI terminology, be associated with Tier 3 or perhaps Tier 2 in some models (Kovaleski & Black, 2010). However, Kovaleski and his colleagues (Kovaleski, 2007; Kovaleski & Glew, 2006) have conceptualized that problem-solving teaming should be utilized in Tier 1 of a multi-tier system to address the needs of larger groups of students and to assist teachers with classwide, gradewide, or even schoolwide instructional changes.

Based on the work of Schmoker (2001), Kovaleski and Pedersen (2008) have operational-ized this process for data analysis teams to identify group trends in meeting proficiency in basic skills and to plan classwide instructional strategies to increase student outcomes. As typically conceptualized, data teams consist of all teachers in a particular grade in one school, the school principal, and specialists, including one person designated to manage the data. The data include results of state tests and, most important, universal screening measures. The basic format of these Tier 1 meetings is to identify the percentages of students at various proficiency levels (e.g., advanced, proficient, basic, below basic) and to identify goals to be accomplished by the next meeting. For example, a typical second-grade target would be to increase the percentage of students scoring in the proficient range on a measure of early reading (e.g., oral reading fluency) by the next measurement occasion (e.g., winter screening). With that goal in mind, the data team then reviews and selects instructional strategies to be implemented by all classroom teachers in that grade. The team also plans the logistics of implementing the strategy, including procedures for ensuring that all teachers are adequately trained and prepared to implement the strategy (e.g., through peer coaching) and have the necessary materials to implement the strategy, and follow up to verify that the strategy is being used as planned. At the next review, usually follow-ing the next universal screening, the data team reviews the students' performance and evalu-ates the efficacy of the selected and implemented strategies. The aim of this process is to assist teams of teachers to gradually identify those instructional strategies that are most effective in facilitating the students' skill acquisition, thereby improving overall instructional effectiveness. Importantly, in classes where gains are not made or are not comparable to the gains obtained in other classrooms, a closer look at the classroom should occur to ensure that the intervention is correctly used and to troubleshoot intervention implementation so that the students in that class can grow at rates comparable to other classrooms in the same grade. Where individual classrooms require this type of intervention implementation troubleshooting, more frequent progress monitoring (e.g., monthly screening) is necessary for decision makers to verify and/or ensure improvements.

A second function of data teams is to identify those students needing interventions beyond basic differentiated instruction at Tier 1. This activity is described below in our consideration of Tier 2 and 3 supports.

Finally, to operate data teams effectively, time must be allocated for collection and manipulation of the data into teacher-friendly formats as well as for the meetings themselves. Many schools set aside blocks of time for data teams to meet at least three times per year, usually immediately after the administration of universal screenings (e.g., fall, winter, spring). Because it is important for all involved staff to be available for these sessions, many schools hold them on days or half-days in the annual calendar during which students are not attending.

Tier 2

The assessment results analyzed during Tier 1 deliberations should be sufficiently robust to identify which students need further assistance to meet proficient performance levels in basic skills. Tier 2 interventions are designed to supplement, and not replace, the core classroom program. These interventions address precise instructional targets and are typically delivered in small-group formats during periods in the school day that are specially allocated for this purpose. Increasingly, to ensure that these supplemental strategies have a strong research base, interventions that use a standard protocol approach (defined below) are emphasized. In addition, the frequency of assessment increases in this tier to monitor students' response to the interventions.

Group Interventions

In general, Tier 2 is an intermediate level of support between general classwide approaches in Tier 1 and more customized, individually designed strategies in Tier 3. Students are identified for small-group interventions in Tier 2 by their performance on universal screening tools. Each group is designed for a specific instructional target based on students' performance. For example, a group of seventh-grade students needing support in reading might be segmented into one subgroup needing assistance with comprehension skills and another needing support with multisyllabic word-analysis skills. The concept of group-based supplemental interventions is based on extensive research that has indicated the efficacy of these approaches (Dickson & Bursuck, 1999; O'Connor, 2000; Torgesen, 2004). As Torgesen has indicated, "the most practical method for increasing instructional intensity for smaller numbers of highly at-risk students is to provide small-group instruction" (p.13). This line of research has shown that interventions using grouping of three to five students have been effective in producing significant outcomes for nonproficient students (Rashotte, MacPhee, & Torgesen, 2001).

Standard Protocols

In contrast to the individualized approach that has been historically used by problem-solving teams in which a unique intervention was planned for each identified student, standard protocol interventions are defined as "interventions for which the components are well specified (i.e., use a protocol) and have been shown to work generally for large numbers of students (i.e., standard)" (VanDerHeyden & Burns, 2010, p. 32). As Reyna (2004) has noted, "Despite the intuitive appeal that 'one size does not fit all,' some educational practices are broadly effective; they can be generalized widely across contexts and populations" (p. 56). Use of standard protocols is a matter of efficiency and efficacy, and they are particularly well suited for use at Tier 2. Many children may require extra support to master essential skills. Use of a packaged intervention that has been shown to work in research reduces the burden on the system in having to find and generate the materials needed to conduct the intervention, increases the likelihood that the intervention procedures used will be effective because they have been shown to work in research settings, and are manualized for training and integrity monitoring. The use of standard protocols in multi-tier models emanates from the extensive research base on the efficacy of instructional interventions (e.g., Vaughn & Fuchs, 2003).

Tier 2 Intervention Intensity

The delivery of standard protocol supplemental intervention depends on a small-group instructional format that allows for enhanced intervention intensity in terms of group size, frequency, and duration, as well as a more explicit and direct teaching style. Tier 2 interventions typically occur multiple times per week (e.g., three to five times) in 20- to 30-minute sessions (Vaughn, Linan-Thompson, & Hickman, 2003). In terms of the climate of the intervention, McMaster, Fuchs, Fuchs, and Compton (2003) used the term "special-education-like instruction" to capture a number of salient teaching procedures (p.4). Tier 2 interventions would include such features as immediate corrective feedback, mastery of content before moving on to the next lesson, more time on activities that are especially difficult, more opportunities to respond, fewer transitions, setting goals and monitoring progress, and a special relationship with the tutor. Intensity at Tier 2 is not defined by the number of minutes of instruction provided, nor the number of sessions per week, nor the number of weeks the intervention is provided, but rather is defined by the type of instruction. Effects of Tier 2 interventions should be evaluated at least biweekly, and students meeting exit criteria should be released from the intervention. Conversely, students who fail to make gains during Tier 2 intervention or who experience frustration and high error rates during the Tier 2 lessons should be moved to Tier 3 intervention immediately rather than enforcing some arbitrary timeline for remaining in Tier 2 intervention.

More Frequent Progress Monitoring

It has long been established that increased monitoring of students' progress produces enhanced instruction, more accurate decision making, and improved student outcomes (Fuchs, 1986). In Tier 2, progress monitoring should occur at least every other week (i.e., twice per month) and should consist of short, repeated measures of critical target skills along with periodic measurement of the "goal" skill. Progress monitoring measures should demonstrate the same characteristics as those described for universal screening. They should be related to important academic attainments, be predictive of future performance, yield reliable scores, be administered efficiently, and be sensitive to small increments of change. Both CBM (e.g., oral reading fluency) and computer-based applications based on item response theory have been demonstrated as effective for ongoing progress monitoring of these skills. Reviews of the psychometric characteristics of these measures are available on current websites of national RTI organizations (e.g., *www.rti4success.org*). Graphs should be used to show a student's progress, so that teachers, students, and parents can track improvements and make adjustments to the intervention. In addition, the calculation of rate of improvement (ROI), which we describe in detail in Chapter 4, is a useful datum on which to make instructional decisions.

Scheduling and Planning for Logistics of Delivery

To accomplish the aforementioned components of Tier 2 interventions, time in the annual school calendar and daily schedule need to be purposefully allocated for Tier 2 instruction. First, as indicated above, time needs to be set aside for data teams to review the group data described in Tier 1 and the progress monitoring data for students receiving tiered intervention. These reviews are important so that the efforts of the remedial tutors and those of the classroom teachers are in sync. Furthermore, these data team sessions will inevitably result in "action" lists that may include in-class coaching or troubleshooting to improve learning rates in whole classes, in Tier 2 sessions, and for students receiving Tier 3 intervention. Time must be provided for adults to follow through on the action list generated when the data team consumes the student data. Second, time should be allocated in the weekly schedule for the actual intervention sessions. These periods have assumed a number of interesting titles, such as "tier time," "power hour," and "what I need (WIN) time." Generally, these periods are scheduled such that all students are engaged in some type of customized activity, with students needing Tier 2 or 3 supports receiving those interventions, while other students are receiving enhanced instruction in content subjects (e.g., acceleration or working on curriculum-related class projects). A depiction of this type of schedule at an elementary school is presented in Figure 2.2. In secondary schools, periods for Tier 2 or 3 interventions are specially arranged into the overall period- or block-based schedule. Importantly, schools must give thought to the needs of all students. Hence, students who do not require Tier 2 or 3 interventions should not be provided with "busywork" during tiered instructional periods. Students who are performing well should experience planned activities that allow them to apply previously mastered concepts and/or interact with more advanced content and instructional targets. Great teachers know that ensuring that all students' needs are met is no small task, and administrators must continually evaluate the degree to which this aspiration is being met, examining the learning gains experienced by all students including those at the top end of the distribution and those at the bottom end of the distribution. Many systems seem to serve those students who are lowest performing or those who are higher performing, but unfortunately, many systems fail to do both.

Tier 3

Tier 3 of a multi-tier RTI system is reserved for those students who fail to make sufficient progress in Tier 2. Frequently, these students need more intense interventions for longer periods of time. Unlike some depictions, our conceptualization of a three-tier model does not equate Tier 3 with special education. Rather, Tier 3 is still considered a general/remedial education activity, with more individualized enhancements in assessment and interventions.

Tier 3 assessment is designed for individual intervention planning. Students needing Tier 3 supports are not responding adequately to the group-based procedures featured in Tier 2.

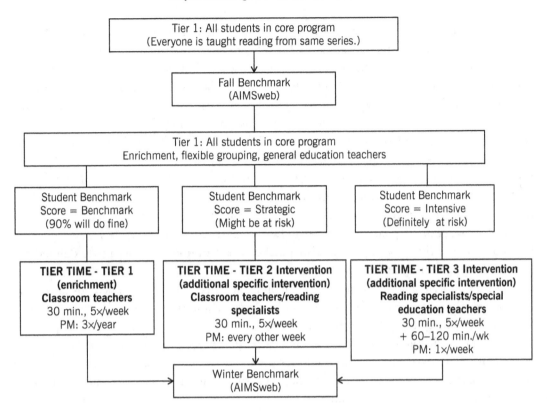

FIGURE 2.2. Example of an organizational structure for a multi-tier system of supports. PM, progress monitoring.

To further analyze the nature of their difficulties, an enhanced assessment of their academic functioning is required. Procedures such as curriculum-based assessment (Gravois & Gickling, 2008) and curriculum-based evaluation (Howell, Hosp, & Kurns, 2008; Howell & Nolet, 2000) have been specifically designed to perform these types of fine-grained skills analyses. Other norm-referenced measures (e.g., CORE Multiple Measures) as well as computer-adaptive tests (e.g., STAR Assessment) are also helpful in identifying enhanced instructional targets and for suggesting alterations in the type of instructional strategies needed for these students. We present more information about these procedures in Chapter 3.

Problem-solving teaming is used in Tier 3. A team format to analyze the results of the aforementioned assessments and to plan a customized intervention is considered best practice at this stage (Hunley & McNamara, 2009). Teaming at Tier 3 most closely resembles the problem-solving format that has been long associated with "prereferral intervention" models. The team here typically consists of a schoolwide group including the student's classroom teacher (or teachers at the secondary level), the school principal, and designated specialists, including the personnel who delivered the intervention at Tier 2. Because students needing Tier 3 support often display more complex needs, school psychologists are seen as important personnel in these deliberations. Based on the analysis of the aforementioned in-depth assessments, the team clarifies the problem identification and creates an individualized plan to increase the student's performance on the target skills as well as her/his overall adjustment to the school environment.

Tier 3 interventions are more intense than interventions at Tier 2. Interventions at Tier 3 occur daily. Although the interventions are intended to be customized per individual, they may still be delivered in group settings, as most schools often find multiple students who display common needs. Cross-grade grouping is often utilized in these situations. Similarly, focus needs to be maintained on identifying research-based interventions, which are best delivered in a standard protocol (i.e., scripted) format. The interventions would be implemented during designated "tier time" with targeted differentiation planned for each student. The difference between Tier 2 and 3 interventions is that individual student assessment data are used to select the intervention and adjustments are made to intervention features to ensure that the intervention will work for that individual student. Key features of Tier 3 intervention include more narrowly defined instructional targets, instruction on lower-level/prerequisite skills, explicit instruction designed to establish accurate responding and conceptual understanding that requires modeling, more involved corrective feedback, and guided practice opportunities with narrowly defined task content that is gradually accelerated based on the individual student's gains.

Tier 3 requires more frequent progress monitoring. Because of the immediacy of the concerns about students at Tier 3, the frequency of progress monitoring needs to increase to the levels frequently associated with special education. Many schools monitor progress once per week at Tier 3, although Fuchs's (1986) review indicated that twice-weekly assessments were most efficacious. The progress monitoring measures are the same as those described above; however, the target of the assessments may change somewhat due to the enhanced assessment data. If not already undertaken at Tier 2, graphing of data and calculation of the student's ROI are particularly critical at Tier 3 because more frequent alterations to the instructional plan are needed.

Assessing Treatment Integrity

As indicated earlier, the determination of a student's RTI is dependent on the extent to which effective core instruction and data-based interventions are delivered with a high degree of integrity.[1] Consequently, a fundamental feature of a fully developed multi-tier system is the planned assessment of the integrity with which core instruction and supplemental interventions are delivered. The use of implementation checklists by principals, instructional coaches, and teachers is recommended to ensure that programs have been implemented as designed. Treatment integrity is essential to the success of any multi-tier system. Because treatment integrity is also directly related to the assessment of the possibility that a student's academic problems are related to a lack of instruction, additional information about the assessment of treatment integrity will be presented in Chapter 6.

Consideration for Referral for Special Education

The goal of a multi-tier system of support is to provide those services and supports so that *all* students succeed in acquiring critical academic skills. When a three-tier model is used at a high level of integrity, in which students' skills are precisely identified and robust interventions pro-

---

[1] We use the terms *integrity, fidelity,* and *implementation accuracy* interchangeably in this book. For a more extensive treatment of implementation integrity, readers are referred to Ganske and Noell (2007) and Sanetti and Kratochwill (2009).

vided in a timely and sufficient fashion, the great majority of students can meet learning expectations within a general educational framework (VanDerHeyden, Witt, & Gilbertson, 2007). However, other students may fail to respond satisfactorily to interventions or may need such intensive interventions to display adequate progress that the existence of a disabling condition and the need for special education may need to be considered. At some point, the school team may need to refer for an evaluation to determine eligibility for special education.

The decision to refer for evaluation, and particularly the timing of that decision, has been an issue of concern regarding the use of multi-tier systems. In a 2011 memorandum to state directors of special education, OSEP addressed the danger of delaying the determination of eligibility for special education, indicating that students who continue to fail in response to robust interventions should not be unduly maintained in those interventions without consideration for special education eligibility. Schools should not fail to identify students who have verifiable disabilities by lingering too long in the tiers. Of course, the "flip side" is the failure to intervene long enough for the student to make meaningful progress, and potentially overidentify students as eligible for special education. Consequently, teams need to specify guidelines as to how long to intervene and what levels of progress (or lack thereof) need to be demonstrated to indicate that special education should be considered. Importantly, in redesigning their referral process to include RTI data, schools should consider the following. First, schools should evaluate the degree to which most students in the school are meeting expected benchmarks at Tier 1. Where high rates of failure occur at Tier 1, special education referral rates will be inflated, and the probability of a false-positive decision error will be high (i.e., a student is referred and made eligible when in fact the student does not have an SLD). If large numbers of students perform in the risk range at screening, then the school should undertake efforts to reduce the number of students at risk over time by adjusting Tier 1 or core instruction. When core instruction is adjusted and most children begin to demonstrate growth, individual children can be identified with greater accuracy for referral for evaluation (VanDerHeyden & Witt, 2005). Second, schools should consider the quality and accuracy with which Tier 2 and Tier 3 interventions are delivered. Large numbers of students failing to respond to intervention provided at Tier 2 and Tier 3 is generally a powerful sign of implementation error (VanDerHeyden & Burns, 2010; VanDerHeyden & Tilly, 2010) and should be interpreted as a red flag indicating that the probability of false-positive errors are inflated when intervention integrity is poor. When intervention integrity is addressed and improved, data from progress due to intervention can be used to accurately identify children in need of referral for special education (Speece, Case, & Molloy, 2003; VanDerHeyden, Witt, & Naquin 2003).

The parameters in making the decision to evaluate for special education are not concrete and likely depend on the student's age, school history, the nature of the interventions provided, and other factors. However, a few guidelines can be offered to assist the decision.

School History

To acquire and maintain critical academic skills, it can be assumed that most students need a stable instructional environment that provides explicit teaching over a number of years, especially in the early grades. Students who have experienced frequent moves during their early school career may need an extended period of stability in their current school to make meaningful progress. Such a situation would constitute a "lack of instruction" that is a disqualifying condition or a rule-out criterion for determination of eligibility for special education in IDEA. We provide further discussion of this important provision in Chapter 6. For now, one indicator for referral for evaluation would be a demonstration of failure in earlier grades in spite of a consistent learning environment. Evidence that would rule out inadequate instruction would include poor performance on universal screening and state tests despite continued enrollment in a system in which the majority of students perform at or above benchmark.

Age

Student age presents a number of dilemmas in deciding on when to refer for evaluation. Some initial research with RTI models has shown that intensive interventions are most efficacious with students in the primary grades (K–3; Shapiro & Kovaleski, 2008). In fact, early intervention has been shown to change the relative position of students in a score distribution and can move children out of the risk range (VanDerHeyden, Snyder, Smith, Sevin, & Longwell, 2005). A good rule of thumb is that interventions that are showing weekly gains on specifically targeted skills should be continued, and "goal skills" should be periodically assessed to ensure that the gains obtained during intervention are carrying over to in-class improvements.

The issue of when to refer for an eligibility evaluation is highly related to consequential validity (Messick, 1995). The concept is that when a student is found to be at risk and fails to respond to intensive and well-implemented interventions, eligibility for special education should be considered. However, a second level of action should also occur. Local decision makers should evaluate the degree to which interventions delivered in special education are improving learning outcomes for those students. Evidence of special education efficacy ensures that identifying the student as eligible for special education is indeed of benefit to the student and therefore has consequential validity. Once a student is deemed eligible for special education, data teams will need to continue, refine, and monitor the effects of individual and small-group intervention provided to that student to ensure that learning gains are attained and sustained.

Students in intermediate grades (e.g., 4–6), who have relatively consistent school histories, have likely established a history of underperformance. For these students, continued lack of progress, even in response to a newly designed intervention, should signal a more rapid referral for evaluation. Particular caution should be taken with students who display a history of school success and then begin to experience failure. In many cases, these students may be reacting to emotional stressors that are creating problems with school adjustment and overall achievement. In other cases, especially at transition grades (e.g., elementary to middle school; middle to high school), the curriculum calls for new skills (e.g., organization, study skills) that have not been required previously and may not have been acquired at earlier grades. Neither of these scenarios suggests the presence of a disability. Rather, they call for an analysis of the presenting problems and interventions directed at those issues.

Sufficiency of the Interventions

The use of a student's RTI as an indicator of a possible disability depends on the efficacy of the intervention and the extent to which it was implemented correctly or with integrity. Although we present more information about this determination in Chapter 6, it should be noted that a consideration for referral for evaluation presumes that the interventions used in Tiers 2 and 3 were matched to the student's needs, were evidence based, and were delivered with sufficient integrity to positively affect the student's skill acquisition. Failure to provide appropriate rigor of intervention invalidates the failed RTI as a marker for eligibility.

Special Education in a Multi-Tier System

A complete description of a multi-tier system requires an articulation of how special education is delivered. In other words, it may be asked, "Where on the triangle is special education?" Some early conceptualizations of RTI equated Tier 3 with special education (e.g., Fuchs & Fuchs, 2001). However, our perspective will conform to what appears to be the majority and contemporary view that Tier 3 is a set of intensive general education interventions as described above. In Chapters 9 and 10, we describe the attributes needed to qualify for special education when using RTI as a core assessment component, as well as guidelines for developing a high-quality IEP based on the data gathered in the evaluation process.

In brief, special education is considered a service (rather than a place) that can and should be delivered in the least restrictive environment, which has been a fundamental requirement of IDEA since its inception. Consequently, special education can be delivered "at any level of the triangle," depending on the needs of the student and the portability of specially designed instruction into the general education setting. Some students may need very intensive interventions delivered in small-group settings for significant portions of the school day, while others may need less intensive interventions for shorter periods or specialized accommodations in general education. A student may receive special education in what looks like a Tier 2 or Tier 3 format. However, the distinguishing feature

> **Special education is considered a service (rather than a place) that can and should be delivered in the least restrictive environment.**

is that the intervention is delivered by special education personnel and is governed by the IEP process. Most critically, what students receive via their IEP is driven by what they need, and an important source of validity evidence is that students provided with special education show gains greater than what they could have attained with general education services alone (including interventions at Tiers 2 and 3). In this sense, RTI is not just a process for ruling out lack of adequate instruction as a cause of poor learning, but rather a call to action and a framework for increasing learning for all students, including those served in special education.

The essential criterion regarding the type and level of service that is appropriate is the determination of the intensity of intervention needed for the student to make meaningful progress according to the goals set forth in the IEP in the least restrictive environment. Both progress and inclusion with nondisabled peers must be effectively balanced. One advantage of using RTI as one component of determining eligibility is that the determination of the appropriate type, level, and duration of intervention in special education is discovered during the provision of three tiers of intervention, rather than "guessed at" as occurs in an ability/achievement-based determination. Second, discussion for IEP planning is guided by student learning outcomes rather than adherence to beliefs about certain instructional processes or availability of resources. We provide explicit guidance on the use of RTI data for IEP development in Chapter 10.

A final point about the provision of special education in a multi-tier system that is frequently heard from beginning implementers of RTI is that the interventions suggested in Tier 3 are as intense as or more intense than what is currently provided in their special education program. This observation reflects the circumstance that exists in some school districts where special education has over the years become "watered down" to the extent that it is far from the robust program that it was designed to be (Zigmond & Baker, 1995). Especially in secondary schools, special education has often become a tutoring service to maintain students in content subjects (e.g., social studies, science) rather than specially designed instruction to help the student overcome deficiencies in basic skills. For example, too many special education programs discontinue explicit reading instruction after the elementary grades. Special education is not simply a re-presentation of the same content at a slower pace. Special education strategies should be the most powerful instructional strategies that can be brought to bear upon student learning with continual adjustments based on the extent to which children are actually learning. To some extent, experience with RTI has helped many school districts identify this systemic problem and implement more robust interventions for students with disabilities.

The Involvement of Parents in a Multi-Tier System

It is perhaps inappropriate to leave the involvement of parents for the last topic in a description of a multi-tier system, as their active participation is universally understood as a foundational principle of a reformed educational system. Furthermore, as we describe in Chapter 8, involving parents of students who are having difficulties acquiring basic skills and who may be evaluated for special education is not just a good idea; it is required by IDEA. The legal provision is that students considered as potentially needing special education must be assessed at repeated intervals and that those results must be communicated to the student's parents. IDEA also requires that the evaluation team document to parents the extent to which appropriate instruction has been provided to the student.

What is clear from these regulatory provisions is the underlying understanding that schooling works best for students experiencing difficulties when parents are an active part of the student's educational program. At minimum, the IDEA regulations suggest that parents be given clear and frequent updates about their child's progress (or lack thereof), as well as the interventions that are being implemented to address the student's needs. However, many practitioners in multi-tier intervention systems know that parental involvement not only keeps parents "in the loop," but also positively affects the student's progress. This enhanced involvement ranges from providing information about the student to providing input during intervention planning meetings to assisting with interventions in the home. The language of IDEA clearly implies that a close parent–teacher relationship facilitates student success and prevents discord.

Administrative Leadership and Support

The provision of a multi-tier instructional system for most schools represents a district-wide effort toward overall school reform or restructuring. Most districts undertake RTI because it is seen as needed for the improvement of the instructional program, and not just as an alternative way to identify students with SLD. Although individual schools have been known to undertake the development of a multi-tier system on their own, a more sustainable practice is to move in this direction with full central office support and leadership in addition to building-level initiative. VanDerHeyden and Tilly (2010) depicted a number of vignettes in which RTI failed to take root because of the lack of a centralized and organized vision and plan. This central leadership can be operationalized as including the involvement of critical stakeholders in the planning and implementation of the project, clear communication of expectations to staff, support for professional development, creation of alternative school schedules, and, most important, contingency planning for overcoming obstacles and expanding to other schools or levels. Vitally important to this effort is the clear articulation of how the multi-tier system fits with other district initiatives, including which procedures or policies are being eliminated and how programs that are being continued interface with the new procedures.

CHAPTER 3

Determining Inadequate Academic Achievement

In this chapter we present the procedures for conducting a comprehensive assessment of the student's academic skills. These assessments fulfill the requirements for the first criterion for the determination of SLD. As depicted in Figure 3.1, this criterion requires that "the child does not achieve adequately for the child's age or to meet State-approved grade-level standards in one or more of the following areas, when provided with learning experiences and instruction appropriate for the child's age or State-approved grade-level standards: oral expression, listening comprehension, written expression, basic reading skill, reading fluency skills, reading comprehension, mathematics calculation, mathematics problem-solving" (§300.309[a][1]). The information gathered during this phase of the evaluation is intended to specify the student's level of performance and determine whether academic achievement is discrepant from what is expected and needed to be successful in general education. To classify a student with SLD, the evaluation team must first demonstrate that achievement is lower than expected. After all, low achievement is the hallmark symptom of SLD. Low achievement should be what prompted initial identification, and changing the student's low achievement for the better is the goal of the assessment and eligibility determination process. In addition to low achievement, students with SLD must be shown to grow at rates that are not sufficient to move them out of the risk range over time (for Criterion 2, when using RTI). How to determine this growth by calculating the student's rate of improvement is described in Chapter 4. These two criteria, inadequate achievement and growth, have been referred to as a dual discrepancy (Fuchs, 2003; Fuchs, Fuchs, & Speece, 2002) and in tandem provide strong evidence that a learning problem exists and that the child will continue to experience academic failure without a change in educational programming.

We will detail procedures for collecting existing data and performing a benchmark gap analysis using the results of universal screening with CBM and computer-adapted assessments and describe how to conduct new assessments that address deficiencies (level) in one or more of

> **Low achievement is the hallmark symptom of SLD.**

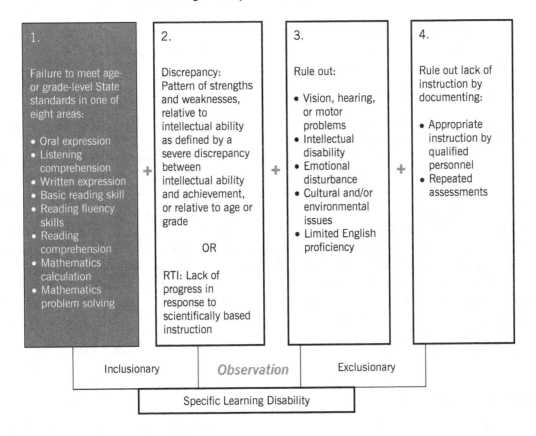

FIGURE 3.1. Schematic diagram of IDEA regulations regarding the criteria for determining SLD, with Criterion 1 highlighted.

the areas identified in the IDEA regulations. Assessment procedures focus on identifying the student's performance on specific skills and subskills to provide information for the eligibility decision and for the development of the eligible student's IEP.

GATHERING EXISTING DATA

As described in Chapter 1, the IDEA regulations specify that as a first step in planning a comprehensive evaluation of a student, the assessment team should review data that already exist regarding the student including "evaluations and information provided by the parents of the child; [c]urrent classroom-based, local, or State assessments, and classroom-based observations; and [o]bservations by teachers and related services providers" (§300.305[a][1]). This provision is particularly salient for schools that are using RTI as part of their eligibility criteria and that have developed the multi-tier infrastructure that is required to effectively and validly determine a student's RTI. As detailed in Chapter 2, a school that has robust procedures for implementing a multi-tier system of supports will have collected during the provision of these supports a wide range of assessment data that not only has informed instruction and intervention but also can be used as important evidence for determining the student's qualifications for special education under the SLD category. This evidence includes the results of state- and/or districtwide tests, universal screening (benchmark testing), and data from progress monitoring.

Statewide and Districtwide Tests

NCLB requires school districts to participate in statewide testing in mathematics and reading or language arts from grades 3 to 8, and at least once from grades 10 to 12. Many states have expanded that mandate to cover additional grades, and many school districts have extended the practice beyond those requirements by purchasing and using commercially available group tests of academic skills. In many locations, students are tested in every grade from 3 to 12. As a result, schools often have a fairly extensive "track record" of an individual student's level of proficiency in reading, mathematics, writing, and some content subjects over a multiyear period. Although each one of these annual results may be suspect given the shortcomings of group-based tests, when taken over multiple years, the trend in the data provides useful evidence. For example, data that indicate that an eighth grader has consistently scored in the proficient range on group tests of reading proficiency from grades 3 to 7 would suggest that "new" academic performance problems in eighth grade would not be the result of an SLD in reading. Again, these data are not conclusive, but can and should be considered as part of the evidence that the evaluation team considers.

Universal Screening

As described in Chapter 2, universal screening of all students on critical academic skills is widely understood to be an important foundation of a multi-tier system of supports and is one of the features that distinguishes an RTI approach from precursor models (Kovaleski & Black, 2010). Universal screenings, typically conducted three times per year, are used to identify students who may be failing to reach proficiency and also usually serve as benchmark testing to determine how students as a group are performing (Kovaleski & Pedersen, 2008). Many schools begin these assessments in kindergarten and continue them through the elementary school years. The availability of these assessments in the primary grades is especially valuable because statewide group testing usually does not begin until third grade. Other school districts extend universal screening beyond the elementary grades into middle and high schools. Although the purpose of screening is to identify students for intervention and to appraise the overall effectiveness of the curriculum and instructional program, the data from screening assessments also serve as another source of useful information about the development of a given student's proficiency in basic skills over a number of years. Like the results of statewide tests, a particular data point may not be conclusive in terms of the extent of the student's deficiencies in relation to grade-level expectations, but the trend in the data over years provides a unique glimpse of how and when the student's difficulties emerged.

Currently, there are technically adequate universal screening instruments in reading, mathematics, and writing. The measures are administered in a number of formats. Perhaps most recognizable are assessments that are based on procedures of CBM, such as AIMSweb (Pearson, 2011), the Dynamic Indicators of Basic Early Literacy Skills (DIBELS) Next (Good et al., 2011), and Easy CBM (Alonzo, Tindal, Ulmer, & Glasgow, 2006). These instruments are typically administered individually, although classwide applications exist for some skills. Another group of measures such as the Classworks Universal Screener (Curriculum Advantage, 1993) allows for group administration and computer scoring. Recently, a number of computer-based approaches that are based on item response theory have emerged, such as STAR Early Literacy (Renaissance Learning, Inc., 2012a), STAR Reading (Renaissance Learning, Inc., 2012c), STAR Mathematics (Renaissance Learning, Inc., 2012b), and the Measures of Academic Progress (Northwest Evaluation Association, 2004). Universal screening of written expression can be conducted with CBM, but this approach appears to be infrequently implemented in the schools at present. There are no current universal screening devices in the other areas of disability as designated by IDEA (i.e., oral expression and listening comprehension). A current list of universal screening instruments, along with ratings of their psychometric characteristics, is maintained by the National Center on Response to Intervention (*www.rti4success.org*).

During each administration of universal screening, students' scores are compared to a benchmark. Benchmarks represent the minimal levels of expected performance, as operationalized through measures of universal screening, progress monitoring, and other procedures. An example of collected oral reading fluency (ORF) data from universal screening over the course of one school year is displayed in Figure 3.2. Benchmark ORF rates in the fall, winter, and spring assessments are 94, 112, and 123 words correct per minute (wcpm) respectively. In contrast, the target (referred) student earned scores of 45, 55, and 61 wcpm on these three assessments. For this student, a clear pattern of deficient performance is evident.

As indicated above, many school districts are currently using computer-adapted testing (CAT) for universal screening. A CAT is a measure that refines the selection of items on the basis of a student's response and provides a mechanism for identifying the particular abilities and potential problem areas within the domain of assessment. The basic concepts on which CAT measures are built are the recognition that there is a progression of skills underlying the academic domain being assessed. Using item response theory to build the measure, a student's competency of specific skills within a domain can be ascertained. The overall scores obtained

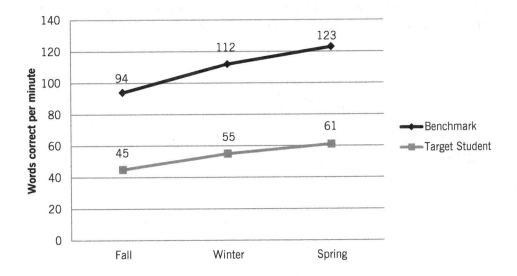

FIGURE 3.2. Example of benchmark assessment of ORF for a fourth-grade student. Norms from Hasbrouck and Tindal (2006) were used to construct the benchmark scores.

on CAT reflect the student's skills in the academic domain of evaluation. Students take CAT measurement systems on computers that are capable of assessing a broad range of student skills in periods as short as 10 to 20 minutes.

CAT measures usually derive a score, typically called a Scaled Score, which defines where on the scale a student's tested abilities fall. In an analogous way, one uses a single metric such as pounds to indicate a person's weight. The same score, pounds, is used to describe weight whether we are measuring a 5-year-old or a 50-year-old individual. However, the weights that are considered "normal" for one's age are different for a 5-year-old and a 50-year-old. Although all individuals are placed on the same metric, the meaning attached to the weight is relative to what is expected for each age. CAT scores are identical in concept. In reading, a student is placed on the scale, and the student's performance is interpreted relative to the expected performance for similar students of the same age or grade. One example of a CAT measure is the Scaled Score derived from STAR Reading (Renaissance Learning, 2012c). On STAR Reading, Scaled Scores range from 0 to 1400 across grade 1 to grade 12. In general, a student scoring at the 40th percentile would be considered to be proficient and one scoring below the 25th percentile would be at risk for academic failure. A score at or below the 10th percentile would be considered a significantly deficient score.

An example of universal screening using CAT (in this case STAR Reading) is presented in Figure 3.3. The benchmark Scaled Scores for fourth grade in fall, winter, and spring are 402, 441, and 470, respectively. The target (referred) student has attained scores of 266, 285, and 310 on these assessments, displaying a clear pattern of deficient performance.

Progress Monitoring Data

As indicated in Chapter 2, a hallmark of multi-tier support systems is the frequent monitoring of students' progress during the course of Tier 2 and 3 interventions. In terms of gathering evidence for the first criterion for SLD determination, the student's scores on a series of progress monitoring measures serves as another piece of data regarding the student's performance level in relation to standards. Procedures for progress monitoring are detailed in Chapter 4.

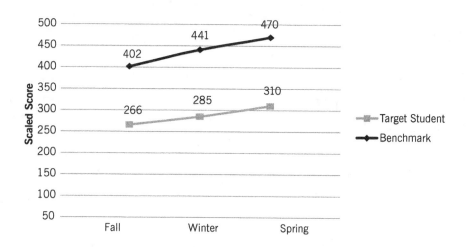

FIGURE 3.3. Example of benchmark assessment using STAR Reading for a fourth-grade student.

USING EXISTING DATA TO QUANTIFY THE EXTENT OF THE ACADEMIC DEFICIENCY: PERFORMING A BENCHMARK GAP ANALYSIS

Once available data have been collected, the evaluation team needs to make an initial determination of the extent of the student's deficiency in his or her academic skills as compared to those of typical students (i.e., the benchmark). A benchmark gap analysis consists of comparing the data collected for the student with what the team determines to constitute proficient performance. The determination of whether this level of deficiency constitutes a qualification for SLD under Criterion 1 is described in Chapter 9. In this section, we describe two examples of conducting a benchmark gap analysis: one with curriculum-based data and one with data from CAT.

Performing a Benchmark Gap Analysis Using CBM

Shinn (2002, 2008) described how CBM data could be used as part of the decision-making process for determining eligibility for special education. The method recommended for CBM data is the calculation of a ratio between the benchmark (proficient) score for the target student's peer group and the score attained by the student. In the following example, ORF data from Hasbrouck and Tindal (2006) are used, with the 50th percentile indicated as proficient performance. As depicted in Figure 3.2, the target student displayed an ORF of 45 wcpm in the fall universal screening. This score could be compared to the average score for the norm group for that grade (94 wcpm) to construct a ratio ([94/45] = 2.1×). That is, the student would be more than two times discrepant from a typically performing student. Following through with the winter and spring assessments, we find that the student's deficiency ratio is 2.0× (112/55) in winter and 2.0× (123/61) in spring. Shinn recommended that 2.0× is a useful parameter for making eligibility decisions for SLD when using CBM. Marston, Muyskens, Lau, and Canter (2003) reported the successful use of this format for identifying students with SLD on a systemwide basis in Minneapolis.

Although this particular format for constructing the deficiency ratio is used on a widespread basis in the CBM literature, it is perhaps more intuitively appealing to reverse the position of the numbers in the numerator and denominator to produce a percentage metric. For example, using the fall scores from above, the ratio would be rendered as 45/94 = 47.8%. The terminology used in this way would indicate that that the gap analysis for this student indicated that he was performing at approximately 48% of what would be expected for his age or grade. The calculations for winter and spring would be (55/112 = 49.1% for winter) and (61/123 = 49.6% for spring). This format may be more understandable for consumers (especially parents).

Performing a Benchmark Gap Analysis Using CAT

A benchmark gap analysis using CAT is performed by a similar procedure to that used for CBM data. In this case, the student's attained Scaled Score is divided by the Scaled Score associated with the 40th percentile. For example, consider a fourth grader who earned a Scaled Score of 266 on STAR Reading in the fall, which is at the 10th percentile (see Figure 3.3). Comparing this Scaled Score with the Scaled Score at the 40th percentile (402) produces the following calculation: 266/402 = 66.2%, which indicates that the student is performing at a level that is approximately 66% of what would be expected for a proficient student. In the winter assessment, the student would have a ratio of (285/441 = 64.6%). In the spring, the ratio would be (310/470 = 66.0%). It should be noted that when using Scaled Scores associated with CAT the reverse ratio (i.e., 2.0×) cannot be used.

CONDUCTING FOLLOW-UP
INDIVIDUAL STUDENT ASSESSMENTS

The existing data sources and the calculation of benchmark gap analyses using the results of universal screening provide an important first step in determining the student's academic deficiencies. Although these analyses give the evaluation team useful information about the student's academic skills in relation to age or state standards, additional in-depth assessment of the student's academic skills is needed for two reasons. First, individual assessment is needed to verify the extent of the deficiency that is suggested by less formal measures (e.g., universal screening). Second, in-depth assessment is needed to fully inform the development of interventions that will be used to rule out lack of instruction in reaching the eligibility decision or to develop the student's IEP, if the student is found to be eligible. In this section, we describe an overall approach to conducting individual academic assessment that not only specifies information about the extent and nature of the academic concern, but also provides a further "drill-down" into the student's academic subskills for intervention planning.

> Individual assessment is needed to verify the extent of the deficiency that is suggested by less formal measures.

The drill-down approach described below is based broadly in the context of the work done over the past 30 years in curriculum-based assessment (CBA; Gickling & Armstrong, 1978; Gickling & Havertape, 1981; Gickling & Rosenfield, 1995), curriculum-based evaluation (CBE; Howell et al., 2008; Howell & Nolet, 2000), and CBM. In a fully formed multi-tier (RTI) model, these types of assessments may have been used prior to consideration for the student's eligibility for special education because they were used to provide data to inform instruction. If the school is using a multi-tier system of support, CBM, CBA and/or CBE data may already be available. If these assessments have not been conducted during the provision of Tier 2 or Tier 3 supports, they should be conducted during the formal evaluation process. We also address the extent to which norm-referenced tests of academic achievement are useful for reaching an eligibility decision and/or planning the IEP if the student is found to be eligible. Historically, norm-referenced tests of academic achievement have been used during the determination of eligibility rather than during the provision of tiered interventions.

CBA Methods

All CBA methods are intended to provide midstream information about student learning to tell the instructor whether instruction is working and what changes need to be made to enhance instructional effects. This approach to assessment can be traced to the seminal work of Deno and Mirkin (1977), whose data-based program modification described a problem-solving approach to the assessment of students' classroom performance problems. In spite of the differences in terminology, there is more overlap between contemporary curriculum-based methods than there are differences. For example, all curriculum-based methods use sets of controlled curriculum materials that reflect (but generally do not come directly from) the student's curriculum. All curriculum-based methods follow standardized administration protocols, allow for repeated assessments to reflect student growth, and provide data useful for planning and adjusting instruction. Readers who are interested in the history of curriculum-based methods and understanding nuanced (and perhaps controversial) distinctions between them are referred to Shinn and Bamonto (1998), Fuchs and Deno (1994), and VanDerHeyden (2005). The distinction between the various curriculum-based methods may be boiled down to a difference in the content that appears on the measure and the time frame within which the instructor/assessor wishes to evaluate learning progress and make adjustments. In our practice, we find that precise measurement of narrowly defined and targeted skills that are taught during intervention and an appraisal of broader competencies that reflect what is needed to be more successful in the curriculum are needed. The content used during assessment depends on the decision the instructor/assessor wishes to make. In the space that follows, we intentionally use CBA as an umbrella term to reflect these methods, which include CBM, CBE, and instructional assessment (Gravois & Gickling, 2008).

Determining the Student's Instructional Level

CBA is intended to embed assessment within the instructional process and to some extent imagines assessment as best conducted during the actual act of instruction. (Gickling [1994] has noted that the Latin root of assess is to "sit beside"; cf. Howell, 2008.) The first step of an individual student assessment using CBA is the determination of the student's instructional level (Betts, 1946). Gickling and his colleagues (Gickling & Armstrong, 1978; Gickling & Thompson, 1985) demonstrated that students made optimal progress when taught at their instructional level as opposed to their frustration or mastery level. Students who were taught at frustration levels grew at slower rates and experienced worse outcomes than those taught at their instructional levels. Gickling and his associates operationalized these levels in terms of the percentage of unknown versus known items in the material to be learned, and they also coded whether the student was being directly instructed or was working independently. As depicted in Table 3.1, when working independently (i.e., without teacher support for correct responding), the percentage of knowns should be between 93 and 97% for optimal learning to occur. In a direct instruction model, where the teacher provides active support for correct responding, there should be 70 to 85% knowns to attain an optimal rate of learning.

The purpose of CBA is to assess the student's current performance in the materials used for instruction to determine whether the student is at mastery, instructional, or frustration level in those materials. If the material is at the frustration level for the student, additional assessment is conducted to determine the level of material that is "workable." That is, the teacher can adjust the level of material to create an appropriate "match" for the student's instructional level. Stated another way, the materials can be made easier in small increments until the student can respond with 93% accuracy for independent work or 70% accuracy on materials for which the teacher will provide direct support during student responding. The student's accuracy of responding is a beacon to the teacher, signaling the type of instructional strategies that will (and will not) be useful given the student's current performance. For example, direct support is needed where

TABLE 3.1. Instructional Ratios of Known to Unknown Material for Mastery, Instructional, and Frustration Levels

Level	Direct instruction	Independent work
Mastery	n/a	> 97%
Instructional	70–85%	93–97%
Frustrational	< 70%	< 93%

student accuracy is low because immediate corrective feedback will be the most useful and important instructional strategy for that student.

Fluency scores (i.e., responses correct per minute) can also be used to determine the instructional level of students. Instructional level can be defined two ways: (1) performance that is at or above the 25th percentile of expected performance within a grade, or (2) performance that is at an empirically identified level that forecasts future success in learning as has been the tradition in precision teaching (Haughton, 1980) and is commonly used in systems that link screening performances to high probabilities of positive outcomes, such as passing the year-end high-stakes test or performing outside of the risk range at the subsequent screening (e.g., DIBELS and iSTEEP [2011]). Using normative data provided by specific products such as AIMSweb (Pearson, 2011), iSTEEP, or aggregated normative data from multiple sources as reported by Hasbrouck and Tindal (2006), the specific fluency level that would define frustration level (i.e., below the 25th percentile) can be identified. For example, based on normative data provided by AIMSweb, for students in the spring of third grade, reading fewer than 92 wcpm on a grade-level passage signifies that the student is at the frustration level. Use of fluency criteria on controlled tasks to determine instructional level might be familiar to readers who have used DIBELS for assessment and who have used Web-based systems like AIMSweb and iSTEEP.

Using the Instructional Hierarchy to Guide Assessment

To plan interventions in a multi-tier system, the assessment team assesses a target skill, one at a time, sampling back through incrementally easier levels of the task, to determine (1) whether the child can respond independently; (2) whether the child's responding is accurate and, if so, fluent; and (3) whether incentives and instructional support allow the child to perform the skill in a more proficient way. The purpose of this assessment is to identify the skills for which the child requires instruction and to identify the type of instruction that will produce the greatest effect on learning. The scientific underpinnings of this procedure come from the instructional hierarchy (Gickling & Armstrong, 1978; Gickling & Thompson, 1985; Haring & Eaton, 1978) and reflect the notion that effective instruction is aligned with the proficiencies and capacities that the child already has. Successful intervention planning involves improving the "fit" between the student and the expectations for learning in the classroom. To improve the fit, instructors must improve the child's skills *and* adjust the task to better support student performance and skill development (Rosenfield, 2002). Children with weak skills often show poor learning in general education instruction simply because the content is too challenging or, stated another way, there is a mismatch between the student's capacity and the environmental supports provided for learning. For example, a teacher may assign three-digit computation with regrouping for independent work in the classroom when most students in the classroom are able to respond accurately without adult assistance. For the struggling student who does not understand how to regroup and perhaps is not fluent with addition facts, independent practice or the instruction provided by the general education teacher is actually contraindicated and may do more harm than good for this struggling student.

As noted by others in the past, the first step is specifying what we expect students to learn and the second step is determining the extent to which students have mastered those skills or require further instruction (Bushell & Baer, 1994). Teachers must map out a sequence of critical learning outcomes at each grade level. Identifying essential skills by grade level is not difficult because of the wide availability of the documents describing curriculum standards. Many states have adopted the Common Core State Standards (National Governors Association Center for Best Practices, 2010), and these provide an excellent starting place to map out the sequence of skills that students are expected to master at each grade level. Each skill that appears in the standards can be further broken down into subskills. For example, in first grade, the Common Core State Standards specify that students should be able to add and subtract within 20 in mathematics. The skill of adding and subtracting within 20 can be broken down into adding to 20 and subtracting with minuends (i.e., first number in the problem) up to 20. These skills can be further broken down to addition with sums to 5, sums to 9, sums to 10, sums to 15, sums to 20, and so on. This map of skills should be arranged beginning at the goal level of performance, with the teacher working backward through incrementally easier tasks as a map for assessment. The purpose of assessment is to find out what stage of learning the student performs at for skills near the goal skill.

The instructional hierarchy (Haring & Eaton, 1978) asserts that skill mastery progresses through four predictable stages of learning including:

- Acquisition
- Fluency
- Generalization
- Adaptation

At the acquisition stage, the skill has not yet been established. The goal of acquisition instruction is to establish correct responding toward conceptual understanding (Harniss, Stein, & Carnine, 2002). Conceptual understanding is apparent when the child can demonstrate understanding of the conditions under which the response is correct and incorrect. Conceptual understanding can be demonstrated in a variety of ways. For example, the teacher can ask the child to draw a picture showing how he or she got an answer, to think aloud when solving a problem, to answer a series of true/false problems, and to change an incorrect answer to a correct one and explain how the change made the answer correct. These approaches provide a window for teachers into the understandings of students so that a teacher can know that a student did not obtain the correct answer by chance or memory alone. Memorized responses are important and can facilitate learning, but only so long as the student understands the conceptual basis for the response. For example, if the student does not under-

> **Four stages of learning:**
>
> - **Acquisition**
> - **Fluency**
> - **Generalization**
> - **Adaptation**

stand how to read a sentence for meaning, use decoding strategies, and finally use context clues to read an unknown word, then simply memorizing the sight word will likely fail the child because all memorized responses are prone to be forgotten. When a memorized response is forgotten, the child must be able to use strategies to obtain the correct response. During acquisition, the teacher should monitor response accuracy on brief tasks attempted without teacher assistance and assess conceptual understanding directly before moving to fluency-building instruction. Once the child is accurate for 90% of responses or better without teacher assistance and the child can demonstrate conceptual understanding, the child is ready for fluency-building instruction on the particular task.

At the fluency-building stage of learning, the skill has been established. In other words, the child understands how to respond correctly or obtain the correct answer. The goal of fluency-building instruction is to increase the ease with which a child can respond correctly. During acquisition instruction, we have monitored accuracy of responding usually measuring the percentage of correct responses. Before moving into fluency-building instruction, the child's performance is near a ceiling on what percent correct can tell us. That is, once a child's performance reaches 100% correct responding, there is nothing more that we can gain from percent correct responding to indicate improved learning. Yet there are important differences in the proficiency of a student who can respond correctly on 100% of problems but whose performance is labored and hesitant compared to the student who can respond 100% correctly but whose performance is automatic. Once a child enters the fluency-building stage of instruction, there must be a timed dimension to performance measurement to detect further gains in proficiency. This can be accomplished using any score reflecting responses correct per minute, which can be obtained from 1-minute timed tests or longer tests that are timed and then divided by the number of minutes to obtain a per-minute estimate of performance (Johnson & Street, 2013).

Once a child's performance speeds up without any losses to accuracy, usually reflected by high rates of responses correct per minute, the child is ready for generalization instruction. In some cases, a student can readily use a learned skill in situations that differ from the training situation. So for example, a student who has learned to add two vertical numbers may respond correctly and easily to the same problem when it is arranged horizontally or within a word problem. Sometimes, however, children (especially those with SLD) may require support to use a learned skill in different contexts or under different task demand arrangements. During generalization instruction, the teacher should closely attend to accuracy of student responding and verify that errors do not reappear.

Once the assessment team has specified a sequence of skills and identified the stage of learning at which the child is performing, the team can plan an individualized intervention and monitor student progress. These data can be used to rule out lack of adequate instruction to determine eligibility for SLD and can also be used to guide development of the IEP (discussed in detail in Chapter 10). Curriculum-based methods create a series of "snapshots," or short assessments, that are embedded within an instructional process and interspersed among teaching trials. The teacher alternately assesses the student and adjusts the next teaching episode depending on the student's response. A sequence of posed questions and decision points allows the teacher/assessor to determine the student's particular knowledge and skills. In reading, for example, this sequence addresses the following skills: language/prior knowledge, word recognition, word study, fluency, responding, comprehension, and metacognition. Although the act of reading is understood as being larger than each of these individual components, the assessment of each of these components is used to conceptualize the student's skills within the reading process, which pinpoints strategies that should be included in the next lesson (Gravois & Gickling, 2008). The applicability of curriculum-based methods to an RTI framework is straightforward, in that the ongoing improvement of instruction is central to the delivery of intensive, supplemental interventions at Tiers 2 and 3.

What typically happens during core instruction in general education is that the teacher often plans "balanced" instruction to support initial skill acquisition, opportunities for guided practice and feedback, checking for understanding, fluency-building practice, and an opportunity to apply the learned skill each day. When teachers introduce new content, they can generally assume that most students in the class will function at the acquisition stage of learning. Once a lesson has been taught, the teacher can verify student understanding, and then assume that most children are ready for fluency-building strategies. Most children will respond over time when this type of instruction is offered even when it is not perfectly aligned with each student's skill proficiency at each moment in time. For some children, however, the instruction will not be a good match with their capacities or proficiencies and they will fall into the risk category at screening. Tier 2 can be very effective in rapidly improving the skills of students so the core instruction is functionally a better match with those students' proficiencies. Students who do not experience success with Tier 2 intervention require individualized assessment to plan an intensive individualized intervention.

Drilling Down to Identify Skill Deficits

In addition to identifying the student's instructional level, additional assessments can be conducted to "drill down" to identify the student's performance on critical subskills within a particular academic domain (i.e., reading, mathematics, written expression). These assessment procedures are best accomplished during the provision of intervention support, but can also be utilized as part of a comprehensive evaluation if the assessments were not conducted earlier. This drill-down approach is based on CBE (Howell et al., 2008; Howell & Nolet, 2000), which is not an assessment type per se, but rather a framework for making instructional decisions in the form of a series of sequentially posed "if–then" questions that are answered by assessment data. By working through conceptual flowcharts, the assessor creates a precise profile of the student's skills in the academic domain and identifies those subskills that are the source of the student's deficiency. For example, in assessing a fifth grader's reading, the assessor might first measure the student's comprehension. If satisfactory, the assessment would end. If not, the student's ORF would be addressed. If ORF is satisfactory, it would be concluded that the student's difficulties lie in comprehension rather than more basic reading subskills. If ORF is not satisfactory, further assessments are sequentially administered to drill down to determine whether the student has difficulties with more basic reading skills, such as accuracy, alphabetic principle, or phonemic awareness. Intervention is planned for the subskills that are the source or cause of the reading problem.

Generally, the assessment sequence begins with measures that appraise performance at higher levels of proficiency, followed by additional brief assessments of the individual component skills or subskills. In early reading (Hosp & MacConnell, 2008), the process might begin with an assessment of ORF or word identification fluency, and proceed "downward" to assess the student's nonsense word fluency, letter-sound fluency, and/or phonemic segmentation fluency. For secondary students who are reading to learn rather than learning to read (Howell, 2008), the process might begin with a number of posed alternative hypotheses that are tested through measures of comprehension (e.g., CBM maze, retell), metacognition (e.g., think-aloud protocols), vocabulary (e.g., vocabulary matching), or reading decoding (e.g., ORF). If the student's reading is satisfactory based on these measures, a likely hypothesis is that the student lacks background knowledge in the content subject of concern, which can be assessed with an analysis of the student's performance on class- and text-related assignments. If one or more of the areas of reading are identified as deficient, assessments are continued until the problematic subskills are identified. For example, because it is not uncommon for secondary students to have difficulty with basic reading skills, assessment of decoding skills might proceed past ORF and downward to assessments of word identification fluency, nonsense word fluency, and so on. A useful commercially available assessment product that incorporates the drill-down format is the CORE Multiple Measures (Consortium on Reading Excellence, 2008), which features a series of short assessments of various reading subskills. The format of this measure is to start with higher-level reading skills (e.g., comprehension) and systematically conduct follow-up assessments depending on the performance of the student on each assessment.

The drill-down process for mathematics is particularly straightforward, given the hierarchical structure of math skills (Kelley, 2008). Depending on the grade level, a survey assessment is constructed that taps many or most of the skills appropriate for that level, with perhaps one or two items composed for each subskill. The results of this survey assessment are then used to create hypotheses about the student's subskills, which are then tested through individual specific-skill assessments. Using the "if–then" decision-making format, these specific assessments continue until a complete picture of the student's mathematics attainments and deficiencies is constructed. Interventions are created to address deficient subskills.

Road-Testing the Intervention before It Is Deployed

In the previous sections, we discussed the wealth of information that can be gleaned from directly assessing the skills students are expected to be able to do to determine whether students conceptually understand, can fluently perform, and can use the learned skill in applied tasks. This information allows data teams to pinpoint the intervention content that will be important, including which skills and subskills should be targeted during intervention and which instructional strategies will be of the greatest benefit to the student (i.e., acquisition strategies, fluency-building strategies, generalization support). Even with all of this information available to plan intervention, there is only one way to be certain that the planned intervention will work if properly used. Since the mid-1980s, a technology has evolved that allows educators to test the effects of certain interventions on learning before the intervention is broadly used. This allows educators to rapidly and directly examine which instructional strategies will improve learning for a given student before large amounts of materials and time are invested using that strategy. This technology has been described as removing the guesswork from intervention planning, providing users with a method to "road test" an intervention before that intervention is used. Knowing that an intervention can work is powerful information that allows an educator to focus on troubleshooting a promising intervention in the classroom to be sure those effects are attained rather than rapidly abandoning the intervention strategy when effects are not obtained right away.

The technology for testing an intervention is called "functional academic assessment" and is based on the science of functional behavioral assessment (Iwata, Dorsey, Slifer, Bauman, & Richman, 1982). In 1986, Lentz and Shapiro detailed how certain environmental variables could be demonstrated to interfere with or maintain correct academic responding. A line of research referred to as brief experimental analysis of academic responding or functional academic assessment ensued, describing procedures for testing the effect of learning accelerators (Daly, Martens, Hamler, Dool, & Eckert, 1999; Daly, Witt, Martens, & Dool, 1997; Noell et al., 1998). Conditions included reducing task difficulty, providing small rewards for performance improvements, and providing instructional supports like listening passage preview or repeated reading. Fluent performance was measured as the conditions were changed using metrics like wcpm or digits correct per 2 minutes. Just like functional behavioral assessment, elevated performance in a given condition demonstrated a functional relationship between instructional conditions and learning. If a child's performance did not improve when small rewards were offered for a higher score, but did improve when task difficulty was reduced, then reducing task difficulty would be identified as an effective strategy to improve that child's performance.

In academic domains, skill-related variables like task difficulty, task novelty, practice with component or prerequisite skills, instructional prompting, and number of opportunities to respond are some examples of instructional conditions that may be tested to see if they improve a child's learning. The conditions that are tested can be greatly narrowed based on the student's stage of learning for a particular skill. If the child is at the acquisition stage of learning, the teacher might test the effects of reducing task difficulty, providing prompts or cues, providing incentives, and providing guided practice opportunities. If the child is at the fluency-building stage of learning for the target skill, the teacher might test the effects of incentives of various types on student performance and the use of timed trials with delayed feedback. Functional academic assessment embodies an ecologic conceptualization of assessment known as ICEL-RIOT (see Figure 3.4; Christ, 2008; Heartland Area Education Agency 11, 2006) in which sources of information about the instructional process, including instruction (I), curriculum (C), environment (E), and the learner (L) are assessed through review (R) of products and records, interview (I), observation (O), and testing (T).

Quantifying the Collected Data

The data derived from curriculum-based methods for use in the eligibility decision-making process consist of a break-down of overall reading, mathematics, or written language performance into their component subskills at the student's grade level. Currently, these data are often conveyed in a statistical, norm-referenced format, through commercially available assessment products (e.g., DIBELS Next, AIMSweb, Easy CBM) or through published sources (e.g., Hasbrouck & Tindal, 2006). For some skills and subskills, data are represented as percentages (e.g., percent of comprehension questions answered correctly, percent of known vs. unknown words). For a student being evaluated for eligibility for special education, data on each of the

> **For a student being evaluated for eligibility for special education, data on each of the subskills can be harvested and used to inform eligibility and plan the IEP.**

subskills can be harvested and used to inform eligibility and plan the IEP. One particular strength of curriculum-based methods of assessment as part of eligibility determination is that

		Multiple Methods of Assessment			
		Review	Interview	Observe	Test
Multiple Sources of Information	Instruction	Permanent products of student's work, records of prior strategies and their effects, lesson plans	Teachers, parents, paraprofessionals, administrators, and peers to describe experiences and perceptions of pace, opportunities to respond, engagement, contingencies, and activities	When and where the problem is most likely and least likely to occur	Systematic manipulations of procedures that include opportunities to respond, repeated practice, durations, contingencies, or activities
	Curriculum	Books, worksheets, software, scope, and sequence	Teachers, parents, paraprofessionals, administrators, and peers to describe content, organization, difficulty, and level	When and where the problem is most likely and least likely to occur	Systematic manipulations of difficulty, stimulus presentation, interspersed materials, and content
	Environment	Seating charts, rules, school layout	Teachers, parents, paraprofessionals, administrators, and peers to describe organization, rules, and set up	When and where the problem is most likely and least likely to occur	Systematic manipulations of praise, contingencies, escape, work completion, criteria for success and failure, seating, and distractions
	Learner	Educational records, health records, prior tests and reports	Teachers, parents, paraprofessionals, administrators, and peers to describe observations and experiences with a specific student or group	When and where the problem is most likely and least likely to occur	

FIGURE 3.4. ICEL/RIOT format of assessment domains. From "Best Practices in Problem Analysis" by T. J. Christ (2008), in *Best Practices in School Psychology V*, p. 169. Copyright 2008 by the National Association of School Psychologists, Bethesda, MD. Reprinted with permission of the publisher. *www.nasponline.org*.

the assessment, by definition, is based on the school's curriculum, which is likely to have extensive overlap with state standards as required by IDEA. Furthermore, data may be available indicating the stage of learning for the target skill (or type of intervention that is likely to be effective) and may provide a direct test of several instructional strategies on student performance. These data allow the evaluation team to rule out lack of instruction in reaching an eligibility decision (see Chapter 6 for more information) and/or construct an IEP if the student is found to be eligible (see Chapter 10).

Norm-Referenced Tests

Traditionally, norm-referenced tests of student's academic skills have been used in the determination of eligibility for special education, particularly the identification of SLD. Norm-referenced tests have been used to determine a student's level of achievement in the ability–achievement discrepancy approach. Instruments such as the Wechsler Individual Achievement

Test (WIAT; Wechsler, 2009) and the Woodcock–Johnson Test of Achievement (Woodcock, McGrew, & Mather, 2001) have been used to assess overall academic achievement as well as performance on subskills and therefore provide users with information useful for identifying skills that should be targeted during intervention. However, norm-referenced achievement tests are not useful in identifying effective intervention strategies and testing interventions before they are used. An interesting question is whether norm-referenced tests of academic achievement may or should be used when RTI is the school district's chosen method of determining eligibility under Criterion 2 of the SLD requirements. We will address the "may" and "should" questions in turn.

In terms of the IDEA statute and regulations, there is nothing to prevent the use of norm-referenced tests of academic achievement (or any other test, for that matter) if a school district is using RTI as part of its eligibility criteria for SLD. Any test that provides useful information about the extent of the student's deficiency in relation to grade and/or state standards or informs the development of the IEP may be used. There is no question that most widely used norm-referenced tests of academic achievement yield reliable and valid scores reflecting a student's competency relative to other same-age peers. However, there is cause to question the extent to which norm-referenced tests are adequate measures of the student's skills in relation to state standards. Understanding a student's competency in relation to state standards is a requirement of IDEA. In a classic study, Jenkins and Pany (1978) determined that there were variable amounts of overlap among items sampled on various tests of academic achievement and corresponding content of various reading curriculum products, a finding that was subsequently corroborated by research by Shapiro and Derr (1987) and Good and Salvia (1988). The implication was that students learning in different reading series would perform differently depending on the test used to measure their reading skills. In other words, students may perform lower on a norm-referenced test, not because they are at greater risk than other students who perform higher, but because they have been taught different skills. This problem creates instability and error in the decision process because concluding a student is low achieving may be an artifact of the assessment tool used rather than "real" risk or low achievement. Hence, in selecting a norm-referenced test, users must verify that the test items are aligned with the state standards. To the extent that test developers incorporate test items that overlap extensively with standards from the state where the test is given, norm-referenced tests may be appropriate in that state.

If norm-referenced tests of academic achievement may be used in an RTI approach to eligibility decision making, should they be used? In this chapter, we have noted that testing should be used to answer questions that have not already been adequately addressed through other means. As we have described, during the provision of multi-tier interventions and supports, extensive data will have been gathered to answer the question as to whether the student's academic skills are deficient in relation to age or state standards. These measures include performance on state and district proficiency tests, universal screening/benchmark measures, progress monitoring, and in-depth academic assessment using curriculum-based methods. As reflected by their name, curriculum-based methods have the strong advantage of being related to standards and therefore have a strong probability of being valid assessments of the student's skills in relation to those standards. The evaluation team needs to decide whether these data are reliable and valid and fully answer the Criterion 1 question. If the team agrees that there is a preponderance of psychometrically sound data that establishes the presence or absence of an academic deficiency in relation to age and state standards, no further assessment, including norm-referenced tests, is indicated. If there is any reason to suspect the accuracy or quality of the data collected during the intervention period, the use of norm-referenced tests may make sense as a means to verify an academic deficiency. In addition, norm-referenced tests such as the WIAT or Woodcock–Johnson Tests of Achievement may be necessary if the SLD is in the area of oral expression or listening comprehension because curriculum-based measures are not available for these competencies. For other areas of SLD eligibility, a decision to conduct a more extensive CBA could be a viable and fruitful alternative to consider using during the evaluation period. We hope that evaluation teams make these decisions based on the needs of the student and the advantages of tests in question. A tenet of appropriate test use is that the test should be selected based on the decision one wishes to make, and there should be available data to indicate that the selected test offers the strongest basis for reaching the desired decision (AERA/APA/NCME, 1999).

> A tenet of appropriate test use is that the test should be selected based on the decision one wishes to make.

SUMMARY

In summary, the collection of data to inform decision making regarding the student's eligibility for special education under Criterion 1 begins with an analysis of existing data, including the student's performance on state proficiency tests and other locally administered assessments. Data collected during universal screening through either curriculum-based methods or CAT provide an important source of information as well as a framework to conduct an initial benchmark gap analysis. Follow-up assessments that address the student's instructional level and the acquisition of skills within an instructional hierarchy provides a basis for knowing which skills and subskills the student has or has not mastered and the types of instructional strategies that are aligned with the student's needs. Beyond the determination of relative deficiency needed as evidence for exceptionality, the many sources of data developed through specific skill assessments may be tested as hypotheses to provide precise data for the development of the IEP, including present educational levels and goals.

CHAPTER 4

Determining Rate of Improvement

In this chapter we present computing rate of improvement (ROI) as part of a comprehensive assessment of the student's RTI. This assessment fulfills the requirements for the second criterion for the determination of SLD. As depicted in Figure 4.1, this criterion requires that "the child does not make sufficient progress to meet age or State-approved grade-level standards . . . when using a process based on the child's response to scientific, research-based intervention" (IDEA Regulations, 2006, §300.309[a][2][i]), and is the alternative to the approach based on the student's pattern of strengths and weaknesses. It also serves as the second part of the so-called dual discrepancy (Fuchs, 2003; Fuchs et al., 2002) described in the Chapter 3.

Perhaps the key decision in determining eligibility for SLD is establishing the rate of change over time of a student's performance. Within an RTI model, at the point where a student is being considered for special education eligibility, the student should have had intensive interventions for a sustained period of time. Throughout the implementation of those interventions within the tiered model, student performance should have been monitored frequently. To determine whether the student is making adequate or inadequate progress, the level of the referred student's growth needs to be compared against grade-level expectations. Understanding the student's rate of growth relative to the rate of growth needed for long-term academic success is the essence of determining whether the student has responded to instruction and intervention. Commonly known as the ROI, a careful method for calculating and interpreting improvement is crucial in using an RTI method for determining the presence of an SLD.

KEY TERMS AND CALCULATION OF BENCHMARK ROI

To fully understand the process of calculating ROI, certain key terms must be understood. *Typical benchmark ROI* refers to the growth rate of a grade-level peer and represents the growth required during the course of typical instruction to meet the minimal level expected of all students. Within an RTI model, universal screening data provide an indication of what level of performance on particular tasks is expected at each grade level in the fall, winter, and

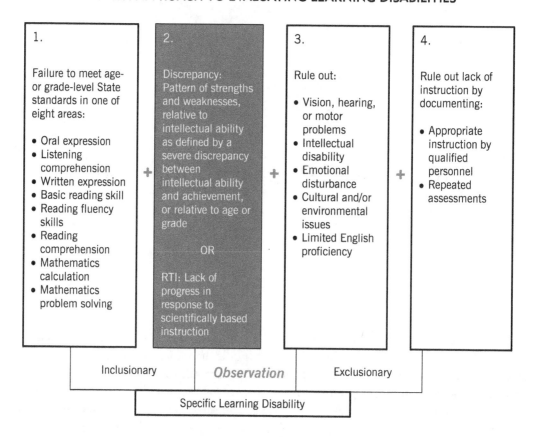

FIGURE 4.1. Schematic diagram of IDEA Regulations regarding the criteria for determining SLD, with Criterion 2 highlighted.

Typical benchmark ROI = growth rate of grade-level peers

Attained benchmark ROI = actual growth rate of referred student

Targeted benchmark ROI = desired growth rate of referred student

spring of a school year. Scores are identified that indicate successful performance on the universal screening measures, and these scores are often referred to as "benchmarks." Using the benchmark levels of typical performing students at each point in time, the ROI can be calculated to show how much growth would be required between screening intervals for students to meet expected learning benchmarks.

For example, Figure 4.2 shows the fall, winter, and spring benchmarks for DIBELS Next for a second-grade student on the measure of ORF. As shown in the figure, the defined benchmark for students at second grade on the measure is 52 wcpm at fall, 72 wcpm at winter, and 87 wcpm at spring. It is important to keep in mind that the methods by which benchmarks are set vary across measures. On the DIBELS Next, the benchmarks (including those for reading CBM) were set based on empirically determined conditional probabilities that predict with 80 to 90% accuracy that students achieving the identified benchmark score in fall would likely achieve the identified benchmark score in winter (Good et al., 2011). In contrast, reading curriculum-based measurement (R-CBM) used by AIMSweb identifies the benchmark scores as a specific point in a normative distribution (Pearson, 2011, *AIMSweb.com*). If one were using AIMSweb, the user would define a specific percentile of the distribution and select that point as representing the benchmark for typical student performance. For example, on AIMSweb R-CBM, the 40th percentile of the distribution for second graders represented scores of 53 wcpm in fall, 80 wcpm at winter, and 96 wcpm at spring. Each measure will have its own set of benchmark scores.

Typical benchmark ROI reflects the growth rate expected of students who begin the year at benchmark and remain at benchmark across the school year. Thus, in the example from Figure 4.2, the typical benchmark ROI is 87 wcpm (spring performance) – 52 wcpm (fall performance)/36 (total weeks of school in a school year) = 0.97 wcpm per week. Thus a typical performing second grader is expected to gain approximately 1 wcpm per week.

The *attained benchmark ROI* refers to the actual level of a student's performance. As indicated on Figure 4.2, the referred student's performance assessed at fall, winter, and spring was 20 wcpm, 37 wcpm, and 50 wcpm, respectively. The target student's "attained benchmark ROI" is calculated by subtracting the end-of-year score from the beginning-of-year score and dividing by the number of weeks in a school year. In the example from Figure 4.2, 50 wcpm (spring performance) – 20 wcpm (fall performance)/36 weeks = 0.83 wcpm per week.

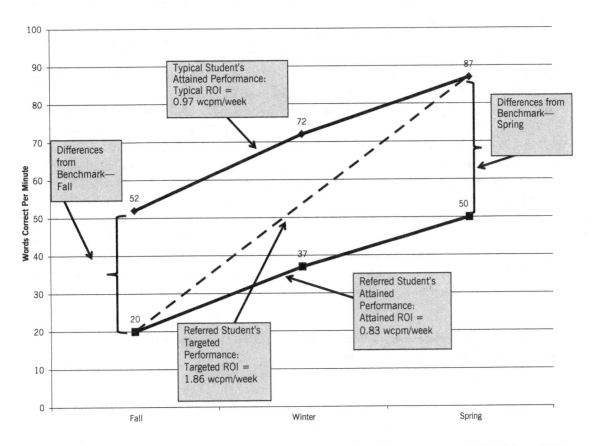

FIGURE 4.2. Second-grade student's typical and attained performance on DIBELS Next ORF across a year.

To understand how much of a gap exists between the target and typical performing student, a third value is calculated, the *targeted benchmark ROI*. This is calculated by using the end-of-year benchmark value of typically performing students, subtracting the attained performance of the referred student at the beginning of the year, and dividing by the number of weeks between the measurements. As illustrated in Figure 4.2, 87 wcpm (end-of-year benchmark performance) − 20 wcpm (beginning-of-year attained performance of target student) / 36 weeks (total weeks in a school year) = 1.86 wcpm per week. This value represents the rate at which the target student needs to progress across the year to completely close the gap with typical peers.

Full-Year or Midyear Benchmark ROI?

There are several key assumptions built into the calculation of benchmark ROI. First, it is assumed that the growth rate from fall to spring across a school year is a linear progression. That is, by subtracting the end of the year from the beginning of the year, we assume that the path from fall to spring that a student grows is a straight line. During the school year in a universal screening model, midyear data are collected. The question of whether the change from fall to spring is really linear can be examined by determining whether the growth from fall to winter is the same as from winter to spring.

Several researchers have examined whether the growth rate across years actually follows a linear trend (Ardoin & Christ, 2008; Christ, Silberglitt, Yeo, & Cormier, 2010; Graney, Missal, Martinez, & Bergstrom, 2009). In general, with few exceptions, greater growth appears to occur from fall to winter than from winter to spring, and this occurs in almost every grade. In addition, AIMSweb provides normative data from large samples of diverse schools using their product in collecting universal screening in reading. Using 36 weeks as the total weeks for a school year and 18 weeks as a half year, Table 4.1 shows the normative performance for students at the 50th percentile for grades 2 and 3 across fall, winter, and spring, with calculations of fall to winter, winter to spring, and fall to spring benchmark ROI. As evident from the table, the growth rates for the fall to spring are substantially higher than winter to spring.

Many reasons are speculated as to why growth rates are not linear throughout the entire academic year. Some suggest that the intensity of instruction is usually greater in the first half of the school year compared to the second half. Anecdotal evidence often shows that interruptions to the school schedule (i.e., field trips, assemblies, vacations) are more common in the spring semester, and such normal aspects of schools can disrupt the efforts to focus on instruction.

TABLE 4.1. Growth Rates from AIMSweb (Pearson, 2011) Normative Data for Grades 2 and 3 at the 50th Percentile on R-CBM

Grade	Benchmark Scores			ROI Fall to Winter	ROI Winter to Spring	ROI Fall to Spring
	Fall	Winter	Spring			
2	62	88	106	1.44	1.00	1.22
3	87	111	127	1.33	0.89	1.11

Another reason often cited is that the state assessments which have become a mandated part of the school year occur in early spring, and efforts to prepare students for the examinations can interrupt the normal instructional process resulting in a slowing of the learning process. Finally, some speculate that following administration of the year-end assessment, more time is allocated to enrichment or end-of-year activities, and there is, in effect, a decrease in instructional time allocations following the year-end assessment.

A fourth reason that has been speculated as to why there seems to be a decline in growth from winter to spring is related to what many term the "summer slide." Over the summer months students may lose some ground in terms of academic performance. Because fall screening often is conducted in the days or weeks at the start of the school year, it is possible that student performance is somewhat lower than would be expected given the loss of performance over the summer break. As such, the growth rate may appear accelerated from fall to winter due primarily to a fall data point that may be somewhat lower than it would be if the fall benchmark data would be collected a month later.

Finally, it is also suggested that the pattern of growth from fall to winter and winter to spring appears to be so universal that it truly represents how students actually acquire the needed knowledge across a school year. That is, students do indeed acquire new knowledge at a rapid pace in the first half of a school year and consolidate that knowledge in the second half of the school year.

Regardless of the reasons for the apparent differential rate of growth across school years, it is important that benchmark ROI be calculated on a half-year basis rather than a full-year basis, to more accurately represent the student's performance against expectations of typically performing students. Thus in our example of the second grade student in Figure 4.2, typical benchmark ROI for fall to winter = 1.11 wcpm/week (i.e., [72 wcpm – 52 wcpm]/18 weeks) and 0.83 wcpm/week (i.e., [87 – 72]/18 weeks) for winter to spring. The target student's fall-to-winter benchmark ROI would be 0.94 wcpm/week (i.e., [37 wcpm – 20 wcpm]/18 weeks) and winter-to-spring would be 0.72 wcpm/week (i.e., [50 wcpm – 37 wcpm]/18 weeks).

Illustrations from a Non-CBM Measure

The same principles and methods described for calculating benchmark ROI for a CBM measure (such as ORF or R-CBM) can also be applied to non-CBM measures. One of those measures is a score based on a computer-adaptive test (CAT). As described in Chapter 3, a CAT is a measure that refines the selection of items on the basis of a student's response, typically using item response theory, and provides a mechanism for identifying the particular abilities and potential problem areas within the domain of assessment. On an academic domain such as mathematics, a student is placed on the scale and the student's performance is interpreted relative to the expected performance for similar students of the same age or grade. One example of a CAT measure is the Scaled Score derived from STAR Math (Renaissance Learning, 2012b). On the STAR, scaled scores range from 0 to 1400 across grade 1 to grade 12. Students in grade 2, for example, are expected to have a fall scaled score between approximately 310 (10th percentile) and 539 (90th percentile; see Figure 4.3). Figure 4.4 illustrates calculations of typical, attained, and targeted benchmark ROI for a second-grade student who began the year at the 10th percentile, compared to typical students at the 40th percentile on the STAR Math measure. The 40th percentile is used, as this often represents a commonly selected level to identify the benchmark performance of students within each grade, with scores falling below the 25th percentile representing the group of students at high risk for academic failure. Schools are free to select performance that is higher or lower than the 40th percentile to represent the level that corresponds to proficient for their particular school and context.

As evident from Figure 4.4, the typical benchmark ROI was calculated by subtracting the spring minus fall scaled score and dividing by total weeks in the school year (i.e., [492–405]/36 weeks = 2.42 SS points/week), for a student starting and ending the year at the 40th percentile, and the attained benchmark ROI was calculated by subtracting the student's actual spring minus fall scaled score and dividing by total weeks in the school year (i.e., [400–310]/36 weeks = 2.50 SS points/week). The targeted benchmark ROI for this student was calculated by subtracting the spring scaled score for the typical student minus the student's fall scaled score and dividing by the number of weeks in the school year (i.e., [492–310]/36 weeks = 5.06 SS points/week). The resulting value represents the ROI needed by the student to close the gap between himself and peers who are at benchmark at the spring assessment. Similar to using CBM, evaluation teams may decide to calculate half-year ROIs rather than full-year ROIs when comparing attained benchmark ROI to typical benchmark ROI using CAT scores.

Grade	Percentile	Fall September Scaled Score	Winter January Scaled Score	Spring May Scaled Score	Moderate Growth Rate Scaled Score /Week
1	10	237	257	286	5.7
	20	263	286	329	4.6
	25	269	299	342	4.6
	40	295	331	376	4.2
	50	307	351	400	3.9
	75	360	405	461	3.4
	90	405	467	513	1.9
2	10	310	363	411	4.4
	20	352	406	448	3.5
	25	363	420	459	3.5
	40	405	454	492	3.2
	50	429	472	511	3.0
	75	484	530	564	2.4
	90	539	578	614	1.7
3	10	423	448	472	3.8
	20	458	487	524	3.4
	25	471	503	542	3.4
	40	507	544	581	3.1
	50	528	566	603	2.9
	75	582	624	657	2.5
	90	632	674	698	1.6

FIGURE 4.3. Normative scaled scores across percentiles for STAR Math. From "STAR Math: Computer-Adaptive Math Test," 2012. Used with permission from Renaissance Learning, Inc.

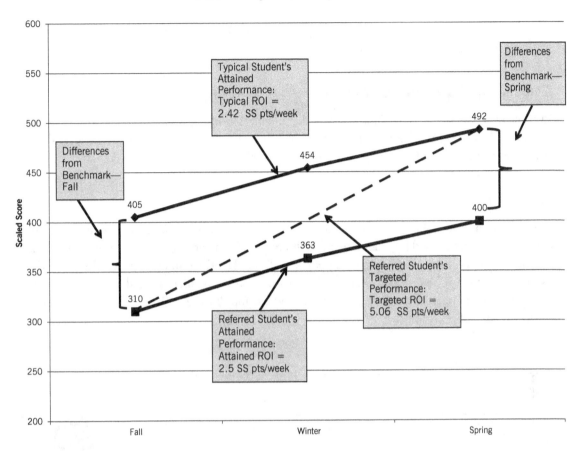

FIGURE 4.4. Second-grade student's typical and attained performance on STAR Math across a year.

PROGRESS MONITORING ROI

When students are provided with supplemental instruction at Tiers 2 or 3, progress monitoring data are collected on a periodic basis. The progress monitoring data offer a perspective on the degree to which the instruction is improving overall student outcomes and how likely a student is to meet the goals set for instruction. *Progress monitoring ROI*, as distinguished from benchmark ROI, is the ROI that occurs from the beginning to the end of the intervention and provides one index of the student's RTI. Determining the progress monitoring ROI offers another important metric that informs the overall special education eligibility decision.

> **Progress monitoring ROI occurs from the beginning to the end of the intervention as calculated by the trend established in the progress monitoring data points.**

As with benchmark ROI, three important terms are considered when examining outcomes—typical progress monitoring ROI, targeted progress monitoring ROI, and attained progress monitoring ROI. The typical benchmark ROI and targeted benchmark ROI as described previously are used as the values against which the student's attained progress monitoring ROI is compared. The major differences for progress monitoring ROI occur with the calculation of the student's attained progress monitoring ROI.

Calculating Attained ROI for Progress Monitoring

ROI for progress monitoring data involves the calculation of the trend established across the progress monitoring data points. Three possible methods are used to calculate the trend: (1) two-point ROI, (2) modified two-point ROI, and (3) ordinary least squares.

Two-Point ROI

Calculating the two-point ROI is the easiest and simplest of the methods and is calculated identically to the process used for calculating benchmark ROI. The ending data point in the series is subtracted from the initial starting data point and divided by the number of weeks between the two data points. As illustrated in Figure 4.5, a two-point ROI calculation would be the final data point (92) minus the data point at the start of progress monitoring (37), divided by the number of weeks (36) = 1.53 wcpm/week.

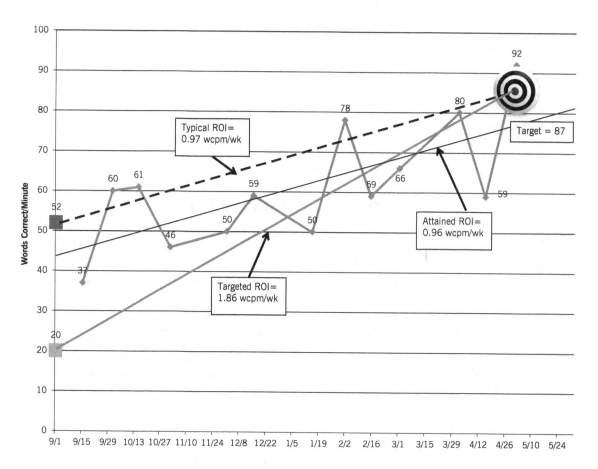

FIGURE 4.5. Example of progress monitoring data for ORF across the year for a second grader.

Although a two-point ROI is simple to calculate, it has many disadvantages. First, it is very vulnerable to outliers (unusual data points). For example, looking at Figure 4.5, one can see that the student went from 59 wcpm in the middle of April to 92 wcpm as the last data point. Such variations in scores are not unusual. Suppose the final data point was 60 wcpm instead of 92. The two-point ROI in this case would have been 0.64 wcpm/week (i.e., [60–37]/36 weeks). Likewise, if the beginning data point was 60 instead of 37, a data point more consistent with scores in October, the two-point ROI would have been 0.89 wcpm/week (i.e., [92–60]/36). The interpretation of a student's ROI would be substantially different for each of these examples. Another disadvantage of a two-point ROI is the fact that the calculation ignores all of the data between the starting and ending points. Establishing a trend across time that ignores what occurred between the start and end of the data series is potentially problematic and may deliver results that do not represent what actually transpired across the school year. Given the potential importance and high stakes given to the progress monitoring data's contribution to deciding whether a student is eligible or not eligible for special education, using such an imprecise measure of trend is not recommended.

Modified Two-Point ROI

The modified two-point ROI involves using the median of the first three starting and ending data points in the series to calculate the ROI. Use of the median or middle score (not the mean or arithmetic average) across the three data points removes any single outlier score that may be evident across the data points. In Figure 4.6, the median values in the circled areas at the beginning and end of the data series would result in an ROI of 0.56 wcpm/week (i.e., [80–60]/36 weeks). The advantages of the modified two-point ROI calculation is that it accounts for potential outliers at the beginning or end of the data set and it is easy to calculate. The disadvantage is that the method still does not account for all data points in the progress monitoring series and may not be as precise a metric as an evaluation team might want for making high-stakes decisions such as SLD determination.

Ordinary Least Squares Regression Line (Slope)

The most precise metric for calculating trend in a progress monitoring data series is the use of the ordinary least squares (OLS) regression line, or slope. This metric examines all the data in a series and calculates the line of best fit across the data series. OLS assumes that there is a linear trend across time or that the student's

> **Ordinary least squares (OLS) regression (slope) is the most precise metric for calculating trend in a progress monitoring data series.**

performance changed over time in a "straight line." Calculation of the OLS is mathematically sophisticated and can be facilitated by the inclusion of the calculation in graphing programs such as Microsoft EXCEL.

Figure 4.5 illustrates the OLS or slope calculation across the same data set as used for the two-point and modified two-point ROI above. In this example, the OLS calculation resulted in a value of 0.96 wcpm/week. The one disadvantage of OLS is the assumption that growth occurred in a straight line, an assumption we know is not accurate when looking across the fall-to-winter and winter-to-spring time periods.

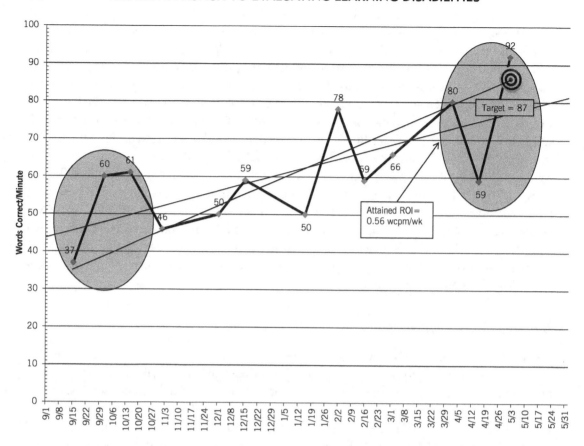

FIGURE 4.6. Example of modified two-point ROI calculation.

Comparing ROI Methods

Table 4.2 shows the outcomes for all three methods of calculating ROI for the progress monitoring data set shown in Figure 4.5. As evident in the table, the three methods resulted in very different calculations that lead to very different interpretations of the ROI for this student. In general, across the methods, the OLS or slope calculation is viewed as the most precise and reliable metric (Christ, Zopluoglo, Monaghen, & Van Norman, 2013). Most software programs that provide ROI based on progress monitoring data use this particular metric as their calculated value. Indeed, we recommend that all practitioners use slope in the process of interpreting the

TABLE 4.2. Comparison of ROI Calculations

Method	ROI
Two-point ROI	1.5 wcpm/week
Modified two-point ROI	0.56 wcpm/week
Ordinary least squares ROI	0.96 wcpm/week

progress monitoring data within an RTI model, especially when eligibility for special education is being considered. Jenkins and Terjeson (2011) found that if measurements are done less frequently, more data points are needed at baseline and follow-up to more accurately calculate a rate of change using non-OLS methods. However, Christ and colleagues (2013), in an extensive set of simulation studies that examined the use of OLS and other methods for calculating the ROI for measures of oral reading fluency, noted that there was strong empirical support that OLS is the only metric that should be used for calculating trends from progress monitoring data. In addition, their research showed that a total of between 8 and 14 data points are required to establish a reliable trend, depending on the quality of the passage set. Indeed, Christ and colleagues as well as Ardoin, Christ, Morena, Cormier, and Klingbeil (2013) noted that the empirical support in general for the decision-making processes using ORF data for progress monitoring is in need of far more research.

Illustrations from a Non-CBM Measure

As described previously with non-CBM benchmark data, the same analysis of growth can be used with non-CBM progress monitoring data. For example, Figure 4.7 shows a progress monitoring example for a third-grade student on STAR Math. His initial fall benchmark score of 458

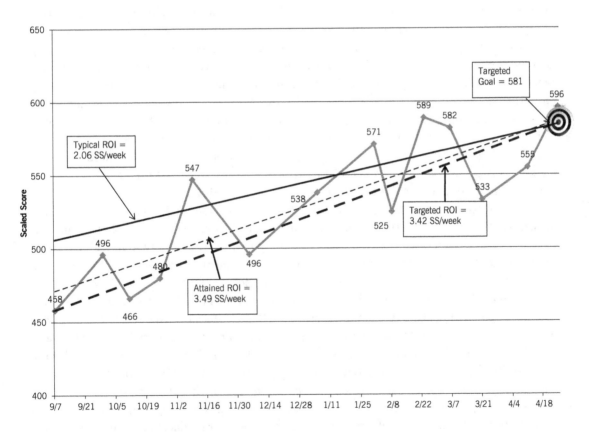

FIGURE 4.7. Progress monitoring example with STAR Math for a third-grade student.

was at the 20th percentile of the normative data provided by STAR Math (see Figure 4.3). The typical progress monitoring ROI was set by examining the expected scaled score of students starting and ending the year at the 40th percentile, the performance level selected as representing benchmark performance for this school. Calculating his typical progress monitoring ROI using a two-point calculation would result in a typical progress monitoring benchmark ROI for the student of 2.06 scaled score points per week (i.e., [581–507]/36 weeks).

A goal of achieving a scaled score by spring of 581, the 40th percentile, was selected. The goal was chosen by the educational team and reflected a need to accelerate learning progress across the year. Calculating the targeted progress monitoring ROI based on a goal of 581 resulted in a targeted progress monitoring ROI of 3.42 scaled score points per week (i.e., [581–458]/36 weeks). The attained progress monitoring ROI for this student (using an OLS calculation) across time was 3.49 scaled score points per week, showing a growth rate higher than the targeted rate.

INTERPRETING ROI: CONDUCTING A GAP ANALYSIS

As discussed and illustrated in Chapter 3, the extent of a student's academic deficiency (i.e., how low) was operationalized as a comparison between the referred student's level of performance to that of his or her peers at the time of referral for evaluation. This comparison is made using the available data, including universal screening and progress monitoring measures, that have been collected over time on all students. The evaluation team conducts a benchmark gap analysis by comparing the referred student's performance against the levels that are expected of typical grade-level peers. As benchmarks represent the minimal levels of expected competency on universal screening measures, comparisons between the referred student's performance on these same measures can offer an empirical method for defining the distance between typical (expected) levels of performance and a student's attained level of performance.

To address the issue of the extent of the student's deficiency in responding to intervention (i.e., the concept of how slow), the evaluation team analyzes the gap between the referred student and his or her peers on the change across time on key indicators of the student's academic performance. In simple terms, the evaluation team needs to determine how slow a student's growth is to determine whether a student qualifies for SLD under Criterion 2. This analysis consists of two procedures: (1) conducting a gap analysis of the student's ROI and (2) determining the impact of the student's current ROI on the attainment of benchmarks. The ROI gap analysis grows out of a procedure that has been used for many years in the CBM literature, the aim line (Hosp, Hosp, & Howell, 2007). The aim line was developed as a tool to facilitate formative use of CBM data. A line was drawn from the student's baseline score to the desired endpoint score (i.e., typical benchmark goal), and ongoing progress monitoring data were examined to determine if the student's progress was on track (at or above the aim line) to meet the end goal by the end of the instructional period. The benchmark ROI can be used the same way. Logically, the ROI gap analysis tells decision makers whether the intervention has been successful to "catch the student up" or not. If the student has not "caught up," there is a high probability that the student will continue to struggle in general education without continued support and intervention.

Progress Monitoring ROI Gap Analysis

The interpretation of progress monitoring ROI incorporates comparisons among the same kind of values as with benchmark ROI. Comparisons of the typical ROI, target ROI, and attained ROI are used together to fully understand the degree to which a student is responding to an intervention. Typical ROI is defined by the expected performance of a student who begins the year performing at benchmark and remains at benchmark through winter and spring assessments. Targeted ROI is the expected ROI for a student who begins the year below the benchmark level and attains benchmark by the end of the year. Finally, attained ROI is the ROI that defines the student's actual performance.

The progress monitoring data of the same second-grade student whose benchmark data were shown in Figure 4.2 is shown in Figure 4.5. Typical ROI (from the DIBELS Next benchmarks for ORF) is 0.97 wcpm/week based on a typical student in grade 2 beginning the year at 52 wcpm and ending at 87 wcpm. The target student started the year at 20 wcpm (prior to the beginning of progress monitoring) with a goal to reach the spring benchmark of 87 wcpm, a targeted ROI of 1.86 wcpm/week. If this student moves at an ROI of 1.86 wcpm/week he will close the gap between himself and his peers. The student's attained progress monitoring ROI (using the OLS calculation) was 0.96 wcpm/week. Examining these three values, one sees that although the targeted student was moving at a rate that approached that expected of typically performing second grade peers, he was not moving at a rate sufficient to fully close the gap between himself and his peers. At the same time, the fact that the target student was moving forward at a rate that approached that of his peers suggests that the student is responding to the intervention to some degree.

The gap analysis using the progress monitoring data is summarized in Table 4.3. Table 4.3 provides the calculations for the example of the second grader whose progress monitoring data are displayed in Figure 4.5. As evident, our student grew at 99.0% of what would be expected for a typical second grader scoring at benchmark across the year, but only at 51.6% of growth that would be expected if our target student were to close the gap between himself and his peers who are performing at expected levels. It should be noted in this scenario that we are using the term "typical second grader" to represent national normative data, and not what may be typi-

TABLE 4.3. Gap Analysis for Progress Monitoring Data of the Second-Grade Student Shown in Figure 4.5

(A) Typical progress monitoring ROI	0.97 wcpm/week
(B) Targeted progress monitoring ROI	1.86 wcpm/week
(C) Attained progress monitoring ROI	0.96 wcpm/week
Progress monitoring ROI gap index (against typical ROI) (C/A × 100)	99.0% of typical ROI
Progress monitoring ROI gap index (against targeted ROI) (C/B × 100)	51.6% of targeted ROI

cal in the target student's class or school. We discuss in Chapter 6 how the performance of the entire local group should be taken into consideration when considering whether the referred student's performance is the result of an SLD or is actually a function of systemic problems (i.e., a lack of instruction that must be ruled out). When the majority of students in a class or grade are in the at-risk range, identifying a particular student who is in the same range as having a disability is problematic.

Benchmark Gap ROI Analysis

The second step of the gap analysis of the student's ROI is to determine the impact of the student's attained rate on the calculated deficit in performance level. As we described in Chapter 3, the distance between the typical and attained levels of performance on universal screening measures can be displayed as a simple ratio, known as the benchmark gap index. The benchmark gap index is calculated by dividing the typical level of performance by the student's attained level of performance. This index provides a measure of how far behind the student is at any given point in time (i.e., level of performance). The question here is whether the student is growing at a rate that closes the gap between himself and his peers. This analysis is conducted by examining the benchmark gaps over time. In the example in Figure 4.2, at the fall benchmark the index shows our target student to be 2.6 times discrepant from his/her peers (52 wcpm/20 wcpm = 2.6×). That is, the typical performing student is 2.6 times higher than the target student. For ease of explanation, the ratio is reversed and multiplied by 100, to determine the percentage of performance achieved by the target student relative to what is expected. A target student achieving at a level equivalent to the typical student would have a benchmark gap index of 100%, indicating that the student is performing 100% of the level and growth expected. Readers might think of this equation like a gas tank where the goal is to be 100% full. In this example, the index would be 20/52 × 100 = 38.5%) indicating that the target student is performing at a level that is only 38.5% of what is achieved by the typical performing student. The same calculations are made at winter and spring to show the change in the benchmark gap index across the year. Thus at the winter assessment, the index would be 37/72 × 100 = 51.4%; at the spring assessment, the index would be 50/87 × 100 = 57.5%.

Table 4.4 summarizes the benchmark gap indices for the example student shown in Figure 4.2 and offers a summary for interpretation. Putting all the indices together, one would conclude that, over the course of the year, the student's benchmark growth against typical-level student performance was just slightly under what would be expected. That is, the student was moving at a rate just slightly under the rate expected of typical performing second graders (0.83 wcpm/week vs. 0.97 wcpm/week). The ROI benchmark gap against typically performing students is 85.6%. However, because the student's fall benchmark gap index was at 38.5% of typical beginning second-grade performance, the targeted ROI was 1.86 wcpm/week (i.e., the rate of growth on which he needed to stay to close the gap between himself and his second-grade peers). The target student's ROI of 0.83 is substantially lower than this target rate. By dividing the attained ROI (0.83) by the targeted ROI (1.86) to compare against the student's rate of progress needed to close the gap, the ROI benchmark index was at 44.6% of targeted growth, indicating that the student moved at a rate that was less than half of what would have been expected across the year. This rate of growth put the student at 51.4% of level in winter and at 57.5% of level in spring, indicating that the student did not make the gains necessary to "catch up" to same-grade

TABLE 4.4. Summary Table of Benchmark Gap Indices for the Second-Grade Student from Figure 4.2

(A) Typical benchmark ROI	0.97 wcpm/week
(B) Attained benchmark ROI for targeted student	0.83 wcpm/week
(C) Target benchmark ROI for targeted student	1.86 wcpm/week
Fall benchmark gap index	38.5% of typical performance
Spring benchmark gap index	57.5% of typical performance
ROI benchmark gap index against typical performers (B/A)	85.6% of typical growth
ROI benchmark gap index against targeted performance (B/C)	44.6% of targeted growth to close gap

peers. Although he was displaying some level of progress, he is not responding to the intervention across the year at an acceptable rate. This conclusion has two implications. First, these data contribute to an eligibility decision in showing that the student's response to intervention has not been sufficient to reduce the student's real risk of failure over time. Second, the intervention needs to be intensified whether it continues in general education or is carried out with special education resources.

Gap Analysis Using CAT

The same kind of analysis using progress monitoring data can be made for CAT measures. As evident from Figure 4.4 and Table 4.5, calculation of benchmark gap indices from the STAR Math measure requires a somewhat different perspective for interpretation than CBM mea-

TABLE 4.5. Summary Table of Benchmark ROI Indices on STAR Math for the Second-Grade Student from Figure 4.4

(A) Typical benchmark ROI (at 40th percentile)	2.42 SS/week
(B) Attained benchmark ROI (at 10th percentile)	2.81 SS/week
(C) Target benchmark ROI with goal to 40th percentile	5.06 SS/week
Fall benchmark gap index	76.5% of typical performance
Spring benchmark gap index	81.3% of typical performance
ROI benchmark gap index against typical performers (B/A)	116.1% of typical growth
ROI benchmark gap index against targeted performance (B/C)	55.5% of targeted growth

sures. Scaled scores between the 10th and 40th percentiles in the fall of grade 2 show a difference of 95 scaled score points, which means that the student at the 10th percentile is performing at a level that is 76.5% of the performance expected for a student at benchmark or the 40th percentile. Thus, to interpret the benchmark gap index shown in Figure 4.4, differences that were greater than 76.5% would be considered very deficient. Likewise, looking at the growth rates across the year, if the student remained at the 10th percentile, he would grow at a rate of 1.53 scaled score points per week, ending the year at a scaled score of 411 (see Figure 4.3), which would still be 83.6% of the typical score. In this example, a growth goal to the 40th percentile or a score of 492 was set by the end of the year, or a targeted ROI of 5.06 scaled score points per week. The student achieved a growth rate of 2.50 scaled score points per week, as reflected in his attained benchmark ROI. Dividing the attained benchmark ROI by the typical benchmark ROI and multiplying by 100 showed that the student in this example grew at 116.1% of what would be expected of a typical performing student; however, against the targeted rate, the student only grew at 55.5% of what would be needed to close the gap.

Table 4.6 shows the summary of these indices for the third-grade student shown in Figure 4.7. As shown in the table and figure, the typical third grader (at the 40th percentile) grows from a scaled score of 507 in the fall to a scaled score of 581 in the spring, averaging 2.06 scaled score points per week during the 36 weeks of school. The target student in this example began the year with a scaled score of 458 (20th percentile) with a target to reach a scaled score of 581 (40th percentile) by the end of the year, a growth rate of 3.42 scaled score points per week. A student who started and ended the year at the 20th percentile grew at a rate of 1.83 scaled score points per week. Over the course of the year, the student attained a growth rate of 3.49 scaled score

TABLE 4.6. Summary Table of Progress Monitoring ROI Indices on STAR Math for the Third-Grade Student from Figure 4.7

(A) Typical progress monitoring ROI for Student at 20th percentile in fall	1.83 SS pts/week
(B) Typical progress monitoring ROI for Student at 40th percentile in fall	2.06 SS pts/week
(C) Targeted progress monitoring ROI for Student with goal to 40th percentile in spring	3.42 SS pts/week
(D) Attained progress monitoring ROI	3.49 SS pts/week
Progress monitoring ROI gap index against student at 20th percentile (D/A)	190.7% of typical growth
Progress monitoring ROI gap index against typical student (40th percentile) (D/B)	169.4% of typical growth
Progress monitoring ROI gap index against targeted progress (D/C)	102.0% of targeted growth to close the gap
Student growth percentile	52

points as reflected in his progress monitoring data. The progress monitoring gap index against typical performing students was 190.7% of what would be projected for a student staying at the 20th percentile and a progress monitoring gap index of 169.4% against typically performing students, with a growth rate against targeted performance of 102.0%. Hence, in this case the student grew more than would be expected and would be predicted to successfully close the gap between his performance and that of his not-at-risk peers.

Interpretations of measures from CAT or similar measures where scaled scores are used require additional understanding for full meaningfulness. For example, Renaissance Learning recently published student growth percentiles (SGP) as a way to better interpret the change over time of students using the STAR measures. An SGP compares a student's growth to that of his or her academic peers nationwide. SGP is reported on a 1–99 scale. For example, if a student has an SGP of 90, it means his growth from one test to another was better than 90 percent of students who started at a similar achievement level in the same grade. In the example shown in Figure 4.7 and Table 4.6, the SGP for this student indicated that the student grew about the same (52nd percentile) across the year as other students who started at the 20th percentile and ended around the 40th percentile. It was encouraging in this case that the student grew more in 1 year than other typical performers starting at the 20th percentile and that they had closed the gap between the targeted student and his/her peers. Ideally, one would like to see student growth percentile rates for those starting at low levels of achievement to have indicated growth that exceeds what would be expected for a typical performing student at the same starting point.

The SGP provides indications of a student's annual growth against the current level of achieved growth and the annual catch-up growth needed to close the gap with peers. A student who starts and ends the year at the same percentile has grown over the year; however, if they do not close the gap between themselves and peers they will be farther behind in subsequent years. At the same time, the amount a gap can typically be closed within a single year is often a function of how far behind or below the peer's level of performance a given student is at the start. The SGP provides an indication of whether the amount of growth demonstrated is far above, at, or below what would be expected of a student starting at the same point in the distribution.

SUMMARY

Calculation of the ROI for student performance becomes one of the key indicators in the decision-making process within an RTI model. The values discussed in this chapter are designed to be simple mathematical representations of how the referred student has done against typical peers who start and end the year at benchmark levels and against the target that focuses on closing the gap between the referred student and peers. Together, the indices offer a rich set of perspectives that empirically define the referred student's responsiveness to the interventions that have been provided.

CHAPTER 5

Ruling Out Other Conditions

In this chapter, we review procedures for ruling out other conditions in the determination of eligibility for special education under the SLD category, which is the third of four criteria for determining SLD. The current IDEA regulations (2006) include the following language: "The group determines that its findings under paragraphs (a)(1) and (2) of this section are not primarily the result of—(i) a visual, hearing, or motor disability; (ii) mental retardation; (iii) emotional disturbance; (iv) cultural factors; (v) environmental or economic disadvantage; or (vi) limited English proficiency" (§300.309[a][3]). This third criterion of the SLD is graphically depicted in Figure 5.1. In this provision (a)(1) and (2) refer to the first two criteria for the determination of SLD. It should be noted that in recent years, the term "mental retardation" has been replaced with the term "intellectual disability," which we use throughout this chapter.

From their inception, the IDEA regulations have included provisions that require multidisciplinary evaluation teams to determine whether a student's academic failure is caused not by SLD, but by other disabling conditions or aspects of the student's life situation. These provisions clearly stemmed from concerns that SLD would become a "catch-all" category for students exhibiting academic problems for a variety of reasons unless the evaluation included specific procedures to rule out other causes of poor academic performance. SLD is a diagnostic category for which we have no definitive rule-in test. In assessment jargon, we would say there is no incontrovertible index or gold standard that tells us whether a person "truly has" or "truly does not have" SLD. The primary symptom of SLD is poor achievement, yet poor achievement can be caused by many factors other than SLD. Hence, poor achievement is not a unique and specific indicator or marker for diagnosing SLD, which has been referred to as a "diagnosis of exclusion" because it involves making a series of rule-out judgments. Where poor achievement is apparent, commonly accepted potential causes of poor achievement must be examined and ruled out first. Once common causes of poor achievement have been ruled out, the evaluation team may conclude that a child has SLD when poor achievement is present. These other common causes of poor academic performance are called the exclusionary criteria under the SLD definition. In this chapter and the next chapter, we consider the two exclusionary criteria. In this chapter we describe procedures for evaluating presence of another disabling condition and situational factors. In Chapter 6, we describe procedures for assessing lack of instruction as an exclusionary criterion for SLD.

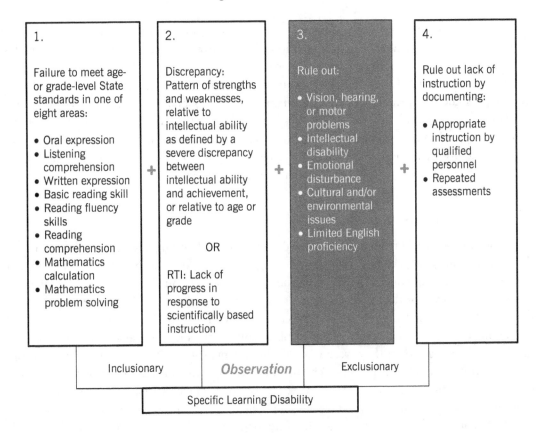

FIGURE 5.1. Schematic diagram of IDEA regulations regarding the criteria for determining SLD, with Criterion 3 highlighted.

GENERAL PROCEDURE FOR RULING OUT OTHER CONDITIONS

The process of ruling out other conditions as the cause of the student's academic failure consists of three parts: (1) screening, (2) evaluation, and (3) verification. Although each of the conditions or factors described in the regulations must be considered as a possible cause of the student's academic problems, a full evaluation may not be needed to rule out their potential influence (Reschly, 2005). Rather, if a screening assessment or procedure makes it clear that the condition being considered is not present, the evaluation team may use that evidence to rule out that condition. If, however, the screening indicates the possibility that the condition may be a causal factor, the team needs to conduct or arrange for more extensive evaluation procedures to verify the causal connection between the condition and the student's academic concerns. To clarify, the first step is to rule out the conditions described below as being causally related to poor academic performance. If another disabling condition or situational factor is not detected upon screening, it can be ruled out as a cause of the student's poor academic performance, and SLD may be considered. When another disabling condition or situational factors are detected, further assessment is necessary to conclude that the disabling condition or situational factors are indeed causing the student's poor academic performance.

When the conditions described below are not detected upon screening, the rule-out decision is easily made. When the conditions described below *are* detected upon screening, the decision is not so straightforward. It is possible that the disabling condition is present, for example, but is not causing the student's poor academic performance. In this case, although the disabling condition is present, it can be ruled out as a cause of poor academic performance, and SLD may still be considered. If, on the other hand, the disabling condition is detected and can be demonstrated to be causally related to the student's poor academic performance, then the exclusionary criterion applies, and the SLD diagnosis cannot be made. We now present procedures for screening and verifying exclusionary factors for SLD.

Visual Impairment

The condition of visual impairment is a useful starting point in exemplifying the rule-out procedure. Visual impairment is one of the 12 disabling conditions for which a child may be found to be eligible for special education. The question to be answered in ruling out visual impairment is straightforward: Are the student's academic problems caused by difficulties seeing the academic materials (e.g., print in textbooks, visual displays on blackboards or projected material)? Screening for visual impairment is commonplace, and most adults can remember participating in vision screenings when they were enrolled in elementary school. Many states require the regular screening of students' vision. The results of these screenings are used by the multidisciplinary evaluation team to determine whether a vision problem exists. If the student is found to have normal vision in the screening, visual impairment can be ruled out as a possible cause of the academic problems. If, however, the screening indicates a possible vision problem, a full evaluation by an optometrist or ophthalmologist would be needed, and the visual impairment should be corrected.

The first question to be answered is whether the student's academic performance would improve if his or her vision was corrected through the use of visual aids (e.g., eyeglasses). We know of one case in which a first grader was identified as having SLD until it was discovered that his eyeglass prescription was incorrect. When the student was fitted with correct eyeglasses, he quickly learned to read and was exited from special education. More significant visual impairment that is not adequately correctable through medical treatment or visual aids would be a potential causal factor in failing to learn basic skills. To exclude SLD and conclude that poor learning was caused by visual impairment, the student's academic growth would have to be monitored to verify that when instructed and provided with visual supports and adapted tasks, the student's learning progress improved. If the student's vision problem was corrected and instruction was provided using properly adapted task materials and the student continued to perform poorly, the evaluation team would rule out visual impairment as causing poor academic problems and the exclusionary criterion would not be met. In other words, the diagnostic team would need to consider SLD as a potential cause of poor performance. For example, a student with blindness who failed to learn Braille may be identified as having SLD as a secondary disability.

Hearing Impairment

Like visual impairment, students are routinely screened for hearing impairment in many states. Hearing impairment is ruled out as causing poor academic performance for all students who pass the hearing screening. Students who fail the hearing screening are evaluated by an audiologist to determine whether hearing aids and/or medical treatments are needed to improve hearing. Evidence for a significant hearing impairment would exclude a student for consideration of SLD until the hearing problem was corrected. A student whose hearing is acceptably corrected for typical instruction who then fails to acquire basic academic skills may be considered for SLD eligibility.

Motor Problems

Students with motor problems may have difficulty with the performance of typical school tasks. For example, a student with an orthopedic impairment that affects handwriting ability may have difficulty with written expression tasks in the classroom. Unlike the sensory impairments, schools are typically not required to screen for motor difficulties. Consequently, multidisciplinary evaluation teams should screen for these issues when conducting a comprehensive evaluation for special education eligibility when the academic performance requires significant motor involvement (e.g., writing). White and Haring (1980) suggested a direct assessment of a student's graphomotor skills that can serve as a screener for motor problems. In this approach, all students in a class are asked to write a letter of the alphabet (e.g., "a") as many times as possible in one minute. The number of recognizable letters produced by the target student can then be compared to that of the rest of the class. If the results are similar in quality and production, a motor disorder (i.e., an orthopedic impairment) can be ruled out as a possible cause of the student's written expression problem. However, if the target student displays difficulty with this screening task in comparison to his or her peers, a further evaluation by a physician or occupational therapist would be indicated. If it is found that the student's writing problems are caused by a motor disorder, SLD could be ruled out. In this case, the student might qualify for special education under the category of orthopedic impairment or other health impairment, or possibly could qualify for accommodations under a Section 504 plan.

Intellectual Disability

IDEA has always required evaluation teams to consider whether the student's failure to learn academic skills might be a result of an intellectual disability (mental retardation in early iterations). An intellectual disability is defined in the IDEA regulations as "significantly subaverage general intellectual functioning, existing concurrently with deficits in adaptive behavior and manifested during the developmental period, that adversely affects a child's educational performance" (§300.8[c][6]). To be identified as having an intellectual disability, a student typically needs to display significant cognitive deficits on a full-scale measure of intelligence as well as concomitant impairment of adaptive behavior on a standardized measure of those skills. Historically, teams have had these data available because school psychologists routinely administered intelligence tests to all students being considered for special education eligibility. With the advent of RTI as an alternative to the ability–achievement discrepancy in the determination of SLD, intelligence tests are no longer required in the basic formulation of SLD identification. Consequently, it might be asked whether intelligence tests are needed in most full and individual evaluations. In regards to the rule-out of intellectual disability, our position is that the screening–evaluation–verification process used for the other conditions pertains to intellectual disability. That is, an evaluation team might use other available data to screen first for intellectual disability rather than automatically conducting a test of cognitive ability. For

> **An evaluation team might use other available data to screen first for intellectual disability rather than automatically conducting a test of cognitive ability.**

example, a student who displays academic achievement in the average range in areas not related to the suspected SLD (e.g., grade-level math achievement for a student with a possible SLD in reading) would not likely display intelligence scores in the range required for intellectual disability if a full cognitive assessment were administered. An evaluation team might be particularly confident in this determination if the student also displayed age-appropriate adaptive behavior. In this scenario, the evaluation team could rule out intellectual disability at the screening level.

If, however, the student did display deficiencies across academic areas and the evaluation team was also concerned about the student's adaptive behavior, a full cognitive evaluation would be indicated. If intellectual disability is suspected, the administration of full-scale measures of intelligence and adaptive behavior is recommended. Students who display consistent scores in the intellectual disability range would be considered for eligibility for special education under the category of intellectual disability and would be excluded from consideration for SLD. Intellectual disability would be ruled out for those students who scored above the intellectual disability cutoff scores on these measures. School psychologists in the Heartland Area Educational Agency in Iowa have used this practice for a number of years. As a result, their use of intelligence tests is sparing, averaging only a few administrations per year (Reschly, 2003). Unlike the previous exclusionary conditions (e.g., vision and hearing impairments, motor disability), intellectual disability and SLD, by definition, cannot co-occur. The presence of intellectual disability effectively rules out the possibility of SLD as a cause of poor academic performance.

Emotional Disturbance

The IDEA regulations also require a consideration of emotional problems as being causally related to a student's academic performance problems. Conceptually, these issues are initially investigated using measures intended for screening of groups of students for emotional and/or behavioral issues. Performance in the typical range on measures such as the Behavioral and Emotional Screening System (Kamphaus & Reynolds, 2007), the Student Risk Screening Scale (Drummond, 1994), and the Systematic Screening for Behavior Disorders (Walker & Severson, 1992) could provide a first-level indication that an emotional disturbance could be ruled out as a cause of the student's deficient academic performance. For students who display emotional and/or behavioral concerns on these measures, a full evaluation of emotional and behavioral problems is indicated. These assessments might include broad-band measures such as behavior rating scales, such as the Behavior Assessment System for Children (BASC; Reynolds & Kamphaus, 2004) or the Child Behavior Checklist (Achenbach & Rescorla, 2000); self-report measures, such as the BASC Self-Report of Personality (Reynolds & Kamphaus, 2004); and semistructured child interviews, such as the Semi-Structured Clinical Interview for Children and Adolescents (McConaughy & Achenbach, 2001). Specific concerns about particular issues such as depression or aggression can be investigated using narrow-band measures such as the Children's Depression Inventory (Kovacs, 1992) and the Adolescent Anger Rating Scale (Burney, 2001), respectively.

Although this general format may be acceptable, evaluation teams might choose to be more thorough in routinely investigating certain types of emotional problems that may not be apparent to teachers, such as childhood depression. Consequently, although full evaluations may not be needed in every case, we recommend that broad-band child behavior checklists be administered to both parents and teachers and used in all evaluations for special education eligibility. Again, scores in the average range on these instruments would rule out emotional concerns as the cause of the student's poor academic performance. Scores in at-risk or clinically significant ranges would signal the need for a more comprehensive assessment of the student's emotional challenges to determine whether the student's academic problems are a function of an emotional disturbance rather than SLD. Where emotional and behavioral concerns cannot be ruled out as causes of poor academic performance, affective and behavioral interventions designed to produce a better fit between demands of the learning environment and the child's behavioral skills and emotional resilience should be initiated with academic progress monitoring to determine whether academic performance improves with appropriate emotional and behavioral supports. Where academic performance improves, SLD cannot be diagnosed. Where academic performance is unimproved, intensive academic intervention is likely to be needed as part of an IEP for services provided under the category of emotional disability or under the category of SLD to ensure adequate learning.

Yet another complicating factor is the situation in which a student displays classroom and other behavior problems as a result of academic frustrations emanating from SLD. That is, the student's behavioral concerns may not be a result of emotional disturbance, but rather by an unidentified SLD. In these cases, the functional academic assessment described in Chapter 3 may be helpful in parsing the causal condition. It is possible that providing an intensive academic intervention (in Tier 3) that is targeted directly at the student's instructional level and uses a robust intervention might not only result in improved performance, but might also ameliorate the behavior concerns, which would give credence to the academic frustration hypothesis. In this situation, if the student's academic gains were minimal, but the behavior improved, an emotional disturbance could be ruled out, and the student could be identified with SLD. Another important source of information is whether the student's behavior problems occur in non-academic environments (e.g., home and community). The absence of behavioral difficulties in those situations would again support a rule-out of emotional disturbance. Nonetheless, it is acknowledged that long-standing behavior problems may not improve over a short-term intervention, and the absence of an identified emotional disturbance does not mean that behavioral concerns will not continue. In those cases, a student with SLD may need both academic and behavioral interventions as part of the special education program.

> **A student with SLD may need both academic and behavioral interventions as part of the special education program.**

Cultural Factors

In this area, the evaluation team needs to determine whether the student's academic deficiencies may be explained by factors related to the student's culture. The scenario envisioned here is that the student's school performance is hampered by factors such as immigration from another country. García-Vázquez (1995) has noted that immigrant students often have difficulty adjusting to the majority culture, which may have an adverse effect on their learning. This phenomenon is particularly pronounced if the emigration was associated with traumatic events in the student's home country (e.g., war, famine). Similarly, some students whose parents are undocumented immigrants may be experiencing stress related to their uncertain immigration status that may adversely affect their academic performance. In addition, immigrant students may experience other situations that adversely affect learning, such as moving frequently, changing households multiple times, having difficulty getting to school consistently, homelessness, and so on. School evaluation teams need to determine whether any of these issues are operative when conducting their evaluations.

A screening for cultural factors might involve administration of instruments such as the Acculturation Quick Screen (Collier, 2000) or the Children's Acculturation Scale (Franco, 1983). A more in-depth assessment would involve taking a family social history. It should be noted here that this assessment is independent from, although frequently closely related to, the process for ruling out limited English proficiency (LEP), which in IDEA is a separate rule-out requirement. Consequently, evaluation teams must take care to determine whether cultural factors are impeding the student's academic performance even whether the student's primary home language is English. If it is determined that the student's learning is primarily affected by cultural factors, the student would be excluded from consideration for SLD determination. If cultural factors are not seen as primarily causative in the student's difficulties, this factor can be ruled out. It is important to develop and deploy strategies designed to attenuate the negative effects of identified cultural factors on a child's academic performance (Artiles, Kozleski, Trent, Osher, & Ortiz, 2010). Such strategies will require the evaluation team to consider community-based services and solutions to troubleshoot ways to increase the child's access to and readiness for school each day. When greater support is provided to the student and the student's family to produce a better fit between the demands of the learning environment and the child and family's capacity to participate fully in that environment and learning improves, SLD is ruled out.

Limited English Proficiency

We will take this consideration out of turn because of its close link to the consideration of cultural factors. It has been a historic concern that students with LEP may be erroneously identified as having a disability, when in fact their academic problems stem from the normal course of

> **Students with LEP may be erroneously identified as having a disability, when in fact their academic problems stem from the normal course of learning English as a second language.**

learning English as a second language (Ortiz, 2008). This concern is exacerbated by how a second language is acquired, in that students may appear to speak English well, but not have the language skills to learn academic subjects. Cummins (1981) identified the now well-known concepts of basic interpersonal communication skills (BICS) to describe those language skills that are required for common, everyday interactions, and cognitive academic language proficiency (CALP) that is needed for learning more complex academic material. Cummins further found that while BICS typically takes 2 years to be acquired, CALP may take 5–7 years. Evaluation teams, therefore, must be particularly careful in determining the language skills of students who are English language learners. Screening for these issues is a federal requirement that requires schools to identify all students whose primary home language is other than English, which is typically accomplished through a home language survey. Schools are responsible to conduct a more thorough evaluation of students' English language skills for those who are identified as having a home language other than English, using instrumentation such as the Assessing Comprehension and Communication in English State to State (ACCESS; WIDA Consortium, 2010) measures. Evaluation teams that are considering a student's eligibility for special education under the SLD category need to access these school records to determine whether the student's academic deficiencies are a function of the process of second-language acquisition, or if these factors can be ruled out. If language support is provided along with academic intervention and learning improves, SLD may be ruled out. If learning does not improve along with a student's language skills and in the face of targeted support for both language development and academic skill development, SLD cannot be ruled out.

Environmental or Economic Disadvantage

The final factor to be considered by evaluation teams under Criterion 3 is whether the student's academic difficulties are a function of environmental or economic disadvantage rather than SLD. It must first be emphasized that it is not assumed that all students whose families have limited incomes (i.e., are below federal poverty levels) are expected to display school failure. Although family income has been consistently demonstrated as being related to school achievement (Duncan, Morris, & Rodrigues, 2011; Duncan, Yeung, Brooks-Gunn, & Smith, 1998; Hart & Risley, 1995), there is ample evidence that children can attain age-appropriate achievement levels in highly effective schools regardless of their level of poverty (Haycock et al., 1999). The task for evaluation teams is to determine whether the family's economic condition is producing situations that are impeding the student's learning. Homelessness and lack of adequate food are two examples of sequelae from economic disadvantage that may affect a student's ability to learn. Similarly, evaluation teams must consider whether other situations that are not related to poverty per se but reflect environmental disadvantage are affecting the student's learning. A tragic but all too common example is child abuse, which is an environmental stressor that can have a deleterious effect on learning and school performance. Evaluation teams are required to take these factors into consideration through interviews with the family and review of school records. These interviews should be a routine aspect of a full and individual evaluation because input from parents is a required component of all evaluations for special education eligibility. When teams are considering the possibility of an SLD, these factors must be ruled out as causing poor academic performance. If appropriate environmental supports are supplied to the student and the family and the student's learning improves, environmental or economic disadvantage cannot be ruled out as the cause of the student's academic difficulties. If these supports along with robust academic interventions (in Tiers 2 and 3) fail to produce an improved rate of learning, environmental or economic disadvantage can be ruled out and the student could be identified with SLD.

SUMMARY

Whereas the process for ruling out other conditions or situations seems logical on the surface, assessing inclusionary and exclusionary factors for SLD can be an extremely error-prone process. If a decision error occurs at one of the multiple rule-out decision points, the final SLD decision may be in error. We can make some recommendations based on diagnostic accuracy data about effective rule-out and rule-in criteria for SLD. If we wish to make a rule-out judgment, it is important to have measures and cut scores that are very sensitive (i.e., have a very low chance of failing to detect a problem that truly exists) for that decision. So for the exclusionary factors, we must use measures that we know are sensitive indicators of whether these conditions exist. The requirement for sensitive measures is easily met for vision impairment, hearing impairment, motor disability, and intellectual disability. This requirement is not so easily met when it comes to ruling out cultural factors and economic or environmental disadvantage. What constitutes environmental disadvantage? How is this criterion operationalized and measured? Ruling out emotional disturbance is technically an easier endeavor than operationalizing and ruling out environmental disadvantage, but it is by no means straightforward or easy. The accuracy with which such a judgment can be made depends on the measurement procedures selected (e.g., data collected through questionnaires, stability of the emotional disturbance over time and thus the capacity of the measure to detect the problem), the cut points used to indicate presence or absence of the emotional disturbance, and the variability of intervention effects for students experiencing emotional disturbance.

In terms of strict diagnostic accuracy conventions, several problems make SLD vulnerable as a diagnostic construct. First, there is no gold standard by which we can know for sure that a student "truly has" or "truly does not have" SLD. For example, there is no lab test that, if administered, can tell us for sure that the student has this condition we call SLD. It is a diagnostic construct that from the moment of its conception was challenged on technical and empirical grounds and was born from advocacy and a desire and need to serve students who struggle in general education but have no readily identifiable "reason" for their struggles (Lyon, 1996). Logically, SLD has been viewed as a way of making children eligible to receive extra assistance to master essential skills and ensure these students have access to a free and appropriate public education. It might be argued that the SLD eligibility decision should be driven by a normative framework where some percentage of the lowest-performing students are made eligible to receive services. Some others have posited that SLD eligibility should be based on the relative certainty of poor academic outcomes in the absence of intensive academic interventions and supports (Vellutino, Scanlon, & Zhang, 2007). Still others believe that there may be a unique group of learners for whom reliable diagnostic criteria can be specified and for whom the diagnostic process will produce information that can be translated into effective intervention via processing strengths and weaknesses (Kavale & Flanagan, 2007). We contend that the meaning of the SLD construct ought to depend on the extent to which identified children show outcomes that are superior to what they would have had had they not received the diagnosis.

Persistently poor academic performance in the face of systematic supports to optimize the fit between student performance and the demands of the learning environment is a unique and specific marker indicating likely sustained failure without more intensive support. Because we cannot know for sure what constitutes "true SLD," we suggest a pragmatic approach to diagnostic decision making that stands upon consequential validity. The goal of the comprehensive evaluation process is to identify learning problems, remove likely barriers to learning, and provide intensive academic supports to improve student learning. This decision process does not end at the SLD identification, but rather, involves continual troubleshooting to improve learning outcomes systemwide and for individual students. Hence, efforts to rule out commonly accepted causes of poor academic achievement should include systematic troubleshooting to minimize the barrier interfering with academic performance and instructional trials to verify whether performance improves. If performance is unimproved, then the school teams must continue to work with the student and the student's family to reduce performance gaps and place the student on a path for long-term learning success.

CHAPTER 6

Ruling Out Inadequate Instruction

In this chapter, the fourth and final criterion for the identification of a specific learning disability (SLD) will be explored (see Figure 6.1). The 2006 IDEA regulations require the following:

> To ensure that underachievement in a child suspected of having a specific learning disability is not due to lack of appropriate instruction in reading or math, the group must consider, as part of the evaluation . . . [d]ata that demonstrate that prior to, or as a part of, the referral process, the child was provided appropriate instruction in regular education settings, delivered by qualified personnel; and [d]ata-based documentation of repeated assessments of achievement at reasonable intervals, reflecting formal assessment of student progress during instruction, which was provided to the child's parents. (§300.309[b])

This language follows from the provision of a "special rule for eligibility determination" in which the regulations indicate that

> a child must not be determined to be a child with a disability . . . if the determining factor for that determination is—lack of appropriate instruction in reading, including the essential components of reading instruction (as defined in section 1208[3] of the ESEA); [l]ack of appropriate instruction in math; or [l]imited English proficiency. (§300.306[b])

It is interesting that the 1997 iteration of IDEA included a similar provision, but only articulated "lack of instruction in reading or math, along with limited English proficiency." The additional language in the 2006 regulations in relation to a lack of instruction in reading refers to that section of NCLB (2001) that defines the essential components of reading instruction as the "big ideas" in reading that we described in Chapter 2. The exact provision in NCLB is: "The term 'essential components of reading instruction' means explicit and systematic instruction in—phonemic awareness; phonics; vocabulary development; reading fluency, including oral reading skills; and reading comprehension strategies" (§1208[3]). Clearly, the framers of NCLB and IDEA emphasized the importance of explicit instruction in basic skills.

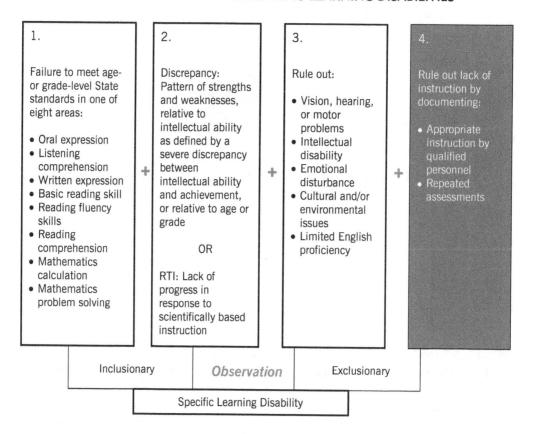

FIGURE 6.1. Schematic diagram of IDEA regulations regarding the criteria for determining SLD, with Criterion 4 highlighted.

One of the primary vulnerabilities of the historical model of referring students for eligibility evaluations is that lack of adequate instruction was not ruled out as a cause of low achievement prior to a student's referral for evaluation. Referral systems relied on "symptoms" like poor achievement to signal a need for eligibility determination, and many children were incorrectly diagnosed with SLD as a result. The problem with low achievement is that it is not a unique and specific marker for the presence of SLD. Stated another way, all children with a learning disability also have low achievement, but not all children who have low achievement have a learning disability. Therefore, relying on low achievement as a marker for SLD is error prone and will result (and did result) in children being misdiagnosed.

> One of the primary vulnerabilities of the historical model of referring students for eligibility evaluations is that lack of adequate instruction was not ruled out as a cause of low achievement.

On the other hand, continued poor achievement when effective instruction has been provided is a powerful marker for the presence of SLD. Classification studies have shown that diagnostic accuracy is improved when RTI systems are used (Compton, Fuchs, Fuchs, & Bryant, 2006; Speece et al., 2003; VanDerHeyden, 2011) to rule out lack of adequate instruction. For example, VanDerHeyden (2011) showed that use of screening data alone did not result in more accurate decision making than could be made by chance alone about which students were at risk or in need of more intensive services. However, screening followed by implementing instructional trials did result in more accurate decision making.

ASSESSING SUFFICIENCY OF TIER 1 OR CORE INSTRUCTION

Universal screening data can be used to evaluate the adequacy of Tier 1 or core instruction. When instruction is not adequate, large numbers of children will perform below criterion or in the risk range. From a measurement validity perspective, judgments about individual students will be highly error prone where performances are similar (i.e., all students are very low performing). From a decision validity perspective, one plausible cause of any individual student's poor performance when many students are low performing is that adequate instruction in the classroom has not occurred. Improving instruction in the classroom as a first step is both necessary to prevent misdiagnosis of individual students and is effort well spent to improve learning for all students (because in fact, many students are at risk for failure in classes where most children fail the screening).

> **One plausible cause of any individual student's poor performance when many students are low performing is that adequate instruction in the classroom has not occurred.**

Collecting and Analyzing Screening Data

The first step in assessing the sufficiency of core instruction is to verify that the screening data are adequate for decision making. For screening data to be used to rule out core instruction problems, screening measures must meet the criteria described in Chapter 2 (i.e., reflect important educational attainments, predict future performance, yield reliable scores, allow for efficient administration, and are sensitive to small changes in student performance). It is important to select a screening measure that assesses a skill that has been taught and on which students are expected to perform well in order to benefit from the instruction that is forthcoming in the scope and sequence at that grade level. There is sometimes a temptation among team members to select a skill that will be easy for the students so student performance will look strong, but this approach leads to inaccurate conclusions. For useful screening decisions to be made, data teams must select measures that assess what students are expected to be able to do, not what we think they can do. This approach allows schools to answer the first step in screening, that is, are most children performing as expected?

To build a sustainable system of universal screening that provides data useful for improving student learning schoolwide and identifying individual students in need of intervention, decision makers must avoid the following common mistakes in universal screening. First, many systems administer too many assessments. Overassessment comes at a direct cost to student achievement. In the case of screening assessment, it is not true that "more is better." The first step that decision makers should take is to complete an assessment inventory for the school. Schools can use the sample inventory in Form 6.1 (at the end of the chapter) to list all existing measures currently used in the school. Where redundant measurement systems are being used, decision makers should choose one system and discontinue the other as a matter of efficiency and efficacy. Universal screening data can be used to:

- Evaluate core instructional effects.
- Evaluate core instructional effects for vulnerable populations.
- Identify students in need of Tier 2 intervention.
- Evaluate long-term effects of interventions at Tiers 2 and 3.
- Inform core resource allocation decisions.

Decision makers should know in advance how each measure will be used to make the above decisions and follow through to ensure the data are used toward that end.

The next step in conducting effective universal screening is to interact with the educational staff at each grade level to review expected learning outcomes for the school year as specified in the state standards and identify an appropriate screening task for universal screening. Teachers should have an opportunity to review available measures and weigh in about preferences for one measure over another to be used for screening. Administrators and implementation leaders should provide a transparent rationale for selecting one screening measure over another and provide a completed assessment inventory so teachers can understand the selection of the screening tool and understand in advance how the data will be used for decision making at their school.

Once the screening measure has been selected and vetted with teachers, the screening procedures can be planned. Universal screening can be conducted during a single school day or across multiple days, depending on the size of the school and the available resources to conduct the screening. VanDerHeyden and Burns (2010) provided a sample single-day screening schedule (see Figure 6.2). Containing screening activities to a single day minimizes time taken away from instruction and allows the school to provide support for accurate screening administration. Implementation leaders should ensure that standard screening administration directions are provided and followed in the collection of screening data. Support should be provided to ensure the obtained data are reliably scored, and the scores should be entered into a database. Because multiple decisions will be based on the screening data, it is important to ensure that the data are collected with minimal threats to reliability and validity. It is also important to organize the data into a database that is easily accessible to decision makers but also protects student confidentiality.

Once the data team leaders have completed an assessment inventory, grade-level faculty meetings are held to review the inventory, provide a rationale for selected assessment measures, and obtain teacher input in selecting particular probes (if applicable) from the range of acceptable measures (e.g., CBM). A screening schedule is provided so each grade level knows when to expect screening to occur at their grade level, and a screening administration script is provided to the teacher so the teacher understands how the screening will be conducted. On screening day, each grade is scheduled in a 1-hour screening block. A trained coach from the school is assigned to each classroom. A coach may be a principal, school psychologist, speech pathologist, special education teacher, Title I support teacher, or basically anyone who can be free from an assigned classroom and can be trained to follow the scripted screening procedures. One coach is needed per class at a given grade level, and the entire team of coaches can be used in subsequent screening-hour intervals to cover all remaining classes. If a given school has five teachers at a grade level, then five coaches are needed for screening day (see Figure 6.2 for a sample screening schedule).

Time	Grade	Teacher Name	Class Location	Coach
7:45–8:45	Grade 1	Teacher A	Room 1-A	Coach 1
		Teacher B	Room 2-A	Coach 2
		Teacher C	Room 3-A	Coach 3
		Teacher D	Room 4-A	Coach 4
9:00–10:00	Grade 3	Teacher I	Room 1-C	Coach 1
		Teacher J	Room 2-C	Coach 2
		Teacher K	Room 3-C	Coach 3
		Teacher L	Room 4-C	Coach 4
10:15–11:15	Grade 2	Teacher E	Room 1-B	Coach 1
		Teacher F	Room 2-B	Coach 2
		Teacher G	Room 3-B	Coach 3
		Teacher H	Room 4-B	Coach 4
11:30–12:30	Grade 5	Teacher Q	Room 1-E	Coach 1
		Teacher R	Room 2-E	Coach 2
		Teacher S	Room 3-E	Coach 3 (Coach 4 organizes data for scoring)
12:30–1:15	Lunch break			
1:15–2:15	Grade 4	Teacher M	Room 1-D	Coach 1
		Teacher N	Room 2-D	Coach 2
		Teacher O	Room 3-D	Coach 3
		Teacher P	Room 4-D	Coach 4
2:15–2:45	Catch up, organize data, and dismissal			

FIGURE 6.2. Sample screening schedule. From A. M. VanDerHeyden & M. K. Burns, "Essentials of Response to Intervention" (2010), in *Essentials of Psychological Assessment*, p. 25. Copyright 2010 by John Wiley and Sons, Inc. Reprinted by permission.

At the appointed time, the coach goes to the assigned classroom with a class roster, the scripted administration procedures, a digital timer, and the screening materials. The coach notes which students are absent and then helps the teacher conduct the screening. If ORF data are being collected, the coach double-scores the first two to five students to ensure that teachers are scoring accurately. At the end of the screening period, all students in the classroom have been screened in reading, mathematics, and writing. At the lower grade levels, the screening may take the full hour if ORF data are collected. At the higher grade levels where measures can be group administered for reading or math, the entire class can be screened in about 15 minutes. Once the screening data are collected, the coach organizes the data. Coaches attend grade-level planning periods the day following screening to help teachers score all the screening measures administered in their classes, and these data are entered into a database by the end of the day. If a computer-based screening tool is being used, similar procedures can be followed to ensure that the computer sessions occur efficiently and without interruption or distraction so that the scores will be meaningful. A sample checklist is provided in Form 6.2 (at the end of the chapter) that data teams may use to verify and document the quality of screening data prior to using screening data for decision making.

Once the data are collected, the more important task of understanding and interpreting the data begins. Scores are organized by classroom as in Figures 6.3 and 6.4. Each child's performance is shown relative to the expected benchmark criterion for performance. Children above the criterion are not at risk, and children below the criterion are at risk. In Figure 6.3, one can see that most children in the class are performing at or above the risk criterion. In this class, there is no classwide problem. When there is no classwide problem, core instruction is considered to be sufficient and is ruled out as a cause of poor performance for students identified as at risk, including those being evaluated for SLD. Where the majority of the class is performing above the risk criterion, small groups of students or individual students may be identified for Tier 2 or 3 interventions.

If the class median score is below the risk benchmark, then a classwide problem is detected and must be addressed prior to singling out individual children for Tier 2 and 3 intervention. Figure 6.4 provides an example of a classwide problem. Most children in this class are performing below the criterion of 40 digits correct in 2 minutes on an expected grade-level skill. When a classwide problem is detected, data teams examine the data to determine whether low performance is a systemic problem affecting many classes, grades, and/or the entire school. The flowchart in Figure 6.5 shows the sequence of decisions that data teams make to determine the scope of detected performance problems. Teams follow the flowchart in Figure 6.5 to determine what type of intervention should be used. For example, if a class median score is below the

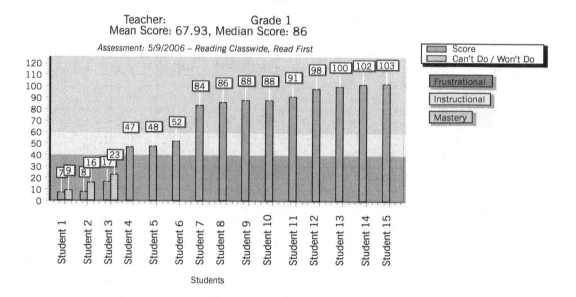

FIGURE 6.3. Performance of all students in the class on the classwide screening. Data teams can conclude that there is no classwide learning problem given the median score (86 wcpm), which is in the mastery range (top horizontal shaded area ranging from 60 to 120 wcpm).

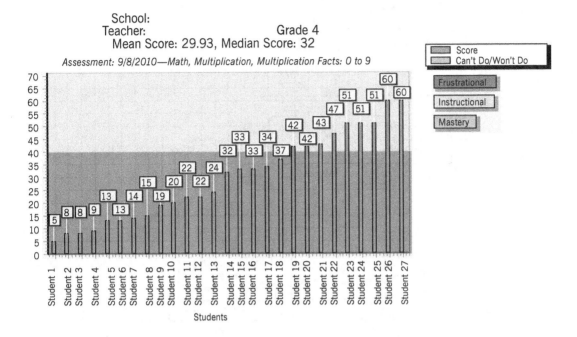

FIGURE 6.4. Performance of all students in the class during classwide screening for mathematics in a fourth-grade classroom. The median score (32 digits correct per 2 minutes) falls in the risk range (0–40 digits correct per 2 minutes) indicating there is a classwide learning problem.

screening criterion, but most classes at that grade level are doing well (i.e., have median scores greater than the screening criterion), then the data team treats the problem as an isolated class-wide performance problem and proceeds with classwide intervention. If, however, more than 50% of classes in a grade have median scores below the screening benchmark, then a gradewide intervention should be planned. Figures 6.6 and 6.7 provide examples of gradewide and school-wide learning problems respectively. In Figure 6.6, all classes at a given grade level are shown. Class 1 has 67% of students below criterion on screening. Class 2 has 86% of students below criterion on screening, and so on. All classes have at least 50% of students performing below the screening benchmark or in the risk range, indicating a gradewide learning problem. When a gradewide problem is detected at a given grade level (fourth grade in Figure 6.6), then data teams should examine the gradewide graphs for the other grade levels in the school to determine where students begin to fall behind performance expectations. In Figure 6.7, gradewide graphs are presented for grades 3, 2, and 1. In all three grades, more than half of the classes have classwide learning problems. When a schoolwide performance problem is detected, it is more effective and efficient to implement systemic solutions that cut across grades. A common error in RTI implementation is trying to treat systemic problems like the one shown in Figure 6.7 as individual student learning problems that rapidly overwhelm the school's capacity to manage intervention and does not produce the kind of widespread instructional changes that are warranted to ensure all students receive the instruction they need to master expected grade-level skills.

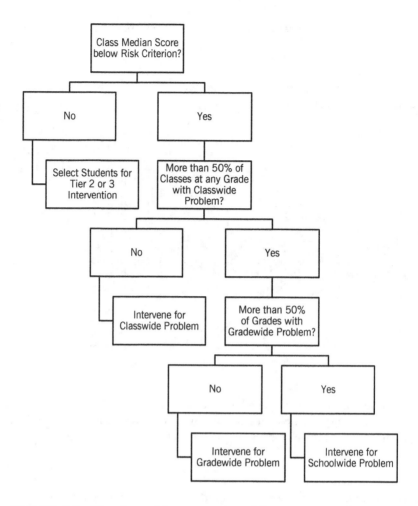

FIGURE 6.5. Flowchart of decision making following universal screening.

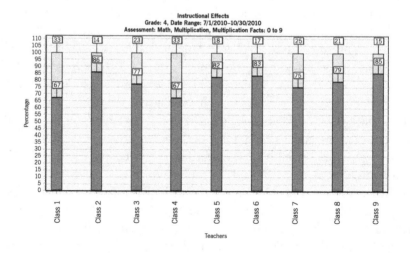

FIGURE 6.6. Performance of all classes at a given grade level (grade 4, in this example). The darker portion of each bar reflects the percentage of students in the risk range. The lighter portion of each bar reflects the percentage of students not in the risk range on screening. In this grade, all classes have a classwide learning problem according to the screening data.

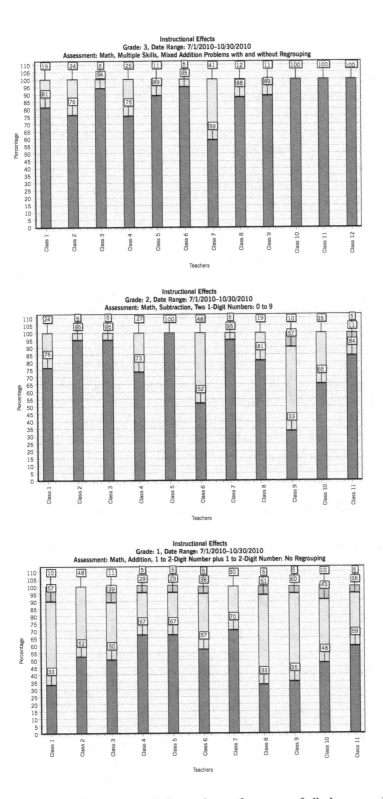

FIGURE 6.7. The top panel of this graph shows the performance of all classes at third grade on the same screening task during universal screening. The middle panel shows the performance of all classes at second grade. The bottom panel shows the performance of all classes at first grade. At all grade levels, classwide learning problems are detected in most, if not all, classes. These screening data indicate the presence of a schoolwide learning problem.

Tier 2 and Tier 3 interventions should be planned and implemented after classwide, grade-wide, and schoolwide learning problems have been addressed. Classwide, gradewide, and schoolwide problems provide evidence that core instruction has not been sufficient. Where core instruction has been found to be insufficient, data teams must focus problem-solving dis-cussion on strategies to verify the adequacy of core instruction and corrective actions that may be taken to improve learning and resolve classwide, gradewide, and schoolwide learning prob-lems. In Table 6.1, a summary of actions and follow-up analyses are provided for data teams to consider when classwide, gradewide, or schoolwide problems are detected. Importantly, whatever corrective actions are taken by the team, subsequent screening data can be used to evaluate whether those corrective actions were successful. Where systemic learning problems are detected, screening can and should be repeated more frequently (e.g., monthly) until the systemic problem is resolved. Data teams can use Table 6.1 to plan the corrective actions and follow-up assessment to determine whether the corrective actions had the desired effect. Imple-menters may find useful research syntheses that summarize instructional strategies that have been found to produce positive learning gains in well-controlled research studies. Interested readers might consult Hattie (2009) and the Center for Data-Driven Reform in Education at Johns Hopkins University (*www.bestevidence.org/index.cfm*). These sources allow implement-ers to determine whether a strategy has been shown to work in research and therefore is an important first step in identifying strategies that can work if they are well aligned with system and student needs and they are implemented with integrity (Burns, Riley-Tillman, & VanDer-Heyden, 2012). See Table 6.2 for a summary of effective intervention programs and strategies for classwide, small-group, and individual intervention.

ASSESSING SUFFICIENCY OF INTERVENTIONS AT TIERS 2 AND 3

RTI implementation requires knowing who is getting intervention, when the intervention is occurring, and what the effects of that intervention are over time. Data teams maintain a log of Tier 2 and Tier 3 interventions in which they record the student's name, grade level, teacher, in-class screening score, start date of the intervention, and whether the intervention has been successful or not. This log can be kept in an Excel file as shown in Figure 6.8.

Evidence of sufficient multi-tier interventions (Tiers 1, 2, and 3) is obtained in two ways. First, most children who receive Tier 2 and 3 intervention should experience success. Research studies can be used to estimate what percentage of students should require tiered intervention. Up to 20% of students may require Tier 2 intervention to master identified learning objectives. Up to 10% of students may require Tier 3 intervention. Of those children exposed to Tier 3 intervention, 1–5% may be expected to have a failed response to intervention, necessitating referral for an eligibility evaluation. These estimates are greatly affected by the overall level of achievement in the school and the extent to which schoolwide academic improvement efforts are implemented. For example, VanDerHeyden, Witt, and Naquin (2003) found that 15% of first- and second-grade students in a school required some type of intervention, and 5% had not experienced intervention success using short-term researcher-implemented intervention. Later, in a districtwide trial using the same assessment procedures and decision rules, Van-DerHeyden, Witt, and Gilbertson (2007) found that only 2% of students required individual intervention when classwide intervention was implemented rigorously in mathematics. Ideally,

TABLE 6.1. Data Team Decision Making

Screening finding	Follow-up actions	Was the corrective action successful?
Classwide Problem	1. Start classwide intervention. 2. Monitor growth weekly until class median reaches criterion. 3. Identify individual students who remain at risk when classwide problem is resolved.	Percentage of classes with classwide problems in subsequent semesters and years of RTI should decrease. Class 2 in Figure 6.9 is an example of a successfully resolved classwide learning problem.
Gradewide problem	1. Examine core instruction procedures (instructional time allocations, use of research-supported curriculum materials, calendar of instruction, understanding and measurement of mastery of specific learning objectives). 2. Begin classwide supplemental intervention to catch students up. Monitor growth weekly in all classes. (Figure 6.9 provides examples of how to monitor classwide interventions.) 3. Conduct vertical teaming meeting with preceding and subsequent grade levels to ensure children attain grade-level expected skills at that grade level in the future.	Percentage of classes with classwide problems in subsequent semesters and years of RTI should decrease. Figure 6.9 is an example of a successfully resolved gradewide learning problem.
Schoolwide problem	1. Examine core instruction materials and procedures (instructional time allocations, use of research-supported curriculum materials, calendar of instruction, understanding and measurement of mastery of specific learning objectives). 2. Establish priorities for improvement and determine timeline for implementation. Add a supplemental instructional program in the prioritized content area with weekly progress monitoring to ensure effects. 3. Conduct data team school improvement meetings to evaluate implementation effects each month and make adjustments to process. Meet with schools in feeder pattern to share data on implementation effects and plan strategies to support long-term success of students.	Percentage of classes with classwide problems should decrease in subsequent semesters and years of RTI. Percentage of students at risk should decrease over time. Percentage of students at risk by demographic categories should become proportionate with performance gaps closing. Percentage of students "on track" on longer-term outcomes in the system (e.g., percentage of students enrolling in and passing algebra, AP enrollment and scores, percent of students taking ACT and meeting ACT benchmarks) should increase.

(continued)

TABLE 6.1. *(continued)*

Screening finding	Follow-up actions	Was the corrective action successful?
Small-group problem	1. Use Tier 2 instructional time to provide more explicit instruction following a standard protocol. 2. Monitor progress of students participating in Tier 2 every other week. Exit students based on postintervention performance in the not-at-risk range on the lesson objectives and the screening measure/criterion. Provide weekly graph to teachers showing growth of students participating in Tier 2. Troubleshoot Tier 2 intervention until most children are showing growth as expected. 3. When most children are successfully responding to Tier 2 intervention, identify children who are not growing and plan Tier 3 intervention for those students.	Most students participating in Tier 2 intervention should meet intervention success criteria (about 90%). Students who met success criteria during Tier 2 intervention should surpass the screening criterion at higher rates on subsequent screenings. Students meeting success criteria on Tier 2 intervention should pass the year-end accountability measure at higher rates.
Individual problem	1. Conduct individual assessment to establish intervention target(s), identify an effective intervention, and specify baseline rates of performance. 2. Prepare all needed materials to conduct the intervention. 3. Monitor intervention performance weekly on the targeted intervention skill and the screening measure. Provide weekly graphs to teachers and parents showing student progress. 4. Troubleshoot the intervention weekly to accelerate student growth.	Most children participating in Tier 3 intervention should respond successfully. No more than 2–5% of the screened population should fail to respond to Tier 3 intervention. An inadequate response to intervention can only be determined when the intervention has been implemented with integrity for a sufficient period of time (e.g., 2 weeks). Growth due to intervention should be apparent within 2 weeks when an intervention is implemented well. Interventions not producing growth should be adjusted. Students meeting success criteria at Tier 3 should appear in the risk range on subsequent screenings at lower rates. Students meeting success criteria at Tier 3 should perform in the proficient range or higher at higher rates on the year-end accountability measure. Children who have a failed response to Tier 3 intervention should qualify for special education services at higher rates. Inadequate response to Tier 3 intervention should be proportionate by demographic categories.

TABLE 6.2. Summary of Effective Intervention Programs and Strategies

Instructional intensity	Name of intervention	Key strategies	Ideal for . . .	Research citation
Tier 1 or 2	Classwide peer tutoring	Maximizes opportunities to respond.	Proficiency or fluency building	Greenwood, Dinwiddie, et al. (1984)
Tier 1 or 2	Peer-assisted learning strategies	Structured support for student corrective feedback, maximizes opportunities to respond, gradual increases in task difficulty.	Proficiency or fluency building	Fuchs, Fuchs, Mathes, & Simmons (1997)
Tier 1 or 2	Classwide math intervention	Guided practice with immediate corrective feedback, content aligned with student performance, gradual increases in task difficulty, maximizes opportunities to respond, student error correction, contingency for improved performance.	Proficiency or fluency building	VanDerHeyden, McLaughlin, Algina, & Snyder (2012)
Tier 1 or 2	HELPS	Repeated reading, content aligned with student performance, immediate corrective feedback, and contingency for improved performance.	Proficiency or fluency building	Begeny et al. (2010)
Tier 3	Cover–copy–compare	Model of correct response, practice responding, immediate error correction.	Acquisition	Skinner, Beatty, Turco, & Rasavage (1989)
Tier 3	Guided practice	Prompting to ensure correct responding, immediate corrective feedback.	Acquisition	Ardoin, Williams, Klubnik, & McCall (2009)
Tier 3	Incremental rehearsal	Systematic increase in exposure to unlearned or unknown items. Content is aligned with student performance very precisely with one unknown item trained each session. Systematic repeated exposure to recently learned items to promote retention.	Acquisition and fluency building. Ideal for skills that must be memorized.	Burns, Zaslofsky Kanive, & Parker, (2012)
Tier 3	Task interspersal	Increases exposure and practice for unknown items by mixing them with known (or easier or preferred) items.	Proficiency	Neef, Iwata, & Page (1977)

Student	Teacher	Grade	Content	Intervention	Final Intervention Score	Successful	Start Date	Date Adjusted	End Date
Student A	Teacher A	2	Math	2-digit subtraction with and without regrouping	53 digits correct/2 min	Yes	1/26/11	2/14/11	3/4/11
Student B	Teacher A	2	Reading	Standard protocol oral reading with comprehension check	72 wcpm	Yes	2/18/11	3/4/11	3/17/11
Student C	Teacher B	3	Math	Multiplication 0–9	59 digits correct/2 min	Yes	3/14/11		3/25/11

FIGURE 6.8. Sample intervention log.

when more than 20% of students appear to need intervention, the need for systemic attention to core instruction is needed. The difficulties that occur when high numbers of students are in need of Tier 2 and/or Tier 3 interventions present serious logistical problems. In schools where more than 20% of students need supplemental intervention, the number of resources needed to provide such interventions are significant. Therefore, a first step is to ensure that 20% or fewer students require Tier 2 and 10% or fewer require Tier 3 intervention.

Although reaching the key level of no more than 20% of students needing Tier 2 or Tier 3 support is an aspirational goal, many implementers of RTI, especially in historically low-performing schools, find that reaching such levels is unlikely in the initial years of RTI model implementation. We have found that if schools have the resources, it is possible to simultaneously address both systemic core instructional weaknesses as well as implement needed Tier 2 and Tier 3 interventions to specific students. For example, Clemens, Shapiro, Hilt-Panahon, and Gischlar (2011) and Zigmond, Kloo, and Stanfa (2011) described RTI implementation in high-need schools where initial levels of students in need of supplemental intervention exceeded the 20% level, but simultaneous addressing of core and supplemental instruction was possible. Both model implementations showed significant improvement over a 3-year period, which approached levels of no more than 20% of students in need of supplemental support to core instruction.

Second, the percentage of students requiring Tier 2 and Tier 3 intervention over time should decrease. Stated another way, when effective multi-tier intervention is provided, the percentage of students at risk should decline across subsequent screening occasions. The top panel in Figure 6.9 shows the percentage of students at risk (and therefore receiving tiered intervention) at fall and winter screenings. Organizing the data in this way allows decision makers to rapidly identify whether interventions are reducing the percentage of students at risk for academic failure and also to identify classes where teachers may require in-class support to provide greater effects for students. In this example, Class 1 has 33% of students below criterion at the fall screening. By winter, only 9% of students remain in the risk range. Class 2 experiences a reduction from 56% of students at risk at fall screening to 5% at winter screening. These reductions are powerful indicators that instructional efforts are paying off with more students experiencing success. Organizing the data in this way allows data teams to rapidly identify classes in which risk reductions are not adequate. In this example, Class 6 does not show a

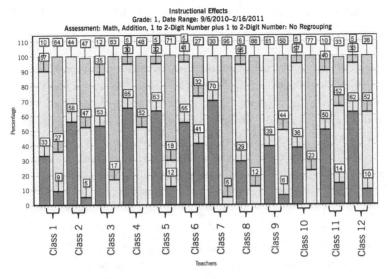

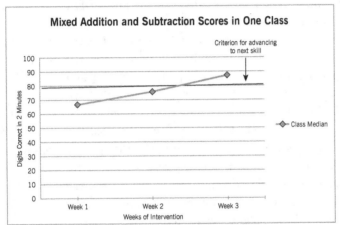

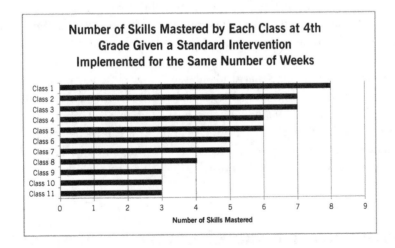

FIGURE 6.9. The top panel shows the percentage of students at risk (and therefore receiving tiered intervention) across subsequent screening occasions within a single grade level. The middle panel shows the median score for a single class across weeks of classwide intervention. The bottom panel shows the number of skills mastered by class within a single grade level where all classes are participating in the same classwide intervention.

strong reduction in the number of students at risk between the fall and winter screening. The data team can engage in a troubleshooting process to identify why Class 6 has not shown results comparable to the other classes (e.g., Is the teacher adhering to the instructional calendar? Is Tier 2 intervention occurring as planned in this class? What changes can be made to accelerate gains for students in this class?). Troubleshooting is likely to require observing intervention implementation in the classroom and more frequent assessment in that classroom to verify that the class begins to make gains. The spring screening can be used to verify that intervention efforts successfully accelerated the progress of students in that classroom.

Student performance data are a powerful tool for discussing overall classwide response to instruction. Schools that understand how to consume and respond to their student performance data can assist all teachers to be successful and highly effective. Data patterns can be used to identify areas in which teachers might benefit from professional development support and/or revisions to curricular goals and materials. Where classwide intervention is initiated, data teams can also examine weekly progress of each class to verify that growth is being made on the targeted skill (middle panel of Figure 6.9). Where gradewide intervention is underway, data teams can use the rate of student mastery of intervention objectives across classes as a powerful indicator of which classes need additional support to ensure that the intervention is successful. The bottom panel of Figure 6.9 shows that Classes 9, 10, and 11 are showing a slower rate of progress relative to other classes at their grade level that are using the same intervention protocol classwide. Data teams can use these data to troubleshoot intervention efforts or make midstream adjustments to the intervention so that the ultimate goal of reducing the number of students at risk in all classes is sure to be obtained by the spring screening.

Another indicator of progress is seen by examining the frequency with which students who have participated in tiered intervention return to the risk range on subsequent screenings. Remaining outside the risk range on subsequent screenings for those who have participated in intervention is powerful evidence of longer-term intervention success. Similarly, schools can look at the probability of passing the year-end accountability test for students who were initially identified as at risk and received tiered intervention. Over time and with effective implementation, one should see the students who receive intervention obtain higher scores on the year-end accountability test.

When collected data indicate that students receiving particular interventions are making meaningful progress (e.g., by high percentages of students leaving the risk range), it is reasonably concluded that an individual student being evaluated for SLD is not displaying a deficient rate of progress because of an insufficient intervention. If it can be demonstrated that the student has been exposed to an effective core instructional program as well as demonstrably effective supplemental interventions, a lack of instruction can be reasonably ruled out as a cause of poor performance.

ASSESSING AND DOCUMENTING TREATMENT INTEGRITY

In addition to analyzing the outcomes of core instruction and supplemental interventions, a potential lack of instruction can be appraised by directly assessing the integrity of instruction and interventions. Sanetti and Kratochwill (2009) describe intervention integrity as a multidimensional construct that includes content, quality, quantity, and process and offer this definition, "Treatment integrity is the extent to which essential intervention components are delivered in a comprehensive and consistent manner by an interventionist trained to deliver the intervention" (p. 448). Teacher report of intervention usage alone is not an adequate basis for measuring actual integrity (Noell et al., 2005; Wickstrom, Jones, Lafleur, & Witt, 1998). Researchers have demonstrated that direct observation of the intervention (Wickstrom et al., 1998), permanent products or written records that occur when the intervention is used (Mortenson & Witt, 1998), and child performance gains (Gilbertson, Witt, Singletary, & VanDerHeyden, 2008; VanDerHeyden, McLaughlin, Algina, & Snyder, in press) may be used to estimate actual intervention integrity.

Perhaps one of the most notable and prevalent threats to the accuracy of RTI decision making is the lack of intervention implementation integrity. Research tells us that poor intervention integrity is the rule rather than the exception (McIntyre, Gresham, DiGennaro, & Reed, 2007). Poor intervention integrity is such a common threat that decision makers must implement practices to both facilitate intervention implementation integrity and directly assess it as part of the intervention success/nonsuccess decision. For the purpose of ruling out incorrect intervention use as a cause of intervention failure, data teams should consider the following. The intervention must have been correctly selected, supported, and consistently and accurately

> **Perhaps one of the most notable and prevalent threats to the accuracy of RTI decision making is the lack of intervention implementation integrity.**

implemented to allow decision makers to determine whether the intervention was successful. In Form 6.3 (at the end of the chapter), an intervention troubleshooting checklist is provided that data teams can use to verify the adequacy of the intervention implementation data prior to determining that an intervention response has been unsuccessful. In addition, treatment integrity checklists that correspond to key features of supplemental standard protocol interventions (including those that are commercially available) may be used to appraise the extent to which a particular intervention is being implemented with integrity. Examples of such checklists can be found on the website of the Heartland (IA) Area Education Agency (*www.aea11.k12.ia.us:16080/ idm/checkists.html*). Because teacher self-monitoring is not sufficient for verifying treatment integrity, we recommend that other staff members who are trained in the intervention (e.g., reading coaches) conduct the integrity check. Ideally, the principal could include formal fidelity checks in her routine observations of teachers delivering both core instruction as well as supplemental interventions.

If the intervention has not been correctly or consistently used, in-class coaching to establish correct intervention use is required, and a period of stable intervention use is necessary to evaluate the effectiveness of the intervention. We recommend that intervention performance data be examined weekly and formatively to determine whether intervention is producing an upward trend toward the learning objective. If an upward trend in student performance is not detected, the intervention session should be observed by a trained coach who can offer feedback and troubleshoot the intervention to maximize intervention effects each week. An intervention should not be considered to be have failed at Tier 2 or Tier 3 unless data teams can answer "yes" to each question in the troubleshooting checklist provided in Form 6.3. If the team cannot answer "yes" to each question, a lack of instruction, or in this case intervention, cannot be ruled out for a student being considered for SLD identification.

DOCUMENTING SUFFICIENCY
OF INSTRUCTION AND INTERVENTION

To be effective in producing student gains, both core instruction and supplemental interventions need to be delivered with sufficient frequency and duration. For core instruction, adequate time must be allocated each day for instruction in the basic skills. Uninterrupted blocks of time are needed to ensure that all aspects of the material to be learned can be accommodated. Sufficient time needs to be available for teacher demonstrations, guided practice, and independent practice for students, while allowing for activities to differentiate for learners' varied needs. Similarly, interventions need to be scheduled during sufficient lengths of time to allow for the delivery of all aspects of the protocol. Failure to schedule adequate intervention time can lead to failed interventions.

Sufficiency of instruction and intervention is documented by subsequent screenings showing that most students perform at or above benchmark, no more than 20% of students require Tier 2 intervention, and no more than 10% require Tier 3 intervention. In those schools starting far below the goal of 80% of students at benchmark, examining a pattern of continuing upward levels of students at benchmark over time also indicates that instruction and intervention are having the desired effect. The percentage of students performing in the risk range should decline or remain very low across screening occasions, and most children exposed to Tier 2 and 3 interventions should experience success with those interventions. When intervention failures occur, direct assessment of integrity is required. Direct assessment of intervention integrity should include direct observation of intervention use or permanent products resulting from intervention use. Failure to deliver interventions with adequate sufficiency is a threat to decision accuracy and prohibits the use of intervention response data to rule out lack of adequate instruction.

SHARING RESULTS OF REPEATED ASSESSMENTS WITH PARENTS

The new provision in the 2006 IDEA regulations that schools provide the parents of a student thought to be SLD "data-based documentation of repeated assessments of achievement at reasonable intervals, reflecting formal assessment of student progress during instruction, which was provided to the child's parents" (§300.309[b]), reflects a continued emphasis in IDEA of the importance of school–parent communication. This communication is especially important when the school uses a multi-tier model of service provision that potentially includes multiple weeks of intervention. One rationale for the notion that schools should monitor students' progress and convey that information explicitly to parents is that interventions take time, and parents should be "in the loop" throughout the many tiers of instruction and intervention. Parents, caregivers, and other stakeholders have a right to see what kind of effects local educational systems are having on student learning in general and for their child in particular, especially when the child is experiencing difficulties.

Given that most systems conduct universal screening and enter those data into Web-based software programs, it is simple and easy to generate graphs and reports on a system's progress to share with stakeholders. Systems can share the percentage of students at risk at each screening occasion or the average score on a screening assessment by content area and by grade level. We suggest that these data be shared on the school website and through the school newsletter. Most schools are probably familiar with the thermometer figure that shows a goal for fundraising and shows how much has been raised up to a given point in time. Such figures are often on display in the entry areas of schools. Schools should give similar prominence to student performance data and provide transparent accounting of the effects of their school improvement and intervention efforts.

Sharing assessment results with parents need not be a cumbersome requirement. Teachers can and should be trained to share classwide screening results at parent–teacher conferences. The teacher can simply cover the names of the other students and show the parent where his or her student is performing compared to other students in the class and the benchmark criterion. Some schools send home the classwide graph with all other student names removed. Other schools provide a brief summary describing what assessment was conducted and provide a student score along with a checkmark in a menu of outcomes that might read as follows: (1) child appears to be doing well, no intervention is needed at this time; (2) child's score is lower than we would like it to be so we will do some follow-up work with the child to be sure that the child does not require intervention; or (3) when a child scores below [specify criterion], the school provides intervention during the regular school day as part of our regular school routine. Suggested wording for this type of announcement would be as follows: "We would like to provide extra help to your child in a small group or one-on-one with a classroom teacher. Please call us to schedule a visit to the school so we can talk about the intervention and answer any questions you may have. We will start the intervention right away, and we can schedule a meeting with you at your convenience. Please call us if you have concerns or questions."

Schools should adopt the routine of sending home performance graphs for students who are participating in Tier 2 or Tier 3 intervention. We suggest that the intervention protocol be copied and paired with the graph of student progress with a handwritten note updating parents on intervention progress and indicating whether the intervention will continue the following week. Parents can be provided with an e-mail address and teacher phone number should they have questions about the intervention.

Sample Universal Screening Assessment Inventory to Be Completed for Each Content Area Screened

Content or Skill Area	Assessment Name	Cost of Measure	Time Required to Administer	Frequency of Administration	What Decision Is Made? (circle one)	Adequacy/Accuracy of Measure?
					• Initial or continued risk/screening • Instruction or intervention development or modification/formative • Intervention effects/progress monitoring • Program evaluation	
					• Initial or continued risk/screening • Instruction or intervention development or modification/formative • Intervention effects/progress monitoring • Program evaluation	
					• Initial or continued risk/screening • Instruction or intervention development or modification/formative • Intervention effects/progress monitoring • Program evaluation	

Checklist for Screening Data Interpretation

Check if true:	Screening Data May Be Used for Decision Making If the Following Conditions Are Met:
	Measure content is aligned with state standards and reflects a skill that students have been taught and must know how to do to benefit from upcoming instruction.
	Scores on measure are predictive of future performance.
	Measure yields reliable scores.
	Measure is brief and efficiently administered.
	Measure yields scores that are sensitive to changes in learning over time.
	Assessment inventory was completed to prevent overassessment.
	Procedures were used to ensure that data collection occurred accurately.
	Graphs were generated for classroom teachers showing each child's performance relative to other children in the same class and a risk benchmark criterion.
	All students participated in screening.
	Schoolwide, gradewide, and classwide patterns of performance were evaluated to identify whether schoolwide, gradewide, or classwide problems were present.

Intervention Troubleshooting Checklist

LEVEL 1: Troubleshoot Problem Definition and Data System	Yes	No
Were all students in the class screened using the same measure?		
Are data of sufficient quality to make decisions (i.e., sensitive to change, reliable, reflect the outcome desired)?		
Was the screening task aligned with instructional expectations according to the state standards?		
Are data available to verify that the screening was correctly conducted?		
Is the screening criterion efficient, accurate, and has it been correctly applied?		
Did teachers receive graphs of student performance by class and by grade?		
Does screening occur three times per year for all classes?		
Summary *If yes is marked in all rows, then the screening data may be used for decision making.* *Proceed to Level 2.*		
LEVEL 2: Troubleshoot Data Interpretation	**Yes**	**No**
Are at least 50% of students performing at or above the screening benchmark (i.e., is the class median score greater than the benchmark)? If not, there is a classwide learning problem.		
Do at least 50% of classes in each grade have class median scores that exceed the screening criterion? If not, there is a gradewide learning problem.		
Do at least 50% of grades in the school have classes with median scores that exceed the screening criterion? If not, there is a schoolwide learning problem.		
Have screening data been organized by poverty status, ethnicity, language status, and gender to verify proportionate numbers of students at risk and growth over time that closes any identified performance gaps?		
Summary *If yes is marked in all rows, then the data have been examined adequately to plan corrective actions at Tiers 1 and 2.*		

(continued)

Adapted from Witt, VanDerHeyden, and Gilbertson (2004) and VanDerHeyden and Burns (2010).

LEVEL 3: Troubleshoot Core and Supplemental Instruction	Yes	No
Does the teacher utilize lesson plans that provide for clear directions, guided practice, frequent opportunities to respond, and feedback?		
Are high-quality research-based curricular materials available to guide instruction?		
Do teachers follow an instructional calendar that specifies a timeline for mastering essential skills at each grade level?		
Are student data collected to verify mastery of essential skills?		
Is Tier 2 intervention sufficient to meet the needs of students who are not mastering essential skills?		
Does Tier 2 intervention involve more explicit instruction (modeling, frequent opportunities to respond, immediate corrective feedback, repetition loops, structured materials that are matched to student instructional level and gradually increased in difficulty as learning progresses)?		
Are student progress data collected weekly with criteria applied for exiting students from Tier 2 and adding new students who are struggling?		
Are fewer than 20% of screened students at risk on subsequent screenings?		

Summary
If yes is marked in all rows, then data are adequate to plan individual interventions at Tier 3.
Proceed to Level 4.

LEVEL 4: Troubleshoot Intervention Integrity	Yes	No
• Intervention was developed based on student assessment.		
Was a functional academic assessment conducted to establish intervention targets and baseline level of performance?		
Was the intervention tested to verify that it produces improved learning when it is correctly used prior to installing it in the classroom?		
• Interventionist support and training was provided.		
Was the intervention developed to ensure that it required minimal classroom time and resources and fit within daily classroom routines?		
Has the teacher accepted and committed to conduct the intervention?		
Are materials (e.g., rewards, worksheets) readily available to the teacher?		
Was a step-by-step protocol describing how to implement the intervention provided?		
Was the teacher shown how to implement the intervention by a "coach"?		
Did the coach observe implementation of the intervention to ensure that the teacher could use the intervention correctly and had all needed materials?		
Was weekly follow-up support provided to the teacher after initial training?		

(continued)

LEVEL 4: Troubleshoot Intervention Integrity *(continued)*	Yes	No
• Integrity of the intervention is monitored.		
Is integrity monitored via permanent products?		
Do permanent products accurately indicate intervention use?		
Are permanent products reviewed with the teacher?		
• Performance management is occurring.		
Are integrity data graphed?		
Are performance data graphed (replacement and problem behavior)?		
Has performance feedback been used?		
Is an administrator involved?		
• Is the intervention occurring daily as planned?		

Summary

If yes is marked in all rows, then the teacher has been adequately trained to use an intervention and intervention integrity is accurately assessed. If the intervention did not change the problem behavior, then proceed to Level 5.

LEVEL 5: Troubleshoot Intervention Design	Yes	No
Is the student making errors during the intervention? If so, has task difficulty been reduced?		
Have incentives been added and adjusted to support improved performance?		
Does the student need acquisition-type learning supports (e.g., more extensive demonstrations of correct and incorrect responding, guided practice with more elaborate feedback)?		
Does the student need fluency-building learning supports (e.g., more opportunities to respond, goal setting, incentives for more fluent performance each day)?		

CHAPTER 7

The Observation Requirement

This chapter provides a discussion of the conceptual rationale and methods for conducting class-room observations, a requirement of completing a comprehensive evaluation. Readers interested in a fuller and more detailed discussion of conducting behavioral observations should see key publications by Hintze and Shapiro (1995), Hintze, Volpe, and Shapiro (2008), Shapiro (2011a), Shapiro and Skinner (1990), Skinner, Rhymer, and McDaniel (2000), and Volpe, DiPerna, Hintze, and Shapiro (2005).

As discussed in Chapter 1, one of the significant provisions in the 2006 IDEA regulations is the requirement that observation of the student in the classroom is considered a required part of a comprehensive evaluation when making a determination of SLD. Specifically, IDEA requires evaluation teams to "use information from an observation in routine classroom instruction and monitoring of the child's performance" (§300.310[b][1]). Observation has typically been a funda-mental (although not required) part of a comprehensive evaluation for students referred because of social or emotional difficulties. However, the explicit requirement of observing classroom behavior for students referred because of learning difficulties has particular implications as to the intent of the policy makers in placing the observational requirement into the law.

First, observing student behavior in the classroom offers opportunities for evaluators to better understand the educational ecology within which learning is occurring. Shapiro (2011a), Lentz and Shapiro (1986), and Greenwood, Horton, and Utley (2002), among many others, have historically linked student academic achievement to specific classroom variables such as rate of active engagement, rate of correct responses to instruction, and opportunities to respond and practice skills (Greenwood, Delquadri, & Hall, 1984; Greenwood, Delquadri, Stanley, Terry, & Hall, 1985; Greenwood et al., 2002; Hall, Delquadri, Greenwood, & Thurston, 1982; Soukup, Wehmeyer, Bashinski, & Boviard, 2007). Indeed, there is a strong literature that shows the under-standing of contextual factors surrounding the learning process can potentially be the strongest explanatory factors about a student's academic success. Many have advocated that assessing the instructional environment needs to play at least an equal role to assessing a student's academic skill development (Christenson & Anderson, 2002; Ysseldyke & Christenson, 1987).

Second, observing classroom behavior provides opportunities to directly assess the qual-ity and nature of the teacher's instructional process. One of the key provisions of conducting a comprehensive evaluation for students being referred for learning problems is to demonstrate that the student is receiving high-quality instruction. Indeed, it is critical to assess whether a student's difficulties are more a function of *how* the student is being taught than the lack of acquisition of skills related to an underlying SLD.

Third, assessing student classroom behavior offers focused examinations of a student's level and nature of engagement with academic tasks. The links between the level and type of engagement during academic instruction have a long and well-documented research history showing the links to academic outcomes for students.

In general, classroom observations of both student behavior and teacher-student interactions can offer important insights into the root causes of academic skills problems. These observations become an essential ingredient in completing a comprehensive evaluation and are critical in determining recommendations likely to lead to improved academic performance. The observation requirement is pertinent to all four of the criteria for SLD. For example, in considering evidence for Criterion 4, classroom observations help to document the rule-out of lack of instruction and the provision of information on repeated assessments to the parents. There is no substitute for direct examination of the learning context to understand what barriers may contribute to a child's learning struggles. This observation is relevant to explain why a planned intervention is successful or not. This observation is also relevant to obtain feedback for improving the effects of intervention, either to rule out SLD or to plan longer-term instruction when SLD is identified. For example, it is possible that a student may have an adequate response to well-controlled intervention, but as the intervention is removed, the student's learning problems return. An observation can provide information about typical instructional conditions in the classroom and whether those conditions offer a good match for the student (i.e., "right" amount of adult support, tasks and content well aligned with student's instructional capabilities). It is also possible that an intervention implemented as part of the eligibility decision may not be implemented correctly or effectively. One of the best ways to determine whether the intervention is being implemented in the strongest way possible is to observe the intervention in the classroom and conduct troubleshooting to improve the intervention's effects. For example, observations can be used to document that the student was well engaged during intervention or, if not, that engagement improved during the intervention. Finally, the differentiation between a performance-based (won't do) and skills-based (can't do) problem is a critical outcome anticipated based on the observational process.

> **Classroom observations of both student behavior and teacher–student interactions can offer important insights into the root causes of academic skills problems.**

KEY BEHAVIORS FOR OBSERVATIONAL ASSESSMENT

Two broad classes of behaviors are critical targets for assessing students' academic behaviors. First, it is crucial to understand fully the level and type of engagement that students have with the assigned academic work. Students who are not fully engaged in the learning process are likely to miss key elements of instruction, resulting in lower academic performance (and lower-performing students are less likely to be academically engaged). Because learning tends to be cumulative, missing elements of the learning process at one point in time is likely to lead to subsequent sustained academic failure due to the fact that students have failed to master the prerequisite skills for learning. Although the particular level of engagement needed for students to succeed can vary greatly depending on student needs as well as the type of task that students are trying to master, students must be engaged in the learning process above some minimum level.

Beyond the level of engagement, the type of engagement is also critical. Academic engagement can be classified into one of two categories: active or passive. Active engagement involves students who are actively taking part in the learning process as evidenced by answering questions, engaging in discussions with the teacher or classmates around the academic problems they are trying to solve, and writing responses to questions. In contrast, students can also be engaged passively by attending to the teacher or classmates, listening to discussions, reading their textbooks, and other nonactive forms of engagement. Research has consistently shown that for students who struggle academically, active engagement produces better learning than passive engagement (Greenwood et al., 2002). Engagement has been measured as "opportunities to respond," which captures a student's response to antecedent cues for student responding such as a task (e.g., worksheet problems) or a teacher question as discrete events or trials. Research has demonstrated that classroom learning structures that increase opportunities to respond (e.g., peer tutoring, reciprocal teaching, cooperative learning) are likely to have stronger links to achievement than classroom structures such as completing worksheets or individual seatwork that rely primarily on more passive interactions (Hattie, 2009). Although passive engagement is important in learning, the weight of interaction for struggling students must be on the side of active learning processes.

A second broad category of behaviors that should be captured in observations are those behaviors that are incompatible with effective learning outcomes and are often termed "off-task" behaviors. Off-task behaviors include out-of-seat, calling out, inappropriate motor behavior, and other similar behaviors. Observations need to capture the level and nature of these behaviors that compete with and prevent successful learning outcomes.

It is important to recognize that collecting observational data on on/off-task behavior alone may not be detailed enough to fully capture the relationship of the academic environment to the student's academic difficulties. Many times, students who appear on task (i.e., passive on task) may actually be "daydreaming" and not really paying close attention to the material being taught. Observations that fail to look carefully underneath the apparent on-task behavior will frequently miss key elements of the learning environment that are not supporting a student's academic behavior. Likewise, a student who appears to be off task to a high degree may actually be paying attention in ways that are not detrimental to the student acquiring and mastering the needed skills. For example, a student may gaze at the ceiling while contemplating a mathematics problem or a question posed by the teacher. Again, unless one obtains details that are beyond the surface collection of on/off-task behavior, full understanding of the relationship between the academic environment and the student's academic problems will not be attained.

METHODS OF OBSERVATION

Procedures for conducting classroom observations can range broadly from simple, macro-level narrative descriptions to the use of complex observational codes designed to capture micro-level events within the classroom structure. The objective for the data collection should be to make sure that the data collected address the critical questions for decision making regarding a student's eligibility for special education. In addition, the data must be sufficiently quantitative to allow objective description of the referred student's behavior, the instructional context in which the student's academic problem is occurring, and to capture the teacher–student and student–student interactions that occur as a natural part of the learning process.

> **The objective for observational data collection should be to make sure that the data collected address the critical questions for decision making regarding a student's eligibility for special education.**

Observational methods for classrooms can be categorized into three broad types: narrative, modified narrative, and systematic direct observation.

Narrative Observations

The simplest and perhaps the most frequently used form of classroom observation is writing a narrative description of the instructional process. Usually, this type of observation involves description with minimal levels of interpretation. The observer watches the student for a specified amount of time and writes a descriptive narrative of the observation. For example, the following observation was conducted of a 13-year-old girl referred for evaluation by her parents because of a suspected learning disability in mathematics. The girl had a trend of failing grades over the past 2 years after a fairly strong and consistent level of performance from kindergarten through fourth grade. The observer conducted the observation during a 30-minute period of mathematics instruction involving a mixture of teacher-directed instruction and small-group practice on math problems.

> During the observation, Pamela was in math class, and the teacher was explaining the new project they would be working on for that day and throughout the semester. Pamela paid close attention to her teacher during the instructions, but showed some off-task behavior during the small-group practice period. Her off-task behaviors included playing with her notebooks, walking around the room without an obvious purpose, and staring out the window. Following the observation, the observer spoke with Pamela's teachers, who reported that off-task behavior was not a concern. The teacher stated that her primary concern is that she does not ask for help with assignments when she does not understand the material and instead turns in assignments that have been completed incorrectly.

The narrative observation for Pamela showed some broad indications that she appeared to be attending to the teacher's instructions but also showed some level of competing behaviors. The teacher's perspective was that the level of the competing behavior was not of sufficient concern. Many details of this narrative observation are missing. For example, exactly what was the empirical level of her attending behavior? How did her level of attending behavior compare to her peers? What specifically were the competing behaviors? How often did these occur? Did her behavior in math vary by the nature of the instructional setting, such as small group, large group, or individual seatwork? Additional questions can be raised about the representativeness of this narrative description to other instructional periods of mathematics. How these questions might be answered for the comparison peer is also important in understanding whether and how Pamela's behavior diverges from that of other students in the same instructional situation.

In a second example of more extensive narrative, this second-grade student had been referred because of suspected learning disabilities in reading. The student was observed during a period of shared group reading where the teacher was leading the instruction.

> During the observation, the class was sitting on the carpet for shared reading. They had just finished reading a story and were searching for the letter combinations that they were talking about that week. Roberto volunteered to answer every time; he often called out "I know." When he was called upon to answer, he was able to correctly identify a word with a double *e* in it, *cheer*. His teacher asked him to read and he tried but he pronounced the *c* as a soft *c*. While he was sitting on the carpet he was fidgety and often moved about. At times he would touch the peers around him on their shirt or their head. During the observation, peers were considerably more on task than Roberto; however, they were engaging in the same fidgety behavior.

As with the first narrative example, broad indications of Roberto's behavior were evident. He appeared to be engaged and attending to the teacher's questions, although the accuracy of his academic response was questionable. Calling out before being called upon was evident throughout the observation, and Roberto did show signs of being fidgety, although the observer did not think Roberto was more fidgety than his peers. Despite these overall generalities, similar questions to the first observation can be asked for both Roberto and his peers. What was the exact level of his attending to the teacher's instructions, and how did this compare to his peers? How often did he call out? When he called out in response to questions, how often did he get the answers right? Was he called on (i.e., reinforced) by the teacher after he called out? How representative were these behaviors from other situations such as large-group instruction or independent seatwork? How representative were these behaviors from instruction during other subjects such as mathematics or writing? Were off-task behaviors more probable on academic tasks that are more challenging for Roberto?

Although the narrative observation offers some broad sense of the events occurring during a classroom observation, this method of observing raises more questions than it answers. Although the content of the observations represents the perspectives of a clinically trained professional, the narrative observation lacks precision and is potentially representing only the subjective views of the observer. Given these limitations, it is strongly recommended that narrative observation *not* be used as the primary method for meeting the observational requirement for conducting a comprehensive evaluation.

Modified Narrative Observations: The ABC Analysis

One process for making narrative recording more objective and empirically grounded is to place the observations within the framework of an analysis of the sequence of events transpiring in classrooms. Typically known as an antecedent–behavior–consequence (ABC) analysis, the observer records the events such that one can better determine the sequential nature of the behavioral responses. Figure 7.1 shows one such ABC analysis form. In this particular form, the observer at specified intervals (every 30 seconds, in this case) records the behavioral events and those events that immediately precede and follow the event. For example, as seen in Figure

Time	Antecedent	Behavior	Consequence
0:00	Teacher asks question.	Roberto calls out.	Teacher tells Roberto to raise hand before calling out.
0:30	Teacher asks question.	Roberto raises hand and answers question incorrectly.	Teacher thanks Roberto for raising his hand and corrects the incorrect response.
1:00	Teacher asks student to read aloud.	Roberto raises hand and says "I want to read."	Teacher tells Roberto he will get a turn soon.
1:30			
2:00			
2:30			
3:00			
3:30			
4:00			
4:30			
5:00			

FIGURE 7.1. ABC analysis form with Roberto using intervals.

7.1, the teacher responded in some way to all of Roberto's behavior, both calling out and hand raising. Such observations, when done over an extended period of time, result in an identified sequence that can provide some insights into student and teacher behavior and provide ideas for adjusting teacher–student interaction for greater behavioral success in the classroom. This type of observation can also be quantified (i.e., how many times across the observation did Roberto interrupt the teacher?) as well as provide a more focused and objective process for narrative recording. Other modifications of narrative observations that attempt to make them more objective would include a simple listing of events in chronological order as they happen in classrooms along with the related consequences that followed the event.

Although the ABC analysis has many advantages over simple narrative recording, the procedure still has substantial difficulties that render this type of observational procedure difficult and more subjective than one would want in conducting a comprehensive evaluation. Many times, the consequences of classroom behaviors are the antecedents for subsequent behaviors. Asking observers to separate these continuous events into discrete ABC units can result in data that are artificial and do not really reflect what is occurring in the natural classroom environment. For example, a sequence of events may involve a teacher asking a child who calls out to "raise your hand before calling out." Immediately after the teacher's response, the student calls out once again without raising his hand. In recording the sequence, the initial event is preceded by a teacher asking a question and followed by the teacher's comment. However, the second event is preceded by what was the consequence of the first event. Such sequences are not uncommon, and separating the consequence from antecedent becomes difficult.

Second, the ABC analysis assumes that the antecedents and consequences are linked temporally to the behavior. In other words, when a student calls out in class, it is assumed that the antecedent was the event immediately preceding, and the consequence is what occurred immediately afterward. At times, the antecedents and consequences of behavior are removed in time from the behavior. Assuming that the events occurring in a sequence are all temporally linked might lead to false conclusions about what is actually causing a student's behavior. For example, a student comes to school in the morning having been bullied on the bus ride just prior to school. When the teacher asks the student a question, the student responds by putting his head on his desk and ignoring the teacher. The teacher then tells the student to pay attention to the questions being asked. What may look like an antecedent of a teacher's question is really the student thinking about the events of the morning bus ride. Clearly, drawing conclusions about antecedents and consequences that are not temporally linked can be very problematic.

In general, although modified narratives offer a much richer picture of a classroom observation than simple narrative descriptions and can be critical in helping to better understand classroom context when conducting observations, such observations are rarely sufficient to meet the requirements of effective classroom observations. ABC analysis often is a precursor to more systematic direct observation, during which more quantifiable data are collected.

Systematic Direct Observation

Perhaps the most frequently recommended method for conducting classroom observations is the use of systematic direct observational procedures that include the collection of quantifiable data. These methods attempt to capture objective data that define the student's behavior in the classroom. The data need to be a direct reflection of what is actually occurring, reported in terms of quantified values that define the student's behavior, the teacher's behavior, and the interactions between teachers, students, and peers.

There are many different approaches to systematic direct observation, but all begin with developing operational definitions of the behavior. A key to developing effective operational definitions is to capture the nature of what is desired to be observed. For example,

> **Methods of systematic direct observation:**
>
> - **Frequency or event recording**
> - **Duration and latency recording**
> - **Time sampling interval recording**

if a classroom observation is designed to describe how a student responds to typical classroom instruction during a math lesson, then the operational behaviors used to define the observation must align with what typically is expected to happen when instruction occurs (i.e., paying attention to the teacher's instructions, writing responses on worksheets, conversing with peers about problems, remaining in one's seat during instruction, raising one's hand to answer questions). An effective operational definition is one that specifies what constitutes an occurrence of the behavior and what does not. A useful rule of thumb when developing an operational definition is that a second observer should be able to read the definition provided and identify occurrences of the behavior reliably. Once the behavior(s) is defined for observation, the way that the data are collected will vary depending on the nature of the behavior being observed. The observation method must be selected in concert with the behavior of interest. Each method of observation can yield somewhat different results, so it is important that the particular method and the resulting data source are fully understood.

Frequency or Event Recording

The recording of frequency or events involves the recording of the number of times a specific behavior occurs. Typically, frequency or event recording is done within a defined time period, allowing the data to be reported as a rate (i.e., number of occurrences/unit of time). For example, the observer might count the number of times a student interrupts a teacher-directed instructional lesson and report the mean number of interruptions across 60-minute instructional lessons. Converting the frequency to a rate (i.e., interruptions per minute) allows the observer to compare outcomes across observations when the amount of time observed varies (e.g., 10 interruptions in 60 minutes can be easily compared to 4 interruptions in 5 minutes when the data are converted to 0.16 interruptions per minute vs. 0.80 interruptions per minute).

Frequency or event recording is most applicable when the behavior of interest has a discrete beginning and end. Throwing paper airplanes, calling out, raising hands, and interruptions are all examples of behavioral events often seen during classroom instruction. Behaviors that persist for a period of time or are continuous are difficult to observe using frequency or event recording. For example, recording a student's academic engagement or on-task behavior would be difficult using frequency or event recording procedures.

Another important consideration in using frequency or event recording is the duration of each behavior. In general, use of frequency or event recording works best when the duration of each behavioral occurrence is approximately equal. For example, if one is counting the number of interruptions during an instructional lesson, it can be problematic if the interruptions vary from a short call-out to a drawn-out tantrum lasting 1 minute or more. Recording events would require a single incident recorded for both kinds of behaviors, whereas there is a clear difference between a single call-out and a tantrum that continues for a minute. In instances where event recording is used with behaviors that vary in length, one might combine event recording with duration recording (i.e., length of the interruption) as described below to better capture the behavior of interest.

A particularly important use of frequency or event recording is when the behavior occurs at a low rate but is an important behavior. Such behavior, while infrequent, would be of interest because of its intensity. For example, a student may refuse to do seatwork and run out of the classroom only once or twice a week, but recording such behaviors is critical to fully capturing the nature of the student's response to classroom requirements. Frequency or event recording represents the simplest and perhaps best method for capturing such behavior.

Methods for recording frequency or events are varied and can range from tallies on a piece of paper to use of recording devices such as mechanical or digital counters. Regardless of the method, any process that keeps track of the frequency of the behavior and records the setting events around the behavior (e.g., the nature of instructional demands, the subject matter, time of observation) is appropriate for recording frequency or events.

Duration and Latency Recording

If the nature of the behavior of interest is such that the amount of time from the start to end of the behavior is important, duration recording can be used. In particular, if one expects through subsequent intervention that the length of the response will be targeted, duration becomes a critical variable likely to reflect the outcomes of an intervention. For example, in terms of classroom observation, if a student is having difficulty completing class assignments within teacher-expected time parameters, it would be important to record how long each assignment takes to complete with a goal to reduce the amount of time while maintaining accuracy in performance.

Likewise, it might also be of interest in some cases to obtain data on how long it takes a student to start assignments once the student receives the direction to begin. This is known as recording latency or the elapsed time between a stimulus or signal (i.e., a verbal instruction to begin the lesson) and the initiation of the behavior (i.e., student starts working on the assignment).

In recording both duration and latency, the behavior of interest must have a well-defined beginning and ending point. Observers must have uniform agreement on what constitutes the stimulus event (i.e., starting point) and the end of the behavioral response. For duration, the end of the response is defined by the end of a period of time in which the behavior occurs. For latency, the end point is defined by the start of the behavioral event, with the beginning point defined as the teacher's prompt to the student to begin.

Methods for recording either duration or latency require precise timing devices. Stopwatches and other similar digital devices are designed for such precision and can easily be used to make these recordings. Technological applications exist for this type of recording as well. The data are reported as the average duration or latency per event.

Difficulties with duration and latency recording include the problem of behaviors that do not lend themselves to discrete starting and ending points, such as classroom engagement in instruction. Therefore, accuracy in duration and event recording can prove problematic since pinpointing the start and end of behaviors is critical to the accuracy of this type of recording.

Time Sampling Interval Recording

Whereas counting the actual occurrence of behaviors using frequency, event, duration, or latency is ideal in trying to accurately determine how often a behavior or set of behaviors occurs in classrooms, the difficulties of these methods to capture more continuous types of behaviors, as well as the practicality of observers having the time to sit in classrooms watching for discrete behavior to occur, present substantial limitations using these methods. As such, the use of time-sampling recording has emerged as probably the most efficient and valuable form of observational data collection for observing classroom instruction. The essential characteristic of time sampling is to select a time period for observation and to systematically sample behaviors in ways that provide data that represent the actual level of the behavioral occurrence. Because the behavior is sampled and not all occurrences of behavior are actually recorded, the data obtained from time sampling result in estimates of the actual occurrences of behavior. However, the nature of the sampling procedures allows for efficient use of observer time as well as mechanisms for systematically collecting quantitative data.

Time sampling procedures typically involve dividing an observational period into equal small units of time within which the behavior is observed. Although the time units can vary depending on the nature of the behavior being observed, typical units of a 30-minute observation would be subdivided into 120 15-second intervals. Within each interval, the presence or absence of the behavior is recorded, depending on which type of interval recording is being used (i.e., whole, partial, or momentary time sampling).

WHOLE-INTERVAL RECORDING

Whole-interval recording requires that the behavior being observed must be present throughout the entire designated interval to be recorded as having occurred. If the behavior ceases to occur at any point during the specified interval, the behavior is recorded as absent. Because the behavior must be present throughout the entire interval, whole-interval recording lends itself either to those behaviors likely to be continuous or to the use of very short intervals (e.g., 5 seconds; Shapiro & Skinner, 1990). For example, if the behavior of interest was sustained engagement in academic performance, use of whole-interval recording would allow the observer to determine whether the student was maintaining his or her attention for long periods of time. In contrast, if the behavior of concern was a competing behavior, such as getting out of seat or calling out, it is unlikely that there would be many intervals where the behavior was present (i.e., the behavior occurred throughout the entire 15-second interval). A short absence of the behavior in any interval would result with the interval being marked as the behavior not occurring. For example, if the child was out of her seat while the teacher was providing whole-group directions for a lesson and the child remained out of her seat for the first 13 seconds of the 15-second recording interval and then sat down for the last 2 seconds, out-of-seat behavior would not be recorded for that interval. Therefore, whole-interval recording tends to underestimate the actual occurrence of behavior.

PARTIAL-INTERVAL RECORDING

Partial-interval recording requires that the behavior being observed must be present during *any* portion of the interval to be recorded. If a behavior begins and ends within an interval, the behavior is recorded as having occurred during that interval. If multiple occurrences of the behavior appear within a single interval, the behavior is only marked that it occurred in that interval. Partial-interval recording is especially sensitive to detecting low-frequency behaviors or those that occur sporadically and for short periods of time because any instance is documented even when the instance is fleeting. An observer would count on-task occurrence for the student who is engaged with academic material for just a few seconds at a time. Because the recording of behavior under partial-interval recording requires that any single or small instance of behavior be recorded, partial-interval recording tends to overestimate the actual occurrence of the behavior.

MOMENTARY TIME SAMPLING

Momentary time sampling requires that the behavior being observed be recorded as present or absent at the specific moment that an interval begins or ends. This procedure involves essentially taking a "snapshot" of the behavior at specific timed intervals and indicating whether the behavior of interest was present or absent at that moment. A trained observer might look down at a timing device for 4 seconds and then looks up only for the 5th second (the last second in a 5-second interval) and records whatever behavior is occurring in that second repeating that process for all remaining intervals in the observation session. The technique is especially valuable when behaviors occur at a moderate level of frequency and are evident throughout the observational period. Momentary time sampling is typically found to result in estimates that are closest to actual rates of behavioral occurrence.

Although any single type of observational method can be used in conducting classroom observations, it is more typical that these methods will be combined in ways that best capture the behavior of interest. For example, if an observer is interested in observing teacher–student interactions, it might be best to devise a system where each instance of a teacher approaching a student is recorded, followed by the student response. When placed into an interval recording device, one could record the interval in which the teacher approached the student (partial-interval format) and whether the student responded to the teacher's approach within the same interval (partial-interval format). Likewise, if an observer is interested in the number of times a teacher approached a student, one could count the frequency of teacher approaches within an interval and thus combine frequency (event) and interval recording procedures. In other words, the observer can use the partial time sampling procedure to code the occurrence of behaviors during an interval (and report as conventional partial interval occurrence such as 20% of intervals containing a teacher approach or converted to 2 teacher approaches per minute) or the observer can code frequency of events within intervals noting potentially more than one teacher approach within a single interval and providing a more sensitive estimate of actual teacher approaches (e.g., 80 discrete teacher approaches during the same 10-minute or 60-interval observation period would equate to 8 approaches per minute). This type of combined recording procedure offers observers much better precision in capturing the behavior of interest because the resulting observation allows teams to understand whether the behavior occurred throughout the observation at similar rates (as opposed to a short burst) and to quantify the behaviors that tended to precede or follow the behavior's occurrence.

Observation Codes

Although observers can certainly design instruments based on their particular interests, researchers have developed a number of observational instruments designed to capture classroom behavior. These instruments offer the ease of already-established observational codes that have been field tested and used in research. Hintze and colleagues (2008) and Volpe and colleagues (2005) provide reviewed lists of instruments found in the literature to be useful in conducting systematic behavioral observations. In particular, Volpe and colleagues focused on measures specifically designed to assess behavior within classrooms.

Among these measures, the Behavioral Observation of Students in Schools (BOSS), developed by Shapiro (2011b), offers observational categories within the code that have characteristics consistent with variables that are most relevant in classrooms. Of high interest in classrooms is how students engage with academic tasks. As noted previously, students can be on task in active or passive ways, and the BOSS code is designed to differentiate both forms of on-task behavior. Several studies have found that the levels of active and passive engaged academic behavior on the BOSS code show differential outcomes as predictors of overall student behavior, particularly students with ADHD (DuPaul et al., 2006; Hosterman, DuPaul, & Jitendra, 2008; Vile Junod, DuPaul, Jitendra, Volpe, & Cleary, 2006).

Beyond differentiating the types of academic engagement, the BOSS code also asks the observer to record a student's competing (i.e., off-task) behavior. Three classifications of off-task behavior are observed: verbal, motor, and passive off-task. Each of these behaviors represents broad groups of competing behaviors often evident during classroom observations. Finally, the BOSS code also examines whether the teacher was engaged in directly instructing students during the observations (teacher-directed instruction [TDI]), collected every fifth interval using a partial-interval recording process. Teacher behavior is recorded to assess in a broad way whether there was active instruction occurring at the time of the observation.

The method of observing using the BOSS code involves dividing the time period into 15-second intervals (see Figure 7.2). At the start of each interval, the nature of a student's on-task behavior is recorded as either active engaged time (AET) or passive engaged time (PET). If the student is off task at the start of each interval, neither of these is recorded. Thus each 15-seconds a student is recorded using a momentary time sample as to whether they are on task and if so, the nature of the on-task behavior. For the remainder of the interval, the observer records the presence or absence of any of the three types of off-task behavior (verbal, motor, passive) as a partial-interval recording process. The combination of momentary and partial-interval recording on the BOSS provides excellent opportunities to assess a student's on- and off-task behavior in an efficient but empirically sound way.

The BOSS code also builds in a very important component of observational data collection. The interpretation of any level of behavior in a classroom is very specific to the instructional context. For example, a student, when observed during a period of reading and language arts

Moment	1	2	3	4	5*	6	7	8	9	10*	11	12	13	14	15*
AET															
PET															
Partial															
OFT-M															
OFT-V															
OFT-P															
TDI															

FIGURE 7.2. Example of a part of the BOSS coding form.

instruction, is found to have a level of AET of 50% of the intervals. To fully understand whether this level of AET is problematic and in need of attention can only be determined by examining the relative levels of AET of nonreferred peers from the same classroom under the identical instructional context. In other words, if the observed level of AET for peers during the same time that the referred student was observed was found to be 45%, the level of AET found for the referred student would not be considered substantially different from peers and therefore represents levels that are most likely viewed by the teacher as acceptable given the context of the instructional period. In contrast, if the referred student's level of AET was only 10% and the peers were at 50%, the referred student's level of AET would be found to be far below that of typical peers.

The conceptual key in making the normative comparison is to recognize that the context defines what is expected. Efforts to provide normative comparisons that go beyond the classroom context where the student is being instructed are likely to result in noninterpretable data. A student who has a level of 85% AET + PET may still be viewed as problematic by a teacher where the normative level for his/her classroom context is 99% (i.e., students in the same classroom during the same instructional activity are on task 99% of the time on average).

Built into the BOSS code is the collection of peer normative data. Every fifth interval, the observer shifts the observation from the referred student to a peer in the classroom. Although there are multiple ways that the peers can be selected (i.e., the observer asks the teacher who in the classroom represents a typical peer, the observer randomly selects a specific peer student), the recommended procedure for the BOSS code is to systematically select a different peer for each of the peer-recorded intervals. Data for the peer comparison intervals is aggregated across intervals to establish what would be viewed as a peer norm. By using a different student for each peer observation, the observer removes the chance that the peer selected by the teacher or at random by the observer did not represent typical performance.

Although the BOSS code provides a very efficient mechanism for conducting classroom observations, the code does not assess teacher–student or student–student interactions in a systematic way. Other codes designed to better capture the interactional nature of classroom behavior are the State–Event Classroom Observation Codes (SECOS; Saudargas, 1997) and the Ecological Behavioral Assessment System (E-BASS; Greenwood et al., 2000). Both systems are more complex than the BOSS, and details of their methods are beyond the scope of this chapter. Likewise, full details for using the BOSS code can be found in Shapiro (2011b).

Logistics of Classroom Observations

When conducting classroom observations, there are a number of important logistical considerations. Observers must consider where the observations should be conducted, how long each observation should be, and how many observations should be collected. Each of these questions are critical to obtaining observational data that can be used effectively in facilitating decisions about a student's eligibility for special education.

Where?

The question of where the observations occur is determined by a careful examination of the key questions that are to be addressed by the observation. Clearly, the academic subject where the student is struggling should be a focal point for conducting classroom observations. If a student is referred because of academic problems in reading, then the instructional process during reading needs to be the focus of observation. However, one also needs to consider the context within reading instruction in determining where observations need to be conducted. For example, a student's instruction in reading may involve a combination of large-group, small-group, and independent seatwork. If a student's behavior in reading varies as a function of these three different types of settings, then classroom observations should be conducted in each of these settings. Likewise, if a referred student's problems are specific to reading but the student is reported to be strong in math, the observer might want to observe in both instructional settings to provide empirical confirmation of what the teacher reports. Selecting the "right" place to observe is a matter of clinical judgment of the trained observer, but is based on obtaining data that can provide quantitative indices about the nature of the student's behavior during various instructional contexts. Data from different instructional conditions (e.g., group size, method of instruction) can provide useful information about those conditions that are most effective in facilitating student progress and which ones are not effective. This information is useful in determining the student's need for special education (see Chapter 9) and for developing the student's IEP.

How Long?

A second logistical question concerns the length of each observation. In general, the length of observation does not need to be extensive, as long as the settings in which the observations are done are carefully considered. Observations of 10–20 minutes are usually sufficient to capture a reasonable perspective of a student's behavior, as long as the instructional process observed is fairly typical of the normal classroom context and technically adequate observation procedures are used to record behavior (i.e., not narrative recording). Longer observations may yield more reliable and potentially stable data, but often there are practical constraints on how much time observers have in their schedules to conduct these observations. Most studies using the BOSS code utilized observations that were usually 15 minutes in length (DuPaul et al., 2006; Vile Junod et al., 2006), with several observations collected over multiple days. Clinically, individuals using the BOSS code often conduct observations of 15–30 minutes across multiple subjects or settings. The key to deciding how long to observe a single observation session is determining whether the data collected through that observation session were sufficient to capture the classroom behavior in question.

How Many?

A third logistical consideration for conducting classroom observations is how many observations are needed to obtain reliable and valid data. There is no direct answer to this question. Observers need to collect enough data to be convinced that the data collected represent the behavior in question and that the observations have captured the nature of the referred problem. One simple strategy for determining the degree to which the data collected during observation represent the student's referred problems is to ask the teacher following the completion of an observation whether what the observer saw was typical of other times the student is instructed. Teachers are often remarkable judges of student behavior and can be very accurate in general ways of judging student performance. Indeed, many studies have shown strong correlations between teachers' judgments of a student's academic behavior and their actual performance on academic tasks (e.g., Feinberg & Shapiro, 2003, 2009). If a teacher indicates that the behavior observed during an instructional period was typical of the student's behavior at other similar instructional periods, then observers may not need to do any additional observations of that particular instructional time. However, if the teacher responds by saying the student's behavior was exceptionally good or poor during the observer's data collection, then additional observations of similar instructional periods would be required. The bottom line for the observer is that the data collected through the classroom observation should represent the student's behavior that is typically seen during that instructional time period.

Technological Supports for Classroom Observations

Over the past decade there has been a substantial increase in available technology to conduct classroom observations. Although paper-and-pencil tools still remain a standard and are frequently used, technological devices exist that can greatly enhance the capacity to conduct classroom observations.

Conducting any systematic direct observation requires both timing and recording devices. Because smartphones and tablets have these built-in capacities, they make ideal devices for collecting observational data. With the addition of specific applications that have been and are being developed for smartphones and tablets, conducting systematic direct observations of classroom behavior is routinely possible. Table 7.1 lists several applications currently available for conducting classroom observations on smartphones and tablets. Interested users should carefully examine each of these potential apps for their classroom observational needs. Some apps were designed primarily for frequency or event recording, while others are geared more toward interval recording. In addition, the BOSS will be released as an app for iPhone, iPad, iPod Touch, and Android devices sometime during the 2013 calendar year. The BOSS app will have the BOSS code built in but also will allow for additional customization by the user.

> **Over the past decade there has been a substantial increase in available technology to conduct classroom observations.**

DOCUMENTING RESULTS OF THE OBSERVATION

When classroom observations are conducted as part of a comprehensive evaluation, the data offer a perspective on the student's actual responses during typical classroom instruction. The following example illustrates how these types of data can be used as part of a comprehensive assessment.[1]

Jadier, a third-grade student, was referred for an evaluation because of persistent problems with reading and language arts. According to his teachers, he had struggled since the beginning of school with reading and writing, and had showed progressively worsening performance since the start of third grade. By contrast, his teachers reported that he was doing very well in math

---

[1] Many thanks to Matt Gormley, a doctoral student in School Psychology at Lehigh University, for the use of his case.

TABLE 7.1. Applications Available for Smartphones and Tablets for Classroom Observations

Name of application/availability	Frequency/ event recording available?	Interval recording available?	Customization by user?
BOSS App (for iPhone, iPod, Android) (BOSS code) (due out in early 2013) Pearson Assessment (estimated $29.95) Will be available from iTunes store.	Limited	Yes	Partially customizable by user
Behavior Tracker Pro (*www.behaviortrackerpro.com*) ($29.99) for iPhone, iPad, iPod Available from iTunes store.	Yes	Yes	Fully customizable by user
iBAA (iPhone Behavioral Assessment Application) (*futurehelpdesigns.com/behavioralapps/ibaa*) ($129.99) Available from iTunes store.	Yes	Yes	Fully customizable by user
ABC Data Pro (*cbtaonline.com/drupal/abcdatapro*) ($27.99) Available from iTunes store.	Yes	Yes	Limited
BehaviorLens (for iPad only) (*www.behaviorlensapp.com*) ($29.99) Available from iTunes store.	Yes	Yes	Partially customizable by user
School Psychology Tools (*www.schoolpsychologytools.com*) ($34.99) Available from iTunes store.	Yes	Yes	Fully customizable by user

and science, demonstrating at or above grade-level performance. When the observer met with the reading/language arts teacher, she indicated that Jadier's behavior was often different in his core instruction block than when he was in his small-group intervention block. The observer decided to conduct observations in both reading/language arts settings (i.e., core instruction and intervention) and to also observe him during a core math instructional time to see whether his behavior was different in that setting compared to reading. The observer used the BOSS observation code to conduct all the observations.

Table 7.2 shows the results of the BOSS observations of Jadier. Results of the BOSS observations for reading and language arts indicated that Jadier exhibited somewhat higher active and passive engagement relative to his peers in the core instruction setting. Conversely, during the intervention group, Jadier spent less than half the amount of time actively engaged relative to his peers and slightly over half the amount of time passively engaged in intervention group activities. In both settings, Jadier exhibited off-task behaviors at equal levels or less relative to his peers. Finally, teacher-directed instruction did not vary greatly between the two settings. Results of the BOSS observation in math demonstrated that Jadier had higher levels of AET and lower levels of PET relative to his peers. Jadier also displayed lower levels of off-task behaviors relative to his classmates. For this observation, the teacher was engaged in TDI during all intervals. Specifically, he worked with each small group of students for a few minutes before moving on to the next group.

Collectively these data demonstrated that Jadier does not engage in high rates of off-task behavior during reading/language arts or math and that he is more engaged both actively and passively during math instruction relative to reading, supporting the teacher's report of Jadier as a motivated and hard-working student who does particularly better during math than reading/language arts.

It is important to note that this example case offers a best-case scenario where the results of the behavioral observation found that Jadier's behavior did not interfere with his overall academic learning process. In many cases, data collected through behavior observation can reveal that a student's off-task behavior can create events that impede the student's ability to benefit from the instructional process. (See additional case studies in Chapter 9.) When the data indicate evidence of potential behavioral interference with learning, it is critical to do a more in-depth examination of the student's potential behavior problems in order to effectively rule out that the student's difficulties in learning are not directly a function of an emotional/behavioral disorder as discussed in Chapter 5.

TABLE 7.2. Results of BOSS Observations for Jadier

	Reading core setting		Reading intervention setting		Math core setting	
	Jadier (139 intervals)	Peers (34 intervals)	Jadier (139 intervals)	Peers (34 intervals)	Jadier (48 intervals)	Peers (48 intervals)
Active engaged time	15.11%	11.77%	16.98%	35.71%	56.25%	25.00%
Passive engaged time	64.03%	52.94%	32.08%	50.00%	29.17%	33.33%
Off-task motor	8.63%	20.59%	5.66%	7.14%	6.25%	8.33%
Off-task verbal	15.11%	17.65%	3.77%	21.43%	10.42%	25.00%
Off-task passive	12.23%	23.53%	0.00%	0.00%	2.08%	8.33%
Teacher-directed instruction		94.12%		92.86%		100%

SUMMARY

As evident from this example, including these types of classroom observations offer a rich source of information about the student that can contribute substantially to the picture painted through a comprehensive evaluation. Including systematic observation that is data driven, empirical, and objective offers important insights into the nature of the instructional context and its influence on a student's behavior. Simple narrative or descriptive observations, so common among practitioners, really do not offer the depth of information provided by the systematic direct observation processes and can be considered insufficient for inclusion in comprehensive evaluation reports.

Certainly, there are many methods and strategies for obtaining classroom observations. Careful reading of the law shows that policy makers wanted to provide opportunities for evaluations of students to fully include an understanding of the instructional context. Research has shown that the nature of the instructional process and environment plays a significant role in influencing student academic outcomes. The importance and time devoted to conducting quality systematic direct observation is equal to all other aspects of assessing the student's academic skills and should not be minimized.

CHAPTER 8

Parent Involvement in an RTI System

As a practitioner or scholar who is focused on obtaining learning improvements for all students and particularly for students who are struggling, it is necessary to make judgments based on data points obtained from brief student assessments. When the data are adequate, decision makers experience a certain level of comfort in trusting those data and reaching decisions about how to distribute resources in a school. After all, experience and science has taught educational leaders that student performance data are the best arbiter in guiding instructional actions in a school. If you are a parent, however, these judgments based on student data are often anxiety provoking and may even be upsetting.

Imagine you are watching a little league baseball game and you see an 8-year-old child come up to bat. He listens to the coach, nods his head, and stands at the plate. His small arms work to hold the bat in the right position, and he is intently focused on the pitch. The coach pitches the ball right into the strike zone, the child swings so hard he almost spins around, and . . . misses the ball. Now imagine watching that happen a second time. A couple of other pitches go by with no swings. Now it is time for the final pitch. Most adults probably find themselves ardently wishing for the child to experience success and hit the ball rather than have to return to the dugout with slumped and defeated shoulders. It seems parents considering the school's and their own child's academic data may feel this same ardent wish to avoid failure at all costs. For the practitioner, a failed score is simply a sign to begin offering assistance or change instructional strategies. To the parent, however, a failed screening may feel bigger or more consequential. For example, parents may worry that poor academic performance may be a sign that the child may not be able to succeed in college or develop a love of learning or may feel so demoralized that he or she does not develop to his or her greatest potential.

Pushing forward as though these fears are not relevant ultimately is less productive than taking the time to build trust between the parent and the school. Too often, parents are viewed as slowing down the decision-making process or being difficult, and this view both dishonors the primary role that parents play in the lives of their children and ultimately weakens the results of a school-based intervention. At worst, not working proactively with parents from the beginning of the process can breed an adversarial relationship that is ultimately unhelpful for all.

There are probably some obstacles to overcome in building productive school–home partnerships in RTI in most places. Imagine how you feel when you visit a physician to obtain results for some medical test you have endured. That physician is probably busy and may pop into the exam room for 3 minutes during which time you are provided the results of a test in language that you may not understand and told to follow up with a specialist. The physician may be gone before you have even gathered your thoughts to ask a question. Similarly, school-based practitioners should carefully monitor their "bedside manner." Often, practitioners should refrain from using jargon when speaking with parents. When we use terms like "DIBELS" or "cut scores" or "benchmark" or "integrity," it can be like talking in a foreign language for parents, and the terms often sound much more "high stakes" than we intend. For parents, using highly technical language makes the discussion difficult to follow at best and alienating at worst. Second, there is a tendency to "stack the room" with school personnel when a parent comes into a meeting with the school, particularly if the parent has asked lots of questions or is perceived as not being very responsive or cooperative with requests from the school. Practitioners should give consideration to the way it feels for parents to walk into a room with as many as 10–15 school personnel, most of whom are strangers, who then communicate sensitive information about the parent's child. The number of school personnel should be limited to those who are most essential for the discussion. Third, school personnel should not allow discussions with parents to wander into territory that is not helpful to intervention planning. Parents are exquisitely sensitive to the notion that they are responsible for any of their child's shortcomings. Asking questions that are not immediately pertinent to intervention planning (e.g., whether the pregnancy was normal) can cause parents to make causal associations that practitioners do not intend. School personnel should keep the discussion on task and focused on planning effective intervention and monitoring the effects of that intervention to make adjustments as needed.

There is a power disequilibrium that operates in school–parent meetings, but practitioners can use RTI data and the process of collecting RTI data to create effective home–school partnerships. When the data are described in nontechnical terms, parents can come to understand that the process of identification and intervention planning is a process that is transparent, replicable, and understandable. Many parents may have learned over the years that the only way to "get help" for their child is through the "gate" of evaluation. Therefore, the tone of the interaction between parent and school may be adversarial from the start with the parent wanting an evaluation and the team feeling frustrated that an evaluation may be unnecessary, unhelpful to improving learning, and ultimately be a costly waste of time for all. It is incumbent on schools to build communitywide understandings of multi-tier systems of intervention and what they mean for struggling students, so that parents will understand that a full psychoeducational evaluation may be important but it is not the starting place in obtaining help for a student who is at risk for academic failure. The onus is on the school to shift understandings that when children fail to respond to instruction, the first step is to change the instruction, rather than to conclude that the child is somehow flawed.

> It is incumbent on schools to build communitywide understandings of multi-tier systems of intervention so that parents will understand that a full psychoeducational evaluation is not the starting place in obtaining help for a student who is at risk for academic failure.

We suggest a more forthright approach that says, "Let's start from scratch." Here are the working assumptions of the team: All children can learn when properly instructed. Instruc-

TABLE 8.1. Typical Goals and Needs of Families

Families want . . .	Families want to know . . .
• Improved learning	• What was my child's score?
• Transparent decisions	• What did you do differently?
• Active system problem solving	• What effect did it have?
• Efficient use of resources	• What are we doing next?

tional failures are not unusual, and as many as 20% of students need instruction that is different from what is provided in the classroom to show optimal growth. When an instructional failure is detected (i.e., the child is performing in the at-risk range), intervention is needed. Most interventions work when used well. As the intervention is used, data will be collected at regular intervals so the adults can see if the intervention is working as planned. If the intervention does not appear to be working, the data team will troubleshoot the intervention. The goal is to find the instructional techniques and strategies that get the child on the right track to long-term success in school. This forthright and pragmatic approach is consonant with the most probable ultimate goals of families (see Table 8.1). We also suggest that systems share data on the effects of their multi-tier or RTI systems through community and school forums, on the school website, and in newsletters. In this chapter we describe concrete steps that systems should take to build positive parent–school RTI partnerships.

ADVISING PARENTS OF RESULTS OF UNIVERSAL SCREENING

Informing parents about the results of universal screening begins even before the screening is administered. The school should provide information to parents at the beginning of the school year parent meeting (sometimes called parent orientation). What parents need to know is that periodic assessment is used at the school to help the school understand whether most students are learning as expected or whether adjustments to the instructional program are needed. Schools might describe academic screening as being similar to checking height and weight periodically at pediatrician visits. The screenings are intended to tell school leaders and teachers whether children are growing academically according to expectations. When problems are detected, the school will plan and implement classwide, small-group and, if needed, individual intervention to catch students up. Parents should be told what to expect during the school year, specifically, that screening will occur three times during the year (or more if problems are detected), that a reliable and valid measure will be used, that results will be shared with parents, and that parents will be kept informed and invited to participate if their child participates in intervention. The National Center for Learning Disabilities has prepared a document available at no cost online entitled "A Parent's Guide to Response to Intervention" that may be accessed at *www. ncld.org/checklists-a-more/parent-advocacy-guides/a-parent-guide-to-rti*. This resource can be printed for parents and/or provided as a link on the school's website.

In summary, before the screening occurs, schools have laid the groundwork with parents about what data will be collected and how those data will be used to improve instruction at the school and to produce learning outcomes for all students. It is important for schools to maintain a positive tone about the screening process, indicating how the data will be used and acknowledging with frankness the limits of those data. For example, typically, screening data are not diagnostic and will not tell users why a child is not performing at the level that is expected. The screening data are, however, a very efficient way to determine whether there are systemic problems that need improvement and whether individual students are likely to fail if they do not receive additional support or intervention. Only when teachers understand the value of the data and how it will be used can they communicate well with parents about the meaning of the data for the school and student. It is important for teachers to understand fully the difference between useful assessment information and productive instructional targets, which are often not one and the same. It is also important for teachers to understand the technical adequacy of the selected measures (i.e., that they are meaningful), how they will be used to reach decisions, and that assessment time is being managed as efficiently as possible. The data team and school leaders should conduct an assessment inventory for the school and review the inventory during beginning-of-the-year faculty meetings. Teachers must have an opportunity to ask questions and have their concerns addressed about all assessments that will be used during the school year. When schools do not ensure that teachers have a substantial understanding of assessment procedures, teachers tend not to use the data well and share their misgivings about the assessment process with parents.

There is one more step to complete before screening occurs. If the school does not have parent representation on a site leadership team or some analogous arrangement, then the school should consider arranging for parent representation on the school-level team, led by the school principal, that sets goals and priorities for the school each year and evaluates progress toward those goals. There is often a tendency to involve parents in schooling in very narrow ways, for example, when community support for a funding initiative is needed. However, a true school–parent partnership is possible only when parents are present at the table when the challenges faced by the school are made apparent, corrective actions are planned, and improvement effects are tracked at follow-up meetings. These leadership team meetings are ideal venues to share schoolwide graphs of student performance and link these data explicitly to instructional planning for the school year. Data on instructional program effects that should be shared in such meetings are discussed below. Importantly, these meetings are an opportunity for stakeholders and leaders to ask questions that can be examined by looking at the student data and other sources of information. For example, a parent may wonder whether the needs of higher-performing students are being met. This question becomes an action plan for the data team to gather the data needed to look at this question and provide an answer in the next parent meeting. These meetings accomplish two objectives: First, the meetings provide an outlet for information that can be shared with other parents and community members. Second, the meeting is a formative process for generating and refining school improvement plans.

WHAT DATA TO PROVIDE TO PARENTS

Screening

There are two types of data that should be provided to parents following screening. First, parents will appreciate a transparent view of data showing the general effects of instruction schoolwide. The principal can generate and share graphs of the percentage of students at risk across grades in content areas, as depicted in Figures 6.7 and 6.9. Parents should be told what actions will be taken by teachers to challenge and accelerate the instruction of those students who are very high performing as well as what actions will be taken to provide more effective instruction to students who are performing in the at-risk range.

The second type of data that should be provided to parents are the data that lead to an "at risk" or "not at risk" judgment for their own children. The simplest way to disseminate these data to parents is to provide a graph of classwide performance with the names of other students removed or covered up as in Figure 8.1. This allows parents to see at a glance where their children are performing relative to the benchmark or screening criterion and where their children are performing relative to all other students in the class. If the child is performing in the risk range, we suggest that the teacher call the parent and also write a note on the screening data report indicating that follow-up assessment will be conducted in the coming week and that the school will invite the parent to come to school to discuss a plan for providing additional instructional support or intervention to the student if needed. It is useful to explain to parents how the benchmark criterion was identified and what it means. For example, parents might be told that the benchmark criterion represents a 100% chance of the child passing the high-stakes test of reading at the end of grade 3. The parent might be told that the criterion was set such that no children who need intervention are missed, but that many children may be considered to need intervention who actually will do fine whether they get intervention or not. The parent might be informed about how follow-up assessments with intervention will allow the school to pinpoint only those students who truly need intervention to succeed. Being precise about intervention need is important because time spent providing unnecessary intervention is time lost to other educational opportunities that the child might experience including enrichment, social interaction with peers, and opportunities to engage in accelerated instruction. Another important theme for schools to share with parents is the notion of efficient assessment and intervention. Efficiency is important even for the individual student because it ultimately allows for a richer overall schooling experience for the child. Another option for schools in sharing student screening data with parents is to prepare a written summary to send home with each student. An example of such a summary is provided in Form 8.1 (at the end of the chapter).

Intervention Planning and Follow-Up

Once children have been identified for intervention, the parent should receive a summary of the intervention plan and a copy of the intervention protocol. Parents should be told who will conduct the intervention, what time of day the intervention will occur, and how many days per week it will be conducted. The data team should tell the parent to expect weekly updates on student progress during intervention that will come home in the child's folder. Throughout the time that an intervention is occurring, the parent should receive a copy of the student's progress graph and a brief note indicating that the intervention is having the desired effect and will continue another week. Forms 8.2 and 8.3 (at the end of the chapter) provide samples of letters that could be sent home to parents to inform them about intervention. Figure 8.2 provides a model for how intervention progress might be shared with parents. This figure shows the progress of a student given individual intervention in mathematics. The graph is sent home to parents each week, and a brief summary is written on the front so parents can anticipate what will happen with the intervention the following week.

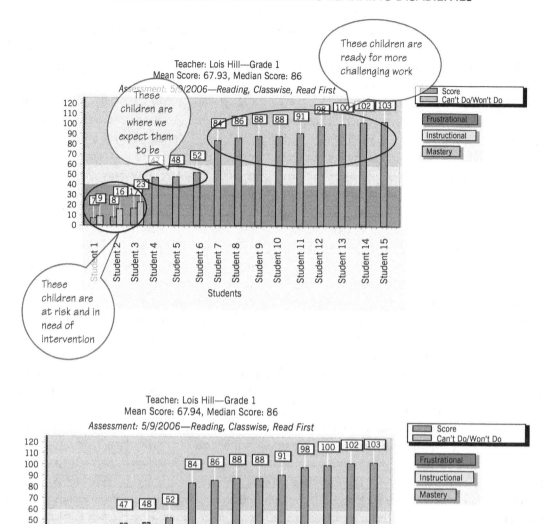

FIGURE 8.1. The top panel shows how the classwide screening data can be interpreted for parents. The bottom panel shows one way of sharing classwide screening data with a parent of an individual child, in this case, a fictional child named "John Adams."

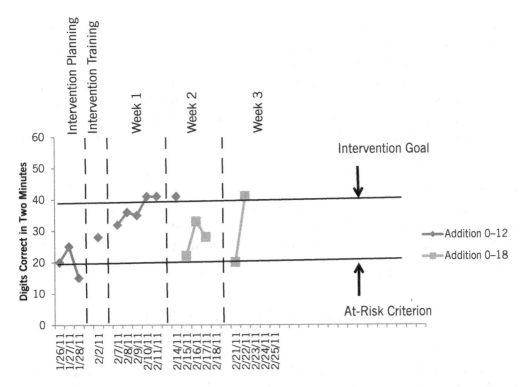

Week 1: Allison showed rapid progress this week and surpassed the goal for mastery for Adding Numbers 0–12. We will continue the intervention for one more day on Monday and if her score remains above the goal, we will increase the difficulty of intervention materials and continue another week.

Week 2: We increased the difficulty this week to Adding Numbers 0–18. Allison only had three days of intervention this week because Friday was a field trip day. We will continue working on this skill in intervention next week.

Week 3: Allison showed rapid progress and reached the intervention goal in two days. We will monitor her progress in the classroom to make sure she remains successful.

FIGURE 8.2. Model for how intervention progress might be shared with parents. Allison's progress during intervention can be shared with parents each week and saved in her permanent file when the intervention is complete.

INVOLVING PARENTS ON INTERVENTION TEAMS

The responsibility for conducting the intervention should fall on the school as a matter of efficacy and practicality. The school is responsible for adjusting instruction to meet the needs of all learners. Children spend most of the day at school, where adherence to schedules and classroom routines should foster consistent intervention delivery. Teachers are trained and tasked with producing learning for all students. Hence, school-based interventions should occur at school. However, schools should make efforts to involve parents as members of the intervention team. The groundwork for parent involvement begins well before there is an identified need for intervention. Before a parent is contacted about starting an intervention for his or her child, the parent should already have

> **Schools should make efforts to involve parents as members of the intervention team.**

an understanding of the purpose of schoolwide screening and whether any system-level problems have been identified. Parents should receive regular updates about efforts to improve learning outcomes for all students at the school.

Parents should be invited to attend the data team session where the student assessment data are used to plan the intervention (especially in Tier 3) and the data team session where a final decision is made about whether the intervention has been successful. Parents should receive a written summary of the assessment data collected and a graph of the student's intervention progress. The purpose of the final data team meeting is to talk about strategies to facilitate continued and more widespread gains in learning at school where the intervention has been determined to be successful. If the intervention has not been successful despite strong implementation and data-based adjustments, then the team should consider requesting parents' permission for an eligibility evaluation to potentially rule out other causes of poor performance and to identify more intensive instructional services that might be provided through special education.

INVOLVING PARENTS IN INTERVENTIONS

In the last section, we asserted that school-based interventions should occur at school. The responsibility for conducting school-based intervention should remain primarily in the hands of the school. However, in many cases parents may have talents and resources to share in designing and delivering more powerful intervention. When an individual child is identified for Tier 2 or 3 intervention, parents should receive a copy of the intervention protocol, a weekly report of the child's progress, and strategies they can use at home to supplement and strengthen intervention effects at school. There are a variety of Web-based tools that can be used from home to provide extra practice for students as long as the child can be motivated to participate and the parent can provide that opportunity without a great deal of struggle or difficulty for the family (e.g., *www.spellingcity.com*; *www.ixl.com*).

> Parents may have talents and resources to share in designing and delivering more powerful intervention.

Intervention data can inform what materials are sent home for practice such that the school is able to provide the parents with instructional materials that the child can complete successfully with only a small amount of adult support. Homework ideally should use tasks and materials with which the child can perform accurately and independently. In reading, knowing the child's proficiency from their assessment data can help schools to provide the parent with materials for shared books and materials that the child can read successfully. Homework should allow the child to practice skills learned in schools to build automaticity; it should not be the occasion for learning new skills. (It is acknowledged that some schools are having success with Internet-based instructional sites such as the Kahn Academy [*www.khanacademy.org*] that provides demonstration lessons that can be used at home, with teachers providing follow-up in class the next day.) In addition to assisting children with practice in learned academic skills, parents are particularly needed to follow through at home on interventions addressing behavioral difficulties. Often behavioral expectations taught in school need to be carried through in the home, and parents can participate in the school's positive behavior support program by delivering reinforcers at home for appropriate school behavior.

APPRISING PARENTS OF THEIR RIGHT
TO A FULL AND INDIVIDUAL EVALUATION

Parents should be aware that they have the right to request that a referral be made for a full individual evaluation through the school system. Whereas some systems interpret this request according to certain local rules (e.g., a parent request is always honored with immediate referral for evaluation), the entitlement that is guaranteed through IDEA is that if a parent requests an evaluation, the school-based evaluation team must determine whether an eligibility evaluation is warranted based on available data.

It is difficult for many practitioners and parents to understand, but when an unwarranted evaluation occurs, there is an increased risk of diagnostic error, and this error carries a risk of harm to the student, which is why parents have due process rights in this regard. Instead, there is often a belief among parents and many practitioners that the assessment carries little risk, and the individual evaluation is often considered a final precautionary step and reflected in a team's decision to "get some testing and see what is really going on." Based on available technical adequacy and treatment utility data, this belief that the testing data will improve outcomes for students is simply unrealistic. Hence, there is little protection in the individual evaluation itself. In medicine, diagnostic tests are not administered unless there is a suspicion that a disease condition is present. Why? Because the tests carry error rates, a test's error rates will be higher if a test is used with individuals who do not meet risk criteria, and the resulting decisions may carry a risk of negative side effects for those who receive the diagnosis (VanDerHeyden, 2011). For example, appendicitis can only truly be diagnosed by removing the appendix through surgery. But because it is not reasonable to remove appendices from all individuals experiencing abdominal pain, diagnostic tests are used to signal a high likelihood of appendicitis. These diagnostic tests include, among other things, computed tomography (CT) scan. The CT scan can be reasonably accurate if used with individuals experiencing the "right" symptoms. The problem arises if diagnosticians wanted to give a CT to everyone who arrived in a medical office, regardless of their symptoms, history, and physical exam findings. There are a certain number of false-positive and false-negative errors that occur with any test, and the rate of errors would be much higher if the test were administered to all rather than the group for which the probability for "real" appendicitis is enriched (i.e., they have active symptoms of appendicitis without other potential causes). Second, the test carries a side effect of radiation exposure that is substantial and can only be justified if the condition needs to be ruled out for the safety of the patient. Third, diagnosis leads to surgery that carries risks for the patient.

This decision-making paradigm is identical whether we are talking about appendicitis or SLD. The tests we use carry risk of false-positive errors (diagnosing a child with SLD when the child really does not have SLD) and false-negative errors (failing to diagnose a child with SLD when the child really does have SLD). The decisions based on those tests (diagnose, do not diagnose) also carry consequences for students. When a full evaluation is needed, it should be conducted without hesitation. What systems have tended to do poorly is use student data to determine whether an evaluation is really needed.

To protect the entitlements of students, schools should attend to the decisions that are made during the school year and the effects that the decisions are having. To what extent do the screening measures accurately identify students in need of intervention? To what extent does intervention reduce student risk for failure over time? How many students receive intervention at Tiers 2 and 3? What percentage of students receiving Tier 2 and 3 interventions are successful? What is the average time between starting intervention and reaching a final decision about intervention success? Do students receiving intervention experience greater school success in subsequent semesters and years? A long delay between decisions is a red flag that RTI implementation is not occurring well. Systems should be able to reach decisions within a single semester as to whether a comprehensive individual evaluation would provide helpful information to rule out alternative causes of poor sustained poor performance (e.g., sensory deficits, intellectual disability) and to aid in the long-term intervention planning that is needed to provide effective instruction to the student.

Parents should also understand at the initial data team meeting that the data being gathered will be used for intervention and instructional planning for the student and that these data could become part of a comprehensive individual eligibility evaluation depending on what is learned during intervention. The parent should understand that their signed permission will be necessary to make an official referral for an individual evaluation and that the evaluation data tend to be most meaningful once the RTI process has been conducted, that the data collected during the course of RTI become part of the evaluation and eligibility decision, and that parents will be kept informed weekly during intervention and will be invited to the final data team meeting to discuss intervention results and plan the next steps. The steps we suggest in this section are designed to avoid the problems described by some parents that the provision of consecutive interventions in a multi-tier (RTI) system created an undue delay in identifying children with a disability. As described in a letter from the Office of Special Education and Remedial Services (OSERS; 2007a), schools using RTI should not inadvertently deny parents' rights to expeditious evaluation and potential identification of a disabling condition and need for special education. As described above, careful and prudent analysis of progress monitoring data and timely communication of this information to parents should adequately address this concern.

SEEKING PERMISSION TO EVALUATE

Again, the groundwork for evaluation begins with schoolwide screening and continues through the intervention process. Once parents are asked to give consent for a comprehensive eligibility evaluation, the parents should understand that their child has shown continued risk for academic failure despite consistent and intensive intervention efforts conducted by the school. The parents should be aware of the need to do something different instructionally because of regular communication from the school showing results of intervention. The rationale for evaluation should be that because inadequate instruction has been ruled out as a cause of poor performance, it is sensible to conduct a comprehensive evaluation that is designed to yield a reliable diagnostic decision as to whether the child has SLD so that the child can be made eligible to receive more intensive intervention services through special education as warranted. Because data are collected prior to referral, the percentage of evaluated students who qualify for special education services should increase and/or remain very high (e.g., greater than 90%; VanDer-Heyden et al., 2007). As described in previous chapters, permission to evaluate in schools using RTI may not include extensive new assessment, especially those tests that are prevalent in a traditional system that uses the ability–achievement discrepancy rather than RTI (in Criterion

2). A permission to evaluate in an RTI system would likely include a post hoc analysis of data generated during the provision of multiple tiers of support (see Chapters 3 and 4) and other techniques to rule out other conditions. It would not likely include a request for permission to administer tests of intelligence unless intellectual disability needed to be ruled out.

DESCRIBING RESULTS
OF THE COMPREHENSIVE EVALUATION USING RTI

We have no blood test for diagnosing SLD. We cannot really ever truly know or not know whether a child "really has" or "really doesn't have" SLD. Hence, SLD is a diagnosis that can only be arrived at when other causes for poor learning are systematically examined and ruled out. Therefore, SLD is often called a "rule-out diagnosis" or a "diagnosis of exclusion." To identify a student with SLD, the evaluation team must provide evidence that the student has deficiencies in level of performance and rate of improvement and must also rule out other conditions. All of these data that are collected and documented during the comprehensive evaluation process must be presented to the parents in a meaningful way both in written reports (see Chapter 9) and in face-to-face meetings.

In addition to providing this information, the IDEA regulations give particular emphasis to communication with parents regarding the requirement to rule out lack of adequate instruction as the reason for the student's academic failure. Information gathered during both core instruction and supplemental interventions (including RTI data) are critical for making this determination, and IDEA specifies that this information should be conveyed to parents. Specifically, data should be presented indicating that most students in the grade and classroom perform at or above the benchmark criterion that forecasts future learning success. Data should be provided indicating that the referred child performs below that benchmark criterion and is among the lowest-performing students in his or her class. Instructional data must be included demonstrating that an effective core program of instruction was sufficiently delivered, that the use of incentives for improved performance did not increase the student's score above criterion, that the use of a research-based Tier 2 intervention delivered with sufficiency and integrity did not increase the student's score above criterion, and that a correctly supported and well-implemented Tier 3 intervention did not increase the student's score to criterion. These data provide the evidentiary support for the determination of SLD and constitute the only way to reliably rule out lack of adequate instruction as a cause for poor academic performance. Most critically, the full and specific communication of this information to parents allows for meaningful compliance with the IDEA regulations.

SUMMARY

In many systems, there has been tension between the desires of the school and the desires of the family. Schools tend to want scores to increase for all students, particularly for vulnerable students. They want to avoid negative annual yearly progress (AYP) labels; they want parents and communities to have confidence in the school; they want all children to have access to the core curriculum; and they want to meet their legal obligations. Parents, on the other hand, often have a broader vantage point and want their children to be happy at school, to learn skills that will help them succeed in life, to develop a lifelong love of learning, and to grow into well-rounded, independent citizens. In the end, both school personnel and parents desire harmonious relations in their pursuit of the shared goals of student academic success and emotional well-being. Unfortunately, over the years, educators and other helping professionals in the school have been part of a system that has failed to achieve this goal. First, parents have developed in many cases unsupported beliefs in the power of extensive test batteries to change child learning outcomes. This belief leads many parents to insist on extensive batteries of testing for their children. Contemporary best practices tell most practitioners that extensive testing is not helpful when effective instruction has not been provided, and in fact may do more harm than good. Second, some parents have come to believe that instruction provided through special education is superior to and will provide superior outcomes than instruction provided through general education. These beliefs are not supported by research findings, but practitioners trying to provide alternate perspectives when they are in the role of gatekeeper can only be perceived as trying to shirk the task of doing the extensive testing or evaluating and finding a child eligible for special education.

The advent of RTI provides an opportunity to reverse this unfortunate dynamic, but does not in and of itself guarantee that parent–school partnerships will function more productively. Changing conceptions about when to evaluate students and what services to provide requires time and trust-building to show that the decisions that are guided by data and the team will continue working until student learning is improved, whether services are provided through general or special education. There are widespread benefits to taking the time to build school–home partnerships through RTI. Student data offer a transparent basis for decision making. The school can use the data to generate school improvement targets and to build community consensus to support the priorities for school improvement set forth for the school. Parents value the role of effective intervention support when they understand that it is, in fact, effective. Parents also have a highly valuable role to play in reminding the school of the "big picture" objectives of education, that is, long-term success inside and outside of the classroom. Parents can be the catalysts that push RTI implementers to examine the degree to which their efforts are changing the long-term odds of student success as measured by those most difficult-to-reach targets like passing entry-level college math or English or entering the career of one's choice. In the short term, the foundation of collaboration and trust that can be built can allow teams to focus on productive targets for improvement rather than very time-consuming tasks that may be less germane to producing optimal student learning outcomes.

Sample Screening Interpretation for Parents

Dear Parent of _____,

All children in our school participate in academic screening. These screenings are brief, requiring only a few minutes, and allow us to see how well our instruction is working and where teachers might need to make changes to get better results.

For reading, we use a timed one-minute reading of a grade-level story. This one-minute timed reading gives us powerful assessment information that we can use to better meet the needs of our students. Even though reading instruction is a much broader undertaking that focuses on the development of reading for meaning and building effective written communication skills, a timed reading indicates which students are likely to become successful readers and which are not.

Our school provides extra help and intervention to students who score in the risk range on our screening.

At your child's grade level, we expect students to read 40 words correctly per minute at this time of year to be on track for reading success.

Expected Score to Indicate Child Is On-Track	Your Child's Score
40 words read correctly per minute	8 without rewards 16 with rewards

_____ Child appears to be doing well—no intervention is needed at this time.

_____ Child's score is lower than we would like it to be, so we will do some follow-up work with the child to be sure that the child does not require intervention.

✓ When a child scores below 40 the school provides intervention during the school day as part of our regular school routine. We would like to provide extra help to your child in a small group or one on one with a classroom teacher. Please call us to schedule a visit to the school so we can talk about the intervention and answer any questions you may have. We will start the intervention right away, and we can schedule a meeting with you at your convenience. Please call us at _____ if you have concerns or questions.

Sample Letter Template

Dear Parent,

Our school is working hard to make sure all students are learning and mastering important skills in reading and mathematics. As part of these efforts, we use brief assessments schoolwide to identify where children, groups of children, or classes of children may need additional instructional support. At our school this year, we found that all classes needed additional instructional support to master our mathematics objectives, and we have been conducting classwide intervention in all classrooms for 15 minutes per day, 5 days per week. This process provides data on student progress so we can identify individual students who may need even more instructional support to master learning objectives. In the area of reading, there has been no need for classwide reading intervention because only a small number of students appear to need support above and beyond what they get during regular reading instruction each day.

For your child, we have noted a need for additional instruction in _____
_____. We have begun working on these skills each day. I will send home a graph of your child's progress each week so that you can see the progress your child is making! Please feel free to call or e-mail if you have any questions.

Sincerely,

[insert signature]

Sample Letter Template

Dear Parent,

Because your child receives special education, your child's educational program is guided by his or her individualized education plan (IEP). We have noted a need for additional instruction in_____
_____. We have begun working on these skills each day.
I will send home a graph of your child's progress each week so that you can see the progress your child is making! Please feel free to call or e-mail if you have any questions.

Sincerely,

[insert signature]

CHAPTER 9

Determining Eligibility for Special Education

Pulling All the Pieces Together in a Comprehensive Evaluation

In Chapters 3 through 7, we provided the assessment procedures for addressing each of the four components of the definition of SLD. In this chapter, we explain how to use the collected data to decide about the student's eligibility for special education under the category of SLD. The IDEA regulations indicate that the qualifying student must be deficient in level (i.e., Criterion 1) and also fail to respond adequately to scientifically based instruction and intervention (i.e., Criterion 2). Put another way, the student must have low performance and slow growth. This chapter addresses the question "How low is low, and how slow is slow?" in terms of meeting eligibility criteria. It should be noted that, because there are no federal guidelines on these indices, our presentation here is guided by what we consider to be demonstrably effective practices at this time. In addition to suggesting eligibility criteria for the first two components of the SLD definition, we also describe procedures for documenting the rule-outs of other conditions or situations (i.e., Criterion 3), the rule-out of the lack of instruction (i.e., Criterion 4), and classroom observations. Finally, we present two case studies of comprehensive evaluations that portray a student who qualifies as SLD and another who does not.

ESTABLISHING QUALIFICATIONS FOR ELIGIBILITY UNDER CRITERION 1: DOCUMENTING DEFICIENCY IN LEVEL

The task of the eligibility determination team is to evaluate the student's qualifications under each of the four criteria described in Chapter 1. For the first criterion, the team must determine whether "the child does not achieve adequately for the child's age or to meet State-approved grade-level standards" (IDEA, 2006, §300.309[a][1]). This evaluation entails four actions: (1) gathering the available data on the student's level of performance, (2) determining the standard against which this level of achievement is to be compared, (3) performing a benchmark gap analysis that compares the student's attained level of achievement to the expected level, and (4) determining the student's qualification under this criterion. This analysis addresses the question "How low is low?"

> **Criterion 1: Documenting deficiency in level**
>
> - **Gather the data.**
> - **Establish points of comparison.**
> - **Perform a benchmark gap analysis.**
> - **Determine if criterion is met.**

Gathering the Data

The evaluation team's first task is to gather the best available data pertaining to the student's level of academic attainment. As we have discussed in past chapters, the team should document the student's performance on statewide and district-administered tests of proficiency, screening/benchmark assessments, terminal scores on progress monitoring measures, the overall trend of student performance during intervention as reflected on progress monitoring, scores obtained when drilling down to the student's skill level, and scores on norm-referenced tests, if applicable. The task of gathering these data entails culling information from teachers, intervention specialists, school psychologists, and parents. Although qualitative information is pertinent, especially for the development of the student's IEP (if found to be eligible), the data that will be most relevant are scores that can be compared to national norms and benchmark criteria that forecast long-term learning success. Scores may be expressed as standard scores, percentiles, rate measures (e.g., wcpm), and raw scores referenced to a benchmark criterion.

Establishing Points of Comparison

The second task of the evaluation team is to determine the benchmarks against which the student's performance should be compared. First, it should be noted that the regulation cited above requires that an achievement comparison be made in reference to the student's age or grade-level standards. This comparison does not consider the student's IQ, regardless of whether IQ was measured. As noted in Chapter 5, an assessment of IQ is relevant only if an intellectual disability is being considered by the team. Unlike previous iterations of IDEA, the standard against which student achievement is compared is simply the student's age or grade. Notably, this criterion—comparison of achievement to age or grade-level standards—is pertinent to all evaluations for SLD, including those that use procedures other than RTI (e.g., pattern of strengths and weaknesses). That is, a student who does not display discrepant achievement in relation to age or grade standards does not qualify for SLD identification.

To establish appropriate points of comparison, the evaluation team must decide what benchmark will be used to determine whether the student meets the low-achievement criterion. A useful starting point is the concept of proficiency, which is a touchstone in NCLB for success in education. Achievement commensurate with age or state standards would be proficient performance. Hence, the comparison point would be the lowest level indicated as proficient performance. The percentile that corresponds to proficiency varies widely both within different grades and measures in a single state and between similar measures across states. For this reason, we propose a combined criterion whereby the student's performance is below the proficiency criterion and the student's performance is among the lowest-performing 10% of students in the norming sample. This decision rule allows for student risk to be determined in a very sensitive way. That is, this criterion (nonproficient and below the 10th percentile) carries very little risk of failing to detect students who may need special education services. This criterion does carry a moderate to high probability of what is called a false-positive error (i.e., suggesting there is SLD where one does not really exist). However, after low achievement is demonstrated, other criteria will be applied, including assessing the student's RTI (Criterion 2), as well as ruling out other conditions that may cause low achievement (Criterion 3) and the lack of adequate instruction (Criterion 4). A full evaluation of all these criteria is essential to reduce the false-positive error rate and reach acceptable levels of diagnostic accuracy.

Currently, approximately 6% of the national student population is identified in the SLD category (USDOE, 2010). Furthermore, research (Torgesen, 2004) has indicated that implementation of robust, evidence-based interventions (similar to what is proposed in Tiers 2 and 3 of a multi-tier system of supports) can produce meaningful progress in reading in 95% or more of *at-risk* students. Lyon (2002) has indicated that current general education procedures can be expected to be successful with all but 2–6% of the student population. This figure is a good target for students in need of special education for SLD because the remainder of the students would be demonstrably successful in meeting benchmarks. Consequently, for this first criterion, a rule of thumb might be that the student's achievement is less than the 10th percentile against national standards, which would allow a further winnowing through the application of the other three criteria. The tactic of percentile comparisons can be used for any assessment measure that provides these types of data, including norm-referenced tests, CBM, or CAT. As we described in previous chapters, it should be noted that some assessment systems (e.g., DIBELS Next) do not calculate benchmarks based on percentiles, but rather on the basis of empirically determined conditional probabilities of achieving the next benchmark. Consequently, the ratio calculation described in Chapters 3 and 4 would apply in these cases.

Our thinking here should not be construed as an arbitrary or capricious way to limit the number of students being identified as needing special education. It is not our desire to recommend denying needy students access to special education. Rather, we take this perspective with the understanding that a fully implemented multi-tier system should produce high percentages of proficient students (i.e., 85–90% or greater) over time and that students failing to respond to effective Tier 1 instruction and research-based Tier 2 and 3 interventions would have the strongest likelihood of having SLD. Furthermore, we believe that the number of students displaying significant deficiencies (i.e., the number of students with SLD) should be rather small. Although we set 85–90% as an aspirational goal for all schools, we recognize that achieving such a goal may be very difficult, especially in historically low-performing schools. It is crucial that the growth over time also be examined as a strong indicator that instruction within Tier 1 is effective. For example, a school with chronically poor reading scores that moves from 35% of students initially at benchmark in the first year of implementation to 70% of students at benchmark after 3 years of RTI implementation and maintains performance at 70–75% over the following 2 years would be viewed as showing substantial improvement. Although not reaching the 85–90% aspirational goal, the improvement and maintenance of these levels of overall student performance is a strong indicator of effective Tier 1 instruction.

Performing a Benchmark Gap Analysis

As described in Chapter 3, the evaluation team would next conduct a benchmark gap analysis by comparing the student's attained academic achievement to that of proficient peers. The extent of the academic deficiency would be documented in percentiles and ratio statements (e.g., 30% of expected level), as described in Chapter 3. This analysis provides a quantitative description of the student's current level of performance relative to normative and benchmark expectations. In general, students qualifying for SLD identification should demonstrate a benchmark gap index that is equal to or less than 50% of proficiency levels.

Determining the Student's Qualifications for SLD under Criterion 1

The final task of the evaluation team in considering the data collected for Criterion 1 is to analyze the data for consistent evidence that the student "does not achieve adequately for the child's age or to meet State-approved grade-level standards" across the various sources of data in reference to the established points of comparison. To meet this criterion for any of the eight areas of academic functioning (i.e., oral expression, listening comprehension, written expression, basic reading skill, reading fluency skills, reading comprehension, mathematics calculation, mathematics problem solving), the preponderance of the data should indicate a deficiency from what would be considered to be proficient functioning. Consequently, low achievement as described above (below benchmark and below the 10th percentile, a benchmark gap index that is 50% or less than expected performance) should be evident in all of the measures included in the analysis, including results of CBM, CAT, state and local tests, drill-down assessments, and the terminal performance on progress monitoring measures. Inconsistencies across data sources should prompt the evaluation team to analyze why the student might display capable performance under some assessment conditions and inadequate performance under others.

The task of the team is to distinguish between classroom performance problems that are not covered under SLD and actual deficiencies in learning basic skills, which are a central aspect of SLD. This first criterion requires verification that the student's inadequate achievement is evident despite being provided with "learning experiences and instruction appropriate for the child's age or State-approved grade-level standards" (IDEA, 2006; §300.309[a][1]). One important source of evidence in ruling out classwide, gradewide, and schoolwide problems is low achievement for the referred student in the face of generally proficient performance in the student's class, grade, and school (see Chapter 6). Teams can apply this decision rule in their early data analysis. If a problem is detected in the student's class or grade, systematic instruction and progress monitoring to verify that the student's problems persist in the face of effective instruction (i.e., instruction that causes other same-grade and same-class peers to improve) is necessary for accurate SLD classification. This long-standing provision of the regulations is the seed concept for the requirement that the evaluation team document that the student's academic deficiencies are not the result of a lack of instruction.

Figure 9.1 provides an example of an excerpt from a comprehensive evaluation report that documents a student's low achievement.

John, a third grader, has scored at the below basic level on districtwide and statewide reading tests since kindergarten. On the most recent universal screening using DIBELS (January), John scored 46 wcpm on ORF. Compared to typical peers for John's age and grade level (92 wcpm), John's benchmark gap index is 50% (2.0× deficient). The Nonsense Word Fluency subtest of DIBELS was also administered. John attained a score of 20 nonsense words correct per minute on this subtest. Compared to the terminal score achieved by first graders (50 wcpm), John has a benchmark gap index of 40% (2.5× deficient). Progress monitoring of John's ORF has indicated that John continues to have difficulty reading in spite of intensive intervention (details provided later in this report). His terminal median score of the most recent three data points during the last week of March was 53 wcpm. John obtained a score of 4 on the DIBELS Daze Test, which places him at the 7th percentile on this measure. In contrast to his performance in reading, John obtained a score of 567 (above the 50th percentile) on the STAR Math computer-assisted testing this winter, which is consistent with his typical performance in mathematics.

FIGURE 9.1. Report excerpt documenting a student's deficiency in level of performance.

ESTABLISHING QUALIFICATIONS FOR ELIGIBILITY UNDER CRITERION 2: DOCUMENTING DEFICIENCY IN THE STUDENT'S RATE OF IMPROVEMENT

For the second criterion, the evaluation team must determine whether "the child does not make sufficient progress to meet age or State-approved grade-level standards . . . when using a process based on the child's response to scientific, research-based intervention" (IDEA, 2006; §300.309[a][2][i]). As with Criterion 1, this evaluation entails four actions: (1) gathering the data on the student's RTI operationalized as rate of improvement (ROI), (2) determining the standard against which this ROI is to be compared, (3) performing progress monitoring ROI and benchmark gap analyses by comparing the student's attained ROIs to those of typically performing students, and (4) determining the student's qualification under this criterion. This analysis addresses the question, "How slow is slow?"

Gathering the Data

As detailed in Chapter 4, as a result of careful progress monitoring during Tiers 2 and 3, a student referred for a comprehensive evaluation enters the process with extensive data on her/his RTI as expressed in the form of graphed data as well as a calculated ROI. Both ways of describing the student's RTI provide an important perspective for the evaluation team and should be documented in the comprehensive evaluation report. As described in Chapter 4, the graph should include the student's data path, the data path of typical students, and fitted trend lines for each. In addition, the graph should include aimlines to depict the targeted ROI and phase change markers denoting intervention changes in Tiers 2 and 3. This graph provides information for the evaluation team and is arguably the best way to share the team's findings and recommendations with parents. At a glance, the team (including parents) can see the student's level of performance relative to risk criteria and whether increasingly intensive interventions were sufficient to move the student out of the risk range.

Although the graphic depiction of the student's ROI is helpful for team decision making, it is not sufficient alone for making a high-stakes decision like the identification of a disability and a determination of eligibility for special education. As we described in Chapter 4, a mathematical calculation of the student's ROI as well as that of typical students is required for this level of decision making. In that chapter, we described different approaches to determining ROI, including benchmark ROI and progress monitoring ROI. Each of these approaches results in an attainment-per-week metric (e.g., wcpm per week, standard score gain per week). There are a number of procedures for calculating the student's attained progress monitoring ROI. Our recommendation and that of other researchers (e.g., Christ et al., 2013) is the use of ordinary least squares regression lines (slope) because it is the most accurate method of representing the totality of the student's performance over time.

Establishing ROIs for Typical Students

To determine whether the student's ROI is substantially deficient to qualify for eligibility, it is necessary to compare the student's ROI to that of her or his peers. In Chapter 4, we described the typical benchmark ROI, which represents the growth required during the course of typical instruction to meet the minimal level expected of all students. The typical benchmark ROI is calculated by subtracting the original benchmark score (e.g., fall) from the terminal benchmark score (e.g., winter or spring) and dividing by the number of weeks in between these two measurements. As with the student's attained ROI, the typical benchmark ROI is expressed in attainments per week. We have also noted the variability between whole-year and half-year calculations of typical benchmark ROI and indicated our preference for half-year calculations because there is typically a difference between fall–winter and winter–spring ROIs. The peer or typical ROI for a metric in a particular grade can often be found in the technical information provided by various assessment products (e.g., DIBELS, DIBELS Next, AIMSweb, STAR).

Conducting Progress Monitoring ROI and Benchmark ROI Gap Analyses

When the student's ROI and that of typical peers is determined, the next step is to compare them to determine whether the student's ROI is substantially deficient from that of the typical students. In Chapter 4, we detailed procedures for first determining whether there is a significant difference between the student's attained progress monitoring ROI and the typical benchmark ROI (i.e., a progress monitoring ROI gap analysis) and then determining the impact of that ROI in terms of reaching the upcoming benchmark (i.e., a benchmark gap ROI analysis). A student who, in the language of the IDEA regulations, does not make sufficient progress to meet age or state-approved grade-level standards will likely display a progress monitoring gap significantly below that of typical peers and because of that discrepancy will be projected to have a significantly deficient benchmark gap in future benchmark assessments.

Determining the Student's Qualifications for SLD under Criterion 2

From the data that have been collected during the provision of multiple tiers of support and documented as part of the comprehensive evaluation of a referred student, the student's level of performance and attained ROI have been well established. However, there are no published empirical guidelines concerning how deficient a student should be in level or ROI to qualify for special education services under the SLD designation. Research has yet to be conducted on what pattern of level and ROI should signal the identification of SLD. Nonetheless, because evaluation teams must currently make this determination, some guidance from our experience with field implementation of RTI can be offered.

When considering the requirement that the student display deficiencies in both Criterion 1 and Criterion 2 (i.e., display the dual discrepancy), a suggested parameter is that a student with SLD would be significantly deficient in level of performance and sufficiently deficient in ROI such that the student would not attain acceptable performance in a reasonable amount of time. The issue then becomes what combination of performance level and ROI will eventually result in acceptable performance. This issue presents two questions: What is acceptable performance, and how long is a reasonable amount of time? We will not endeavor to answer these questions here; rather, both of these questions need to be addressed on a case-by-case basis by the evaluation team, including the parents. Again, however, some guidance is in order.

> A student with SLD would be significantly deficient in level of performance and sufficiently deficient in ROI such that the student would not attain acceptable performance in a reasonable amount of time.

Regarding the first question, a simple answer is that acceptable performance is proficiency on the assessed skill (e.g., the 40th percentile). Some teams might set that outcome as the aim for the student. Alternatively, it can be argued that, while proficient performance is the ultimate goal, an acceptable level of performance might be that level at which the student is no longer below the threshold that signals a significant deficiency (e.g., the 25th percentile).

The second question is how long should it take for a student to reach either of the aforementioned levels (25th or 40th percentile) based on the student's current level of performance and attained ROI. Evaluation teams will need to make that determination based on a number of factors including the student's age, school history, and current RTI. For example, for a fourth-grade student who has experienced a significant lack of instruction because of sustained homelessness and relocations, the team might determine that it will realistically take 3 years for the student to reach an acceptable level of performance. For this student, it can be projected as to whether his current level of performance and attained ROI will allow him to reach that level in 3 years. If it does, the team might determine that the current course of a robust core instructional program and supplemental interventions are sufficient and would not identify the student as eligible for special education. If the student's current attained ROI does not project him to reach the designated level within that time period (i.e., it would take much longer than 3 years), the student would meet Criterion 2 for identification as SLD and in need of special education.

Figure 9.2 depicts the ROI trajectories for such a student who is performing at 50% of benchmark level in the winter assessment in fourth grade. Projecting 3 years (to the winter of seventh grade) indicates that he would need an attained ROI of 0.49 wcpm/week to reach the 25th percentile and an attained ROI of 0.74 wcpm/week to reach the 50th percentile.[1] Depending on the level designated by the evaluation team, the student would need to sustain or increase this projected ROI during that time period. Consequently, if the student's current attained

---

[1] Although the 40th percentile is typically identified as indicating proficient performance on many assessment measures, the 50th percentile is used in the following examples because of data availability issues.

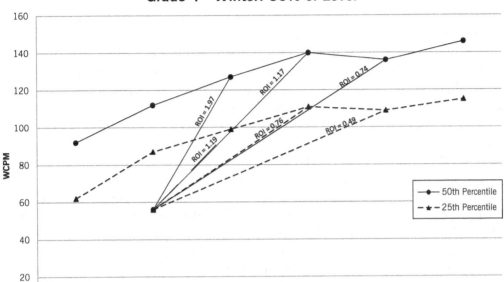

FIGURE 9.2. Graphic depiction of trajectories of attained ROIs used in examples.

ROI was lower than 0.49 wcpm/week (using the 25th percentile target), the student would meet the Criterion 2 for identification as SLD. If the student's attained ROI was greater than 0.49 wcpm/week and it was believed by the evaluation team that that ROI could be sustained through tiered interventions, the student would not be designated as in need of special education because the current general education interventions were sufficient to allow him to surpass the targeted level. Of course, an attained ROI that would allow the student to reach the higher target (50th percentile) in 3 years or the lower target in a shorter amount of time would allow the evaluation team to be more confident in its decision.

In contrast, for a fourth-grade student who has had consistent and explicit instruction in the same school since kindergarten, the evaluation team might examine whether the student's current level of performance and attained ROI will allow him to reach the designated acceptable level in 1 or 2 years. If the student's current attained ROI when projected to 1 year later indicates that the student will not reach the desired level within that time period, he would meet Criterion 2 for identification as a student with SLD. If his attained ROI would allow him to reach the designated level, the team would determine that the current interventions were not only working well, but they also indicate a lack of need for special education; hence, the student would not be designated as eligible for special education as SLD. In this example, if the fourth grader performs at 50% of level in the winter benchmark test (see Figure 9.2), he would need to achieve an attained ROI of 1.19 wcpm/week to attain the 25th percentile of level and an attained ROI 1.97 wcpm/week to attain the 50th percentile of level by winter of fifth grade (1-year projection). A less ambitious (2-year) projection would require the student to achieve an ROI of 0.76 wcpm/week to attain the 25th percentile of level and an ROI of 1.17 wcpm/week to attain the 50th percentile of level. So, the student would meet Criterion 2 if his attained ROI was less than 1.19 wcpm/week using the 1-year projection to the 25th percentile, and would not meet the criterion if his attained ROI was greater than 1.19 wcpm/week.

Table 9.1 depicts ROI calculations that are based on ORF benchmarks provided by Hasbrouck and Tindal (2006). These benchmarks are aggregated normative levels calculated from across multiple reported studies. They do not represent an actually collected set or normative data. Because they are data from across multiple studies, they offer users an "averaged" set of performance indicators. For each grade level, ROI trajectories are provided for students performing at 25%, 50%, and 75% of the typical level for that grade in terms of the ROI needed to attain the 25th or 50th percentile in 1–3 years.

It is our purpose here to provide evaluation teams with some guidelines and principles to improve their decision-making process. Consequently, in lieu of the availability of empirically established parameters that indicate the extent of the deficiency in level of performance or ROI that signal identification as SLD, when making the decision regarding the extent of the gap between the student's ROI and that of typically performing peers, we recommend that the evaluation team compare the student's attained ROI to the ROI that would be needed for the student to attain proficiency, or at least make sufficient progress to function at a level that would surpass the eligibility requirements under Criterion 1.

The concept is that a student who is deficient in level and who displays an attained ROI that is lower than what would allow him or her to attain the targeted level in the projected year would qualify for eligibility for SLD (under the Criteria 1 and 2). Conversely, a student who is deficient in level, but who has an attained ROI that, if sustained, would allow him to hit the projected mark in the designated time frame would not be eligible because at that point the student would not qualify under Criterion 1. Of course, the team would have to be confident that the intervention provided would be sufficiently robust to allow for the ROI to be sustained during this period of time, and regular progress monitoring would be needed to ascertain whether the desired ROI was being sustained. As indicated above, the decision as to how many years to project and what marker to target (25th, 40th, or 50th percentile) would be the prerogative of the evaluation team and would depend on numerous factors that pertain to the individual student. An advantage of this approach is that parents, as critical members of the decision-making team, would have a clear depiction of how far behind the student is performing, how fast he is catching up, whether current interventions are working, and how long it might take to reach a reasonable level of proficiency. We believe that this perspective is currently impossible to attain with traditional testing procedures and causes parents much confusion and consternation.

Figure 9.3 provides an example of an excerpt from a comprehensive evaluation report that documents a student's deficiency in ROI (i.e., his RTI).

ESTABLISHING QUALIFICATIONS FOR ELIGIBILITY UNDER CRITERION 3: DOCUMENTING THE RULE-OUT OF OTHER CONDITIONS

The documentation for Criterion 3, the rule-out of other conditions, is straightforward. As described in Chapter 5, the evaluation team uses screening procedures to rule out certain conditions including a visual, hearing, or motor disability; intellectual disability; emotional distur-

TABLE 9.1. ROIs Needed to Reach the 50th and 25th Percentiles of ORF in 1–3 Years When Starting at 25%, 50%, and 75% of Benchmark Level

Grade 1: Winter ORF

Percent of level	Target percentile	Grade 2	Grade 3	Grade 4
75%	50	1.52	1.04	0.88
(17.25 wcpm)	25	0.69	0.62	0.65
50%	50	1.68	1.12	0.93
(11.5 wcpm)	25	0.85	0.70	0.70
25%	50	1.84	1.20	0.98
(5.75 wcpm)	25	1.01	0.78	0.75

Grade 2: Winter ORF

Percent of level	Target percentile	Grade 3	Grade 4	Grade 5
75%	50	1.06	0.81	0.68
(54 wcpm)	25	0.22	0.46	0.42
50%	50	1.56	1.06	0.84
(36 wcpm)	25	0.72	0.71	0.58
25%	50	2.06	1.31	1.01
(18 wcpm)	25	1.22	0.96	0.75

Grade 3: Winter ORF

Percent of level	Target percentile	Grade 4	Grade 5	Grade 6
75%	50	1.19	0.81	0.66
(69 wcpm)	25	0.50	0.42	0.39
50%	50	1.83	1.13	0.87
(46 wcpm)	25	1.14	0.74	0.60
25%	50	2.47	1.44	1.08
(23 wcpm)	25	1.78	1.06	0.81

Grade 4: Winter ORF

Percent of level	Target percentile	Grade 5	Grade 6	Grade 7
75%	50	1.19	0.78	0.48
(84 wcpm)	25	0.42	0.38	0.23
50%	50	1.97	1.17	0.74
(56 wcpm)	25	1.19	0.76	0.49
25%	50	2.75	1.56	1.00
(28 wcpm)	25	1.97	1.15	0.75

(continued)

TABLE 9.1. *(continued)*

Grade 5: Winter ORF

Percent of level	Target percentile	Grade 6	Grade 7	Grade 8
75%	50	1.24	0.57	0.47
(95.25 wcpm)	25	0.44	0.19	0.18
50%	50	2.13	1.01	0.76
(63.5 wcpm)	25	1.32	0.63	0.48
25%	50	3.01	1.45	1.06
(31.75 wcpm)	25	2.20	1.07	0.77

Grade 6: Winter ORF

Percent of level	Target percentile	Grade 7	Grade 8	Grade 9*
75%	50	0.86	0.57	0.38
(105 wcpm)	25	0.11	0.14	0.09
50%	50	1.83	1.06	0.70
(70 wcpm)	25	1.08	0.63	0.42
25%	50	2.81	1.54	1.03
(35 wcpm)	25	2.06	1.11	0.74

Note. *, Grade 8 norms used for the 3-year projections. ORF figures derived from Hasbrouck and Tindal (2006).

Throughout the current intervention period, John has displayed little progress. At the beginning of the intervention, John scored 43 wcpm on ORF probes. The median of his last three scores at the end of 10 weeks of the Tier 3 intervention was 46 wcpm. John's attained progress monitoring ROI during this period was 0.3 wcpm/week. Compared to the typical ROI for students in John's grade (0.9 wcpm/week), John is 33% (3.0× deficient). If John continued at his current ROI, in 1 year he would be reading at 58 wcpm, which is below the 10th percentile for fourth graders. To reach the 25th percentile by this time next year, John would need to attain and sustain a progress monitoring ROI of 1.13 wcpm/week. To reach the 25th percentile in 2 years, John would need to attain and sustain a progress monitoring ROI of 0.73 wcpm/week. John's current ROI of 0.33 is not sufficient to allow him to meet minimal benchmarks of proficiency in the near future. The intervention that was provided to John was developed using functional academic assessment, included direct instruction on grade-level passages, was monitored for correct use, and intensified weekly to attempt to obtain stronger effects on learning. Although some improvement in growth was noted midway through the intervention, the overall progress monitoring ROI and the final ROI (best ROI computed on last 4 weeks of intervention) is not sufficient to move John out of the risk range.

FIGURE 9.3. Report excerpt documenting a student's deficiency in ROI.

bance; cultural factors; environmental or economic disadvantage; or limited English proficiency. Alternatively, if a condition cannot be ruled out and may be the cause of the student's academic problems, a more formal evaluation of that condition is needed. The evaluation team must consider each of the eight conditions or situations and provide evidence that each of them can be ruled out. Failure to rule out any condition or situation would lead to a finding that the student did not have SLD.

The documentation appropriate for this section consists of a report of the results of the screening or follow-up evaluation that was conducted to analyze whether the condition is determined by the evaluation team to be the cause of the student's academic performance problems. Again, if any of these conditions are judged to be causal, SLD may not be identified. Figure 9.4 provides an example of an excerpt from a comprehensive evaluation report that documents the rule-out of the eight conditions.

Sensory Impairments: John's vision has been screened annually by the school. No visual problems have been detected (give most recent date). Vision problems are ruled out as a possible reason for John's academic difficulties. John's hearing has also been screened annually by the school. No hearing problems have been detected (give most recent date). Hearing problems are ruled out as a possible reason for John's academic difficulties.

Motor Problems: John does not display motor problems in the classroom, as indicated by reports of his teacher and by the observation conducted by the school psychologist. No motor problems have been identified by the school nurse or during school-sponsored physical examination that is conducted on all students in second grade, and in which John participated. John's "tool movements," as assessed by calculating the number of letters he can write in 1 minute, were commensurate with those of his classmates. Based on this information, motor problems may be ruled out as a possible reason for John's academic difficulties.

Intellectual Disability: John displays many indications of typical intellectual ability. His scores on tests of arithmetic skills have been in the proficient range since kindergarten, including state tests and universal screenings. His developmental milestones were age-appropriate and he displays adaptive skills that are appropriate for his age and grade level. Based on this information, intellectual disability can be ruled out as a possible reason for John's academic difficulties.

Emotional Disturbance: John displays appropriate behavior in the classroom. He is attentive and tries hard. He gets along well with his peers and teachers. According to the results of the Behavior Assessment System for Children–Second Edition (BASC-2), his parents and teacher report typical behavior on both externalizing and internalizing subscales. John is often frustrated by his difficulties in learning to read, but these emotions appear to be secondary to his learning problems. Based on these data, emotional disturbance can be ruled out as a possible reason for John's academic difficulties.

Culture and Language: John is an African American student whose primary home language is English. John's culture and language are not seen as related to his academic concerns. It is not believed that acculturation, language, or environmental circumstances are the primary cause of John's academic difficulties.

Economic/Environmental Disadvantage: Although John participates in the Free and Reduced Lunch Program, the limited income of John's family is not believed to be related to his academic problems. He is a well-cared-for child who attends school regularly and has all the materials needed to do his work. Economic/environmental disadvantage is ruled out as a primary cause of John's learning difficulties.

FIGURE 9.4. Report excerpt documenting the rule-out of other disabilities and conditions.

ESTABLISHING QUALIFICATIONS FOR ELIGIBILITY UNDER CRITERION 4: DOCUMENTING THE RULE-OUT OF LACK OF INSTRUCTION AND THE PROVISION OF INFORMATION ON REPEATED ASSESSMENTS TO THE PARENTS

In this section of the comprehensive report, the evaluation team must rule out the possibility that a lack of instruction is the cause of the student's academic problems. To conduct this rule-out procedure, the team must document that appropriate instruction has been provided in the student's general education program by qualified personnel. The team must provide evidence that the core instructional program that the student has received is based on scientific research and has been delivered with sufficient integrity so that students acquire the requisite skills. The 2006 IDEA regulations are particularly specific about the area of reading, linking this analysis to "the essential components of reading instruction (as defined in section 1208[3] of the ESEA" (§300.306[b]). As we described in Chapter 6, the evaluation team must document these essential components by describing how the student has been systematically taught the "big ideas" of reading. That is, the team should articulate how the student's core instructional program explicitly taught phonemic awareness, phonics, vocabulary, fluency, and comprehension. Although not explicitly stated in the regulations, a similar analysis of the school's mathematics and writing curriculum and instructional program should be undertaken if the student displays deficits in those areas. The evaluation team should further indicate methods that were undertaken to ensure the integrity with which the student's teachers have implemented this instruction, including the use of integrity checklists and other methods of assessment used by school personnel during classroom observations of core instruction. Finally, the report should note how long the student has participated in this instruction. The documentation should take two forms: a description of how this particular student was exposed to effective core instruction, including the appraisal of implementation integrity; and an overall indication that the school's instructional program has led to proficiency for the majority of its students.

In addition to the documentation of effective core instruction, the evaluation team should describe and evaluate the interventions implemented for this student during Tiers 2 and 3. As with the analysis of core instruction, the interventions used with the student should be evaluated on the extent to which they are research based (i.e., there is empirical support demonstrating intervention effectiveness with struggling students) and delivered by qualified personnel. The team should also document efforts to appraise the integrity with which the interventions were implemented, especially through observations using integrity checklists. Finally, the interventions should be evaluated in terms of their sufficiency: were they implemented with sufficient frequency and duration to produce gain for the student? Again, the documentation takes two forms: a description of the interventions that were used with the student, including the appraisal of implementation integrity; and data showing that the intervention has worked for other students with similar needs, both in this school and in empirical studies. One important source of systemic evidence of high-quality RTI implementation (and therefore accurate decision making) is the demonstration that most children receiving Tiers 2 and 3 interventions in the school have successful responses. Figure 9.5 provides an example of an excerpt from a comprehensive evaluation report that documents the rule-out of lack of instruction.

John has received appropriate instruction in reading throughout his 4 years at Lincoln Elementary School (K–3). Since kindergarten, John's teachers have used the SRA Reading Mastery reading series, which uses explicit instructional procedures to teach the "big ideas" in reading. This research-based program has been successful in bringing 80% of the current third graders to proficiency. All of John's teachers have had extensive training with SRA. Fidelity checks conducted by reading coaches and the school principal indicate that the SRA program has been used with a high degree of implementation fidelity. (Documentation of the fidelity checks are on file in the principal's office.)

John has been provided with intensive reading interventions at Tiers 2 and 3 of Lincoln's three-tier model since September 2008. He has been provided with small-group interventions to address his difficulties in phonemic awareness and decoding skills, using the Early Reading Intervention (ERI) program (Scott Foresman). ERI has been identified by the Florida Center for Reading Research as a research-based practice and has been shown to significantly increase the proficiency of students at Tiers 2 and 3 in Lincoln School. Fidelity checks conducted by the district's reading coordinator indicate that the reading teachers who implemented the ERI program have done so with a high degree of fidelity. (Documentation of the fidelity checks are on file in the principal's office.)

FIGURE 9.5. Report excerpt documenting the rule-out of lack of instruction.

The second required documentation in this section of the IDEA regulations is the report on the school's adherence to the required use of repeated assessments with the referred student and the extent that the results of these assessments were communicated to the student's parents. At minimum, these assessments would include the universal screenings in which the student participated and the progress monitoring that was conducted during interventions in Tiers 2 and 3. The reports of the universal screening to the parents should have occurred after each screening (e.g., three times per year). The frequency with which reports of the progress monitoring is provided to parents varies and often is a function of the frequency of teacher–parent conferences during the school year. In general, the frequency of reports to parents should correspond with the frequency of assessment. If progress monitoring occurs every other week in Tier 2 and weekly in Tier 3, reports to parents should be on the same schedule. Generally, the results of these assessments (i.e., the data) would have been reported in previous sections of the comprehensive evaluation report as part of the evidence regarding the student's deficiencies in relation to level (Criterion 1) and RTI (Criterion 2). Consequently, this section does not call for a repeat of the data, but rather would include documentation of what data were reported to the parents and at what frequency. Figure 9.6 provides an example of an excerpt from a comprehensive evaluation report that documents the provision of information about repeated assessments of the student's performance to parents.

Since kindergarten, John has been assessed during the universal screening in reading three times per year (fall, winter, spring). Reports of John's performance on these assessments were provided to parents as an addendum to the report card, which is distributed two weeks after each screening. Since his involvement with Tier 2 and 3 interventions this year, John's progress has been monitored using CBM on a weekly basis. Results of progress monitoring have been provided to his parents through written monthly reports (including graphed data) and in team meetings that were attended by the parents.

FIGURE 9.6. Report excerpt documenting the provision of repeated measures of assessment.

DOCUMENTING INFORMATION
OBTAINED DURING THE CLASSROOM OBSERVATION

As described in Chapter 7, a classroom observation of a student referred for a comprehensive evaluation under the SLD category is an important aspect of the process, informs the decision about eligibility, and provides useful information about the relative effectiveness of various interventions. In that chapter, we advocated for the use of systematic behavioral observation techniques using formatted codes such as the Behavioral Observation of Students in Schools (BOSS; Shapiro, 2011b) to ensure that a complete observation of the student's performance in response to various instructional conditions could be observed and recorded. Referred students should be observed in core instruction in those areas (subjects) of concern as well as in areas in which the student does not display difficulties. Observations during Tier 2 and 3 interventions are also useful. A comparison of the student's behavior in these various instructional settings provides useful information about how the student's skill deficiencies are affecting his attention to instruction and overall on-task behavior. Documenting specific data regarding the student's on- and off-task behavior as well as the frequency (rate) of interfering behaviors in response to instruction in various instructional conditions informs both the determination of SLD and those interventions that should be incorporated into the IEP.

DETERMINING THAT THE STUDENT NEEDS SPECIAL EDUCATION

The determination of eligibility for special education involves two key issues: does the student have a disability, and if so, does the student need special education? The guidelines we have presented in this chapter so far inform the first of these questions. Assuming that the evaluation team determines that the student meets SLD criteria using the four criteria that we have been discussing, along with supporting information gleaned from the classroom observation and from the parents, the next step is to determine whether the student needs special education. The critical issue is whether the student needs the specially designed instruction that is only available through special education programs and services to make meaningful progress in the acquisition of basic skills. It is theoretically possible that a student might be identified as having an SLD but not need special education to make meaningful progress. In such a case, the student would not be determined to be eligible for special education.

The issue as to whether a student needs special education is particularly challenging because many multi-tier systems of support provide extensive interventions, especially at Tier 3. As we mentioned in previous chapters, it is not uncommon to hear practitioners argue that some Tier 3 interventions are more intensive in terms of frequency, duration, and/or intensity than the existing special education programs. In essence, the question here is "What is special about special education?" That is, what programs and services will be delivered through special education that are necessary for the student to make meaningful progress and are beyond what can be provided through general (and remedial) education? Grimes and Kurns (2003) noted that the student's needs are beyond what

> The student's needs are beyond what can be addressed in general education when the curriculum, instruction, or environmental conditions needed for student growth are different than that needed for typical students.

can be addressed in general education when the curriculum, instruction, or environmental conditions needed for student growth are different than that needed for typical students. Hardman, McDonnell, and Welch (1997) argued that specially designed instruction requires sustained effort, time, or resources to be sustained; is provided extensively or throughout the school day; and requires preplanning and special resources.

Perhaps the most comprehensive view of the gradations of intervention intensity was provided by Barnett, Daly, Jones, and Lenz (2004), who defined intervention intensity as "qualities of time, effort, or resources that make intervention support in typical environments difficult as intensity increases, establishing a clear role for specialized services" (p. 68). Barnett and colleagues further defined the logistical characteristics related to increases in intervention intensity as consisting of enhancements to management and planning, modifications to typical classroom routines, and types of intervention episodes, materials, and change agents. Although these authors did not indicate a dividing line between general and special education, their framework can be used to inform decision making in regard to student's needs. Enhancements to management and planning in special education would include more frequent monitoring of student responding, more frequent progress monitoring, more explicit teacher prompting, and more frequent and detailed communication with parents and professionals. Modifications to typical classroom routines would involve different types of instructional tasks and assessments, increased assistance to students during instruction, additional practice opportunities, enhanced feedback to students about performance, and unique contingencies for meeting expectations. In special education, one would also expect to see different instructional formats such as social skills instruction and explicit teaching over sustained periods of time. Instructional materials that allow explicit teaching of basic skills as well as ample practice opportunities are also basic requirements for effective special education instruction. Finally, providing special education presupposes that teaching staff are specially trained to deliver highly explicit instruction and make instructional adjustments based on students' responding.

In considering the student's need for special education, these parameters become critical. An identified student is eligible for special education to the extent that these special instructional and logistic features are necessary for the student to make meaningful progress. A detailed analysis of these features will also help practitioners to create the level of intensity that is needed for the student to make such progress. The full intent of special education is to devise a program of instruction that will accelerate the student's progress beyond that which was realized during the provision of multi-tier supports. For some school districts, the examination of these features may lead to a reconsideration of the question "What is special about special education?" For some, additional levels of intensity beyond what is currently provided may be necessary to meet students' needs (i.e., to accelerate their rates of learning), and these criteria may become an action list for improving the intensity of instruction provided through special education.

CASE STUDIES

Candice

Candice is a third-grade student who excels in reading, but has struggled for several years in mathematics. Her parents report that math is a "problem area" for Candice, and they have sought summer tutoring and assisted her with homework during the school year. In prior grades, she has earned a passing grade in math but is described by her parents as being "unable to keep up" with math at third grade. Candice scored in the nonproficient range on the most recent (end of second grade) school-administered standardized test in mathematics. A referral for evaluation was made in March of third grade, after the winter administration of universal screening. Data for this school year (third grade) for Candice as compared to benchmark scores on AIMSweb Math Computation are presented in Figure 9.7. (Spring data are also depicted and will be discussed later in the case study.) As can be seen in the figure, Candice's math computation skills were significantly deficient in relation to these benchmarks. Benchmark testing on AIMSweb Mathematics Concepts and Applications was also conducted, and Candice's performance in relation to benchmarks is presented in Figure 9.8. Again, Candice was significantly below expectations on this skill in both fall and winter administrations. In fact, Candice's scores on both assessments were at or below the 10th percentile on both fall and winter administrations.

Based on these data, additional assessment was conducted to drill down and identify the prerequisite skills that Candice had and had not mastered. Assessment findings indicated that Candice had not mastered single-digit addition and subtraction facts, multidigit addition and subtraction with and without regrouping, which indicated an inadequate conceptual understanding of place value, a poor understanding of the procedures required for regrouping, and a general dysfluency with addition and subtraction (indicating a lack of fluency for rapid comparison of quantities, and combining and decomposing numbers). A conceptual understanding of addition was demonstrated by Candice's ability to correct incorrect addition and subtraction problems and draw pictures to solve addition and subtraction problems. However, in solving addition and subtraction problems, her answers were slow and labored.

Schoolwide data using locally developed individual skill probes indicate that most students in the grade are mastering multiplication, which is an essential outcome of winter instruction in mathematics at third grade. As indicated in Figure 9.9, when comparing the winter and spring screening data, the number of students in the risk range (darker portion of each bar) is greatly reduced from winter to spring as the skill is taught and students show benefit from that instruction. Candice is enrolled in Class 9 in Figure 9.9. At the spring screening, only 5% of students

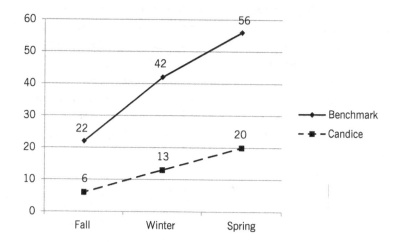

FIGURE 9.7. Results of benchmark assessment using AIMSweb Math Computation for a third grader (Candice in case study). Data are expressed in correct digits.

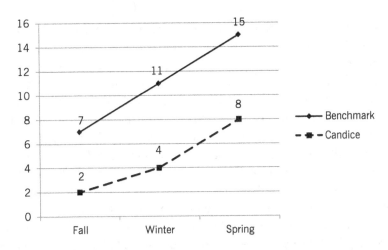

FIGURE 9.8. Results of benchmark assessment using AIMSweb Mathematics Concepts and Applications for a third grader (Candice in case study). Data are expressed in total points.

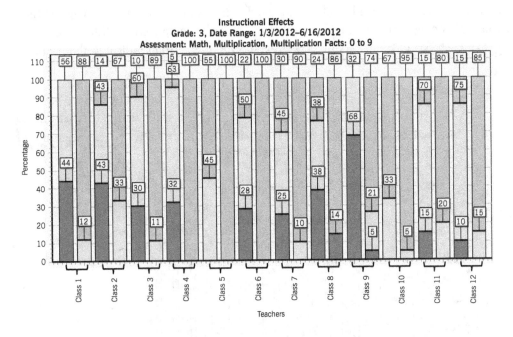

FIGURE 9.9. Class proficiencies in multiplication facts (Candice's class in case study). The winter and spring screening is shown for each class. The bottom-shaded area of the bar represents the percentage of students below criterion during screening. The middle area represents the percentage of students in the instructional range or not at risk. The top-shaded area of the bar represents the percentage of students at mastery on the assessed skill or skills. This graph was created on iSTEEP.

are in the risk range. Figure 9.10 shows Candice's performance in her class at the spring screening. Candice is the lowest-performing student in her class and in the risk range. A double-digit subtraction with regrouping probe was also administered to her class for screening, and Candice was the second lowest-performing student in her class, again performing in the risk range (see Figure 9.11). Taken together, these data indicate that Candice's difficulties are not a result of a classwide instructional problem, and because Candice has been in this school since kindergarten, are also evidence that Candice is not hampered by a lack of appropriate instruction.

Based on the drill-down analysis, a Tier 3 intervention was developed to build fluency in addition facts. Intervention began in January with addition facts 0–20, and Candice rapidly reached and maintained fluent performance on that skill with intervention (see Figure 9.12). The intervention was adjusted in February to target multidigit addition with regrouping. Candice demonstrated conceptual understanding of regrouping and could explain when and why regrouping was required. Daily intervention was conducted following an intervention protocol that involved guided practice completing multidigit addition problems with immediate corrective feedback and assistance provided by her teacher to ensure 100% correct responding. Following the practice interval, Candice completed a timed worksheet to try to beat her last best score. After 2 weeks of intervention, Candice's performance was not sufficiently improved. An intervention coach conducted an observation of the intervention and determined that the intervention was being correctly implemented. In addition, a completed worksheet and score was available each day of the preceding 2 weeks, and the observation indicated that Candice was

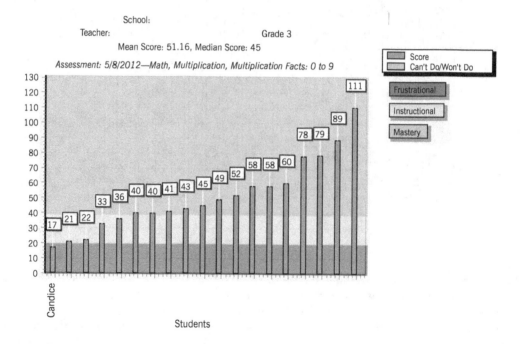

FIGURE 9.10. Performance of all students in Candice's class (in case study) on the multiplication 0–9 probe. Most students are performing in the instructional (middle-shaded background ranging from 20–40 digits correct per 2 minutes, not at risk) and mastery (top-shaded background, not at risk) range. Candice is in the risk range and is the lowest-performing student in her class. This graph was created on iSTEEP.

School:
Teacher: Grade 3
Mean Score: 32.95, Median Score: 34

Assessment: 5/8/2012—Math, Subtraction, 3-digit number from a 3-digit number: regrouping from 10s column only

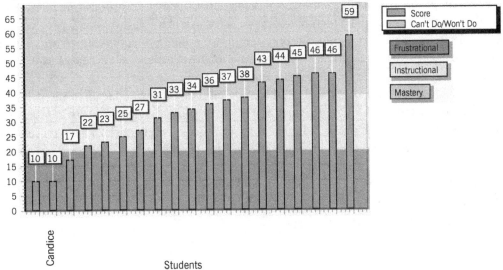

FIGURE 9.11. Performance of target student (Candice in case study) in relation to peers. Candice is the lowest-performing student on a multidigit subtraction probe. This graph was created on iSTEEP.

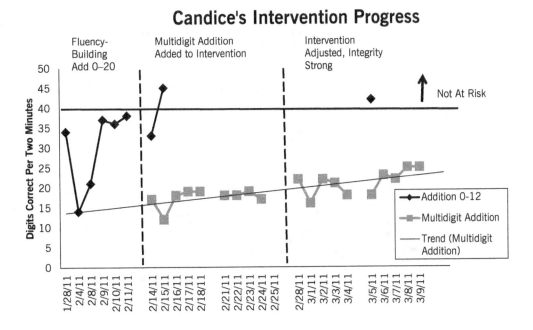

FIGURE 9.12. Progress monitoring data on specific skills (Candice in case study). Intervention began on addition 0–20. Once Candice reached 40 digits correct in 2 minutes, the intervention content was advanced to multidigit addition. Following a period of flat growth, the intervention was observed by a trained coach, and troubleshooting occurred to improve the intervention's effects. In the final phase, intervention continues for multidigit addition. The linear trend of growth is fitted through the data points to show the student's ROI.

fully engaged during the intervention and appeared to give her best effort by working diligently the entire time. The observation and scores indicated that Candice's error rate remained around 10%. Based on these data, the intervention was adjusted to include only two-digit problems with regrouping in the ones column only (as opposed to three-digit problems with regrouping possible in the ones and/or tens column). The intervention was changed to a cover–copy–compare format with teacher support for correct responding.

Because Candice was being evaluated for eligibility for special education, the evaluation team also conducted weekly progress monitoring on a general outcome measure (AIMSweb Math Computations). As depicted in Figure 9.13, Candice's weekly performance on this measure was very poor, as indicated by her attained ROI of 0.49 correct digits/week. Candice's attained ROI was 45% of the ROI of typical students (0.49/1.08) and 15% of the ROI in comparison with the targeted ROI that Candice would have needed to reach proficient performance (0.49/3.31).

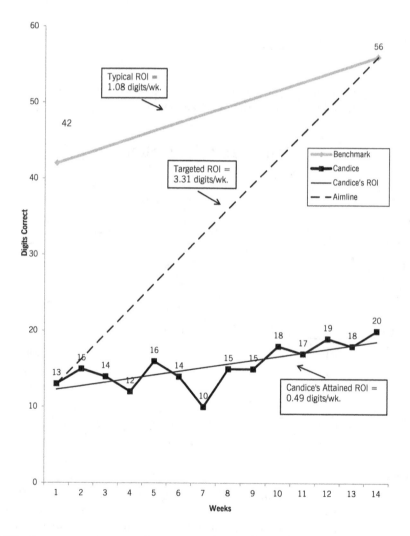

FIGURE 9.13. Progress monitoring data using AIMSweb Mathematics Calculations for a third grader (Candice in case study). Data are expressed in correct digits.

During the course of the evaluation, Candice participated in the spring universal screening. As indicated in Figure 9.7 and 9.8, Candice continued to perform far below the benchmark level, scoring at or below the 10th percentile. The evaluation team conducted a benchmark gap analysis of the spring screening data for both Math Computation and Mathematics Concepts and Applications. Results of the benchmark gap analysis of the Math Computation indicated that Candice's performance was 3.2× (42/13) discrepant in level from her peers before intervention (winter). That is, she scored at 31% (13/42) of typical performance at that time. Following intervention, Candice was 2.8× (56/20) discrepant, or scoring only 36% (20/56) of what she needed to score to move out of the academic risk range. Results of the benchmark gap analysis of the Math Concepts and Application assessment indicated that Candice's performance before intervention (winter) was 2.8× (11/4) discrepant, or at 37% (4/11) of typical performance. After the intervention (spring), Candice was 1.9× (15/8) discrepant, or at 53% (8/15) of typical. Although Candice made some progress from winter to spring after an intensive intervention, she was still significantly behind her peers.

Candice is enrolled in a class that has shown growth during general mathematics instruction, and there is no systemic learning problem in mathematics. She has not shown sufficient growth given an evidence-based intervention that was matched to her learning needs and delivered with integrity, despite intervention adjustments. The rate of progress established by Candice was not sufficient to reduce her risk of long-term mathematical failure or to close the gap between her current performance and that needed to ensure successful learning in her general education environment. Candice needs to make much more rapid progress on this skill so that she does not fall farther behind her peers in the overall mathematics curriculum. Based on these data, Candice would meet the first two criteria for SLD.

Candice was observed using the BOSS by the school psychologist in reading and math classes and during her math remediation period. In reading class, Candice was on task for 90% of the intervals observed as compared to an 87% on-task level displayed by her peers. Off-task behaviors were unremarkable and did not interfere with her performance. In contrast, in her math core instructional class, she was on task only 50% of the observed intervals in comparison to her peers, who were on task 85% of the intervals. Motor off-task behaviors were observed during 20% of the intervals, with off-task verbal behaviors occurring in 20% of the intervals, and off-task passive behaviors during 10% of the intervals. She was more on task in her math remediation period, displaying on-task behavior during 80% of the observed intervals (compared to 85% for her peers). In general, these observations are convergent with her academic performance; she is generally on task during instruction in which she excels (reading) or when she receives explicit instruction (math remediation), and is significantly off task in a challenging area when she is not provided with individualized supports (core math instruction).

Exclusionary criteria can now be considered. Candice has participated in routine sensory screenings at her school. At the last screening in the current academic school year, no visual or hearing impairments were detected. No motor problems are suspected. Candice's parents and teacher report that Candice's work is very neat and she routinely completes writing tasks on time and earns scores in the above-average range in handwriting. Intellectual disability is not suspected, as Candice is reading in the above-average range for her grade level and has adaptive skills that are age appropriate. Emotional disability is not suspected, as Candice earns high conduct marks and gets along well with her peers. Candice has expressed frustration during homework and during math lessons at school that are commensurate with the level of challenge faced given her mathematics skill deficiencies and the demands of her mathematics learning environment (there is a mismatch between her current skills and the performance that is expected of her). Candice is a Caucasian female whose primary language is English. Culture and language barriers are not suspected. Economic and environmental disadvantage are not suspected, as Candice does not qualify for free or reduced lunch and her parents have sought and paid for outside tutoring assistance for her mathematics learning problems. Lack of instruction has been ruled out, as Candice showed some growth given a well-controlled intervention aligned to her learning needs, but the growth was not sufficient to close her learning gap.

Candice has demonstrated low achievement in mathematics that is persistent in the face of intervention. Candice has demonstrated a need for special education because she has demonstrated a need for more intensive sustained mathematics instruction concentrating on below-grade-level skills with frequent progress monitoring and adjustments to stimulate and sustain learning gains. Without intervention, Candice is likely to experience long-term failure in mathematics.

Sam

Sam, a third grader, was referred for comprehensive evaluation because of significant difficulties in learning to read. In contrast, his teachers see him as having strong skills in mathematics, and he has consistently been above benchmark on universal math screening. He has had good school attendance and receives satisfactory grades in work habits and study skills. The school where Sam has attended for the past 3 years uses a "guided reading model" that features a literature-based, whole-language approach to the teaching of reading. Explicit teaching of letter-sound correspondence and phonetic decoding is not carried out in this program; rather, these skills are embedded in contextualized reading, and students are assumed to acquire the skills indirectly. Sam's ORF scores from first to third grade are presented in Table 9.2. The district's reading specialist administered the CORE Multiple Measures, including the CORE Phonics Survey. Results indicated that Sam had difficulties with rapid, automatic decoding and

TABLE 9.2. Fall, Winter, and Spring Benchmark Scores and ROIs for DIBELS Next ORF for a Third Grader (Sam in Case Study) as Compared with Benchmarks

Grade	ORF Scores			ROI		
	Fall	Winter	Spring	Fall to Winter	Winter to Spring	Fall to Spring
1 (benchmark)	n/a	23	47	n/a	1.33	n/a
1 (Sam)	n/a	10	20	n/a	0.56	n/a
2 (benchmark)	52	72	87	1.11	0.83	0.97
2 (Sam)	21	30	38	0.50	0.44	0.47
3 (benchmark)	70	86	100	0.89	0.78	0.83
3 (Sam)	34	71	n/a	2.06	n/a	n/a

Note. ORF scores are expressed in words correct per minute (wcpm). ROIs are expressed in words correct per minute per week (wcpm/week).

word analysis skills. He made frequent single- and double-vowel confusions and had particular difficulties with double vowels *oo* and *ea*, double consonants *sh* and *gh*, and with the final-*e* pattern.

In response to these difficulties, the data team developed a package of interventions that included explicit instruction in letter-sound correspondence, with particular emphasis on Sam's identified errors; explicit instruction in sounding-out and blending phonemes; systematic introduction of new letter sounds; discrimination training to distinguish new letter-sound cor-respondences from previously learned ones; and the use of decodable stories with controlled vocabulary for contextualized reading. These interventions were initiated in September and were conducted in 30-minute sessions four times per week in addition to the core language arts instruction.

The evaluation team conducted a progress monitoring gap analysis of Sam's response to these interventions (see Figure 9.14). His progress monitoring ROI (based on OLS) of 1.90 wcpm/week was 213% of the rate displayed by typical third graders (0.89 wcpm/week.). Sam needed to progress at 2.88 wcpm/week to reach benchmark by winter. His ROI of 1.90 was 66% of the targeted rate, which was judged by the evaluation team to be very ambitious. The evaluation team then conducted a benchmark gap analysis of Sam's fall and winter benchmark scores. From fall to winter, Sam increased from 49% of benchmark (34/71; 2.1× deficient) to 83% of benchmark (71/86; 1.2× deficient). While still below benchmark, Sam was now above the at-risk level of 68 wcpm. Projecting Sam's ROI to this time next year indicated that if Sam could maintain the same ROI (1.90 wcpm/week), he would increase by 68 wcpm and reach 139 wcpm by the winter benchmark assessment, which would be well above the 103 wcpm rate at

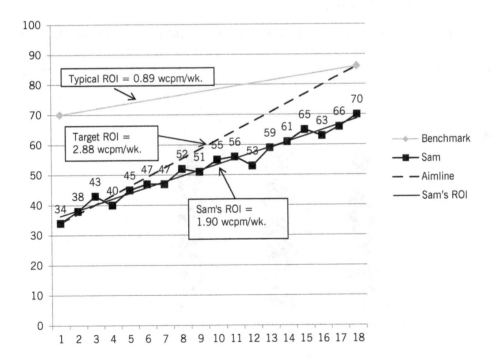

FIGURE 9.14. Progress monitoring data using DIBELS Next ORF for a third grader (Sam in case study).

that time. In fact, if Sam progressed at the typical ROI (0.83 wcpm/week) for the next year, he would be just under the winter benchmark (101 compared to 103 wcpm).

Sam was also observed by the school psychologist prior to and after the intervention in both core instruction and during the tiered intervention using a time-sampling behavioral assessment in which on-task and off-task behavior was recorded in comparison with typical peers. As depicted in Figure 9.15, Sam was on task during only half of the observed intervals in core instruction prior to the intervention, compared to largely on-task behavior of the comparison peers. His on-task behavior increased substantially in the intervention environment, with both Sam and the comparison peer on task for more than 80% of the observed intervals. After the intervention, Sam also improved his on-task behavior during core instruction compared to comparison peers.

The evaluation team interpreted these data as indicative of a student who improved dramatically after receiving a highly robust intervention that was targeted to his particular instructional needs. They concluded that, as a result of the successful intervention, Sam did not qualify for SLD identification under Criterion 1 (level) or Criterion 2 (RTI). Because Sam no longer displayed a deficiency in relation to grade or state standards, there was no need to rule out other conditions as causal for the previous problems. Rather, it appears likely that Sam's previous poor performance could be attributed to a lack of explicit instruction in basic reading skills in the earlier grades. The evaluation team recommended that Sam continue in tiered intervention until he reached benchmark, and that his progress be reported to his parents via weekly reports using graphed data.

Discussion of Case Studies

In these case studies, we presented two scenarios: one in which the student displayed the dual discrepancy required for identification as SLD, and a second in which the student's positive RTI eliminated the need for identification as eligible for special education. Results of these

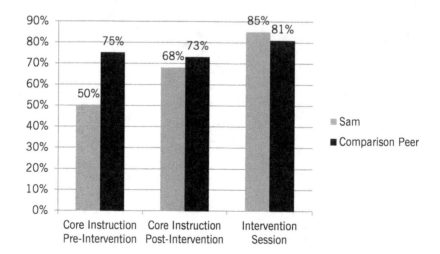

FIGURE 9.15. On-task behavior for target student (Sam in case study) and comparison peers across three instructional conditions.

studies are illustrated in Table 9.3. In the first study (Candice), the student displayed a significant deficiency both before and after intervention in relation to level (Math Computations) and displayed a poor ROI during the intervention. The evaluation team determined that the intervention was effective for other students, ruling out a lack of instruction, and further determined that the student's math deficiencies were not due to other disabilities or other conditions. In the second case (Sam), the student was referred for evaluation after 2 years of difficulties in acquiring basic reading skills. A drill-down assessment indicated specific phonetic weaknesses, which served as the basis for a multifaceted intervention that was implemented during supplemental periods and also included accommodations during core instruction. The student responded robustly to this intervention package, attaining an ROI that was substantially greater than that displayed by typical students. After 18 weeks of intervention, the student had not reached benchmark but had significantly closed the gap and appeared to be on the way to proficient performance within the next calendar year. As a result, the evaluation team found this student not to meet diagnostic criteria for SLD. It should be noted that we present these case studies in terms of what would occur once a student is referred for a comprehensive evaluation for a potential disability. In a school that has as strong infrastructure for RTI in place, it is likely that

TABLE 9.3. Summary of Case Studies

	Candice	Sam
Target area	Math	Reading
Pre-intervention benchmark gap	31% (3.2×)	49% (2.1×)
Post-intervention benchmark gap	36% (2.8×)	83% (1.2×)
Drill-down assessment	Informal math assessment	CORE Multiple Measures
Intervention	Fluency building with math facts and multidigit addition	Explicit phonics instruction
Progress monitoring ROI	0.49 correct digits/week	1.90 wcpm/week
Progress monitoring ROI gap (compared to typical ROI)	45% of typical ROI	213% of typical ROI
Observation data	50% on task in core math instruction; 80% on task during intervention	≥80% on task behavior postintervention in core and supplemental reading instruction
Rule-out of other disabilities and conditions	Other disabilities and conditions ruled out	Not applicable; student no longer displayed deficiency
Rule-out of lack of instruction	Lack of instruction ruled out	Lack of instruction likely
Determination	SLD (math)	Not eligible

Sam's positive RTI would have been noted by the team, and a referral for evaluation would not have been indicated.

Both case studies illustrate the key principles for decision making. Evaluation teams used multiple sources of data to reach their conclusion, followed guidelines that looked at the predicted outcomes if instructional processes continued with the same intensity with which they were implemented through the tiered process, and considered the student's behavior within the context of their classroom through direct, systematic observation. Data from both universal screening and progress monitoring were examined, as well other data sources obtained during the intervention process. Together, evaluation teams used these data to provide empirically supportable decisions using the four key criteria for SLD determination.

CHAPTER 10

Using RTI Data to Build an IEP

As described in Chapter 9, some students who receive a comprehensive evaluation will be found eligible for special education. Since 1975 when it was first enacted, IDEA has always mandated that the comprehensive evaluation produce two outcomes: a decision as to the eligibility of the student under one of a number of categories and extensive information to drive the development of an individualized education plan (IEP) that would result in a high-quality special education program. RTI processes provide one way to improve diagnostic accuracy in specifying who needs to receive services through special education under the category of SLD. Once children are made eligible to receive services for SLD, the goal shifts to improving the instructional intensity and student learning outcomes obtained for students served in special education. Special education instruction (i.e., specially designed instruction) should represent the most intensive instruction the school can deliver. Table 10.1 summarizes instructional strategies that are effective and intensive and that should be used in special education. There is also wide variability across schools and systems as to the quality and effects of instruction provided through special education.

As a rule, data teams should follow children receiving special education services to verify that their growth improves with specialized instruction and that their risk of academic failure is decreased over time. Following all children receiving intensive intervention is part and parcel of obtaining improved learning for all students, but this approach may represent a paradigm shift for some systems. Special education is not an endpoint of RTI; rather, it is a way of making instructional resources available to permit more intensive intervention.

If RTI was well conducted, then the special educator should have access to information specifying what instructional strategies were attempted and what effect those strategies had on student learning. The special educator would also have access to extensive assessment data that were generated during the provision of multiple tiers of instruction and intervention (see Chapter 3). This information allows the special educator to place the child's performance on a skill hierarchy and specify what additional assessment is needed to plan instruction and set goals for instruction. If an intervention was identified and used that produced a positive effect on student learning but was not sufficient to move the student out of the risk range, then the intervention planning will likely involve providing a more intense dose of that instruction with

TABLE 10.1. Characteristics of Intensive Instruction

Intervention is linked to child assessment

- An analysis of skill mastery has been conducted to identify target skills and generalized outcomes for instruction.
- The child's performance on the target skills has been assessed to determine the rate of errors and fluency with which the child can perform the skill.
- The intervention is planned to establish correct responding, build fluent responding, or facilitate generalization.

Instruction has the following features

- Methodical demonstrations of correct and incorrect responding.
- Guided practice responding with immediate corrective feedback and systematic prompts to ensure correct responding.
- Use of repetition loop when errors occur (i.e., error is detected immediately, response is corrected, and problem is presented to student again).
- Multiple opportunities to respond with delayed corrective feedback once the student's error rate is low.
- Systematic fading of antecedent supports including prompting and modeling.
- Systematic increases in task difficulty across instructional sessions depending on student performance.
- Systematic fading of controlled task materials to those that are used in the general education classroom.
- Use of motivating strategies including goal setting, graphing progress, small rewards or privileges for "beating last best score," bonus rewards, mystery motivators, interspersal of easy tasks with more challenging tasks.
- Daily assessment of student progress and weekly adjustment to instructional plan.
- Graphs shared with general education teachers on the student's team and parents.

more frequent progress monitoring. However, a different process will be needed for students who experienced a failed RTI and did not show growth in response to instructional strategies attempted. In this chapter, we provide step-by-step suggestions for using student data to specify present level of performance, to plan intervention, to adjust intervention, and to measure special education effects over time to inform system improvements. In some cases, these data will be available from the RTI efforts already conducted. In other cases, what follows is a guide for data teams to use in collecting the data needed to plan effective special education services for children identified with SLD.

SPECIFYING PRESENT LEVELS OF PERFORMANCE

Understanding what students have mastered is fundamental to planning instruction. The data gathered in the comprehensive evaluation can be highly useful if an RTI system was well utilized. If RTI data are available, then the comprehensive evaluation can inform the IEP team as to what skills students are expected to be able to do to signify adequate response to general education (i.e., the screening tasks across semesters and grade levels) and what the student's peers are capable of doing (i.e., screening data). Furthermore, the IEP team should access all results of the precise analysis of skills and subskills that were conducted during the provision of multi-tier supports. For instructional planning, this analysis allows the special educator to situate the child's learning within a task hierarchy or skill hierarchy. A skill hierarchy is one way to map out target skills (e.g., skills represented on the screening task) and work backward to specify all underlying skills that the child must master to be able to perform the "end" or goal skill. This skill hierarchy becomes a map for translating the existing assessment to plan special education instruction, set goals for performance, monitor progress, and make adjustments to ensure that students grow.

SETTING IEP GOALS

The screening data collected during universal screening provide a framework within which to establish a sequence of expected skills. Data collected during the comprehensive evaluation can be used to specify intervention targets and identify whether the child's stage of learning is at the acquisition, fluency-building, generalization, or adaptation stage so that effective instructional strategies can be identified. Table 10.2 summarizes typical performance patterns for students at these various stages of learning as well as effective instructional strategies at each stage. Follow-up (drill-down) assessment, conducted during the provision of multi-tier supports and collected during the evaluation process (see Chapter 3), provides a basis for knowing which skills and subskills the student has or had not mastered and the types of instructional strategies that are aligned with the student's needs. In setting IEP goals, it is helpful to specify skill-specific short-term goals (e.g., student will reach mastery criterion for sums to 20) and goals that reflect generalized progress and better overall adaptation (e.g., reduced risk status on screening over time, increased year-end test scores). Figure 10.1 displays examples of IEP goals that follow from an in-depth skills analysis.

DESIGNING SPECIALIZED INSTRUCTION

When educators and advocates talk about the importance of granting all children access to the general education curriculum, it is critical to keep in mind that access for the struggling student must be systematic, incrementally provided, with support for accurate and fluent performance, and progress must be monitored to ensure that the struggling student is learning well. This notion of providing instruction at the right level of difficulty is distinct from simply providing easier content. Equity for students served in special education is about equity of results or outcomes, not providing identical content and instruction. Students receiving special education services should get what is needed instructionally to grow at paces comparable to students in general education (VanDerHeyden & Harvey, in press). Tiers 2 and 3 can be very effective in rapidly improving the skills of students so that the core instruction is functionally a better match with their proficiencies. Readers might think of this as adjusting the learner to improve the learner's fit with the demands of the learning environment. Useful Tier 2 and Tier 3 strategies often target proficiency for prerequisite skills

> **Students receiving special education services should get what is needed instructionally to grow at paces comparable to students in general education.**

TABLE 10.2. Effective Instructional Strategies Appropriate for Various Stages of Learning for Typical Students

Student performance . . .	Instructional strategies should include . . .
Acquisition	
is slow and hesitant. Error rate is greater than 10%.	• Verification that child has mastered prerequisite tasks. • Use of well-controlled instructional materials. • Support for correct responding including modeling, prompting, and guided practice with corrective feedback. • More elaborate corrective feedback. • Use of repetition loops. • Monitoring response accuracy. • Gradual increases in task difficulty based on improved student performance. • Verification that student conceptually understands the conditions under which the response is correct and incorrect.
Fluency building	
is accurate but slow. Child responding is 90% accurate or better.	• Multiple opportunities to respond. • Delayed corrective feedback. • Well-controlled instructional materials to which the child can accurately and independently respond. • Goal setting and motivational strategies to encourage more fluent performance. • Monitoring responses correct per minute. • Systematic increases in task difficulty based on student performance improvements.
Generalization and adaptation	
is fluent (accurate + speeded) under conditions that differ from training conditions.	• Intentional variation of task materials (e.g., slight increases in difficulty, changes in problem format, introduction of unpracticed materials). • Continued monitoring of responses correct per minute when variations are made to materials.

using systematic preview and practice strategies. However, children who experience poor learning when Tier 1 and 2 instruction is provided well are students who require much more precision in what instruction is provided to obtain strong learning gains. Stated another way, children who respond well to core instruction are generally children who are capable of learning in less well-controlled instructional conditions. In a nutshell, this is why simply repeating the lesson that was delivered during general education and hoping it will suddenly be effective at establishing the skill in the special education classroom is a futile and fruitless approach.

If students should not receive the exact same content, how then is the content of their instruction determined? As described in Chapter 3, understanding the student's stage of learning for particular skills is a highly useful and effective heuristic for instructional planning. Knowing a student's stage of learning tells the teacher what type of instruction, practice, and feedback is needed, when to increase difficulty or accelerate task presentation, and how to maximize instructional effects that can be obtained during the instruction period.

Demonstrating Conceptual Understanding

Problem: 6 × 7

- **Child can draw the answer.** Child can draw six sets of 7 or seven sets of 6. Child can express the problem as an addition problem (e.g., 7 + 7 + 7 + 7 + 7 + 7).
- **Child can "think aloud" to explain the solution or "teach the teacher" to get a solution.** Child can explain that the problem involves a case of counting, joining sets, or generating sums. Child can identify an "easier" product (e.g., 5 × 6 = 30) and then add or count forward two more sets of 7 or can explain the answer as (5 × 6) + 7 + 7 or (5 × 6) + 14.
- **Child can identify correct and incorrect (true or false) answers from a set of questions.** Child can indicate whether quantitative comparisons are true or false (e.g., [6 × 7] < [6 × 8]). Child can indicate that 6 × 7 = 7 × 6 is a true statement. Child can indicate that 6 × 7 is one set of 6 greater than 6 × 6.
- **Child can correct an incorrect answer and explain what made it correct and why**. Child can change related product equations to make them equivalent or to indicate that one quantity is greater or less than another quantity. Child can specify why 6 × 7 ≠ 36, indicate the correct answer, and draw hash marks to show why the first solution was incorrect and to verify the accuracy of the second solution.

Demonstrating Fluent Performance

- Given randomly presented multiplication problems using numbers ranging from 0 to 12, child can complete 80 digits correct in 2 minutes.

Demonstrating Generalized performance

- Child can solve word problems requiring computing products. Child can use product knowledge to solve applied problems like computing area.
- Child can "fill in the missing number" to solve using fact family knowledge or knowledge of inverse operations (e.g., ____ × 7 = 42). Child can write two formulas from a single multiplication product to show the inverse relationship.
- Child can compute the related division problem.
- Child can identify factors for 42.

FIGURE 10.1. Examples of IEP goals following from an in-depth skills analysis.

At the acquisition stage, the skill has not yet been established. The goal of acquisition instruction is to establish conceptual understanding (Harniss et al., 2002). Acquisition strategies are designed to establish correct responding and conceptual understanding and include strategies such as modeling correct and incorrect responding and providing guided practice opportunities to respond with structured prompts and immediate corrective feedback. Corrective feedback during acquisition instruction is often fairly elaborate, providing an explanation for why one response is correct and another is not. Feedback during acquisition usually emphasizes repetition loops such that if the student's response is incorrect, the response is interrupted, the child is guided to the correct response, and the problem is repeated so that the child can provide the correct answer independently. For example, if the teacher is providing guided practice reading text and the child misreads a word, the teacher may prompt the child by providing the first sound in the word. The child may then repeat the first sound in the word and attempt the middle sound, making an error. The teacher would then prompt the child by pointing to the middle letter and saying, "What sound does this letter make when there is an *e* at the end of the word?" and if the child does not respond, the teacher may say, "Remember, the *e* at the end makes the vowel say its name," and if the child still does not respond, the teacher may provide the middle sound. When the word has been sounded out with support, the teacher will point to the beginning of the word indicating the child should say the word again aloud. Having the child read the word aloud independently after corrective assistance has been provided is a powerful strategy to establish correct and independent responding. During acquisition, the teacher should monitor performance accuracy on brief tasks attempted without teacher assistance and assess conceptual understanding directly before moving to fluency-building instruction. Once the child is accurate for 90% of responses or better without teacher assistance and the child can demonstrate conceptual understanding, the child is ready for fluency-building instruction on that task.

At the fluency-building stage of learning, the skill has been established. In other words, the child understands how to respond correctly or obtain the correct answer. The goal of fluency-building instruction is to increase the ease with which a child can respond correctly. During acquisition instruction, we have monitored accuracy of responding, usually measuring the percentage of correct responses. Once a child enters the fluency-building stage of instruction, there must be a timed dimension to performance measurement to detect further gains in proficiency, and this can be accomplished using any score reflecting responses correct per minute, which can be obtained from 1-minute timed tests or longer tests that are timed and then divided by the number of minutes to obtain a per-minute estimate of performance.

At the fluency-building stage of instruction, one of the most important instructional strategies is providing effective practice. Because the child is responding accurately, delays between the child's response and teacher-provided corrective feedback can be tolerated and actually are desirable because interrupting the child's performance to tell the child that he or she is responding correctly (remember, by definition, skills at the fluency-building stage are skills that the student can perform accurately and independently) is not helpful and has the effect of reducing practice opportunities. An analogy can be made to athletics. Athletes understand the importance of practice to building fluency and the importance of fluency to attaining mastery. For example, great runners understand that to become a better runner (greater endurance and speed), one must run consistently. Academic proficiency is no different. A learned skill must be practiced to be mastered. Effective instructional strategies at the fluency-building stage of instruction include providing multiple opportunities to respond, using delayed corrective feedback strategies where feedback is provided after the practice interval has concluded, monitoring responses correct per minute per practice session, setting goals for more fluent performance, and using small rewards and privileges to facilitate more fluent performance. In many classrooms, a very common instructional error is that teachers introduce new content but do not ensure that students reach mastery for what has been introduced before moving on to more advanced work (National Council for Teachers of Mathematics, 2006). Effective fluency-building instruction results in learned skills that are remembered, that endure over longer intervals of time, and can be applied in different contexts to solve novel problems (Haughton, 1980). These instructional outcomes are referred to as REAPS (retention, endurance, application performance standards; Binder, 1996). REAPS are functional goals of instruction that suggest that a skill has been mastered to a level that it can be of use in the student's future learning. Once a child's performance is speeded without any losses to accuracy, usually reflected by high rates of responses correct per minute, the child is ready for generalization instruction.

In some cases, a student can readily use a learned skill in situations that differ from the training situation. So for example, a student who has learned to add two vertical numbers may respond correctly and easily to the same problem when it is arranged horizontally or within a word problem. Sometimes, however, children (especially those with SLD) may require support to use a learned skill in different contexts or under different task-demand arrangements. Effective teachers provide children with systematic opportunities to use learned skills in situations that differ from those used during training. Generalization is important because it is not feasible to teach every possible variation of a trained skill that a student might encounter, and it is not necessary in most cases. Generalization instruction involves the teacher providing opportunities for the student to use the learned skill in situations or to solve tasks that differ from those encountered during training conditions. If a child has been taught a decoding rule for handling long vowels using the long-*a* sound, providing a child with a word that contains a long *o* and seeing whether the child can apply the learned rule (when the word ends with *e* the vowel says its name), is an opportunity for the child to generalize the learned long-vowel rule. Similarly, at the adaptation stage of learning, the child learns to alter the learned response to solve novel problems. If a child has learned to count by 10's and has a fluent understanding of ordinal position, the child might be able to solve 20 plus 19 by adding two sets of 20 and counting backward by 1 to obtain the answer of 39 well before double-digit addition has been introduced. Providing opportunities for the student to explain his or her answers and reasoning are important instructional strategies at the generalization and adaptation stages of learning. During generalization instruction, the teacher should closely attend to accuracy of student responding and verify that errors do not reappear.

IDENTIFYING AND USING PROGRESS MONITORING MEASURES TO GUIDE INSTRUCTION AND TO EVALUATE ANNUAL PROGRESS OF STUDENTS RECEIVING SPECIAL EDUCATION SERVICES

To serve students receiving special education well, we must have data to make several types of decisions as shown in Table 10.3. First, as discussed above, we must have data to determine the student's present level of performance and to set goals for instructional outcomes. Second, we must have data to evaluate the effects of the interventions for establishing targeted skills and producing broader, more distal, and comprehensive learning gains. We suggest frequent assessment of the skills that are being targeted during instruction. Daily measures may be taken as part of the instructional session, and instructional changes might be made weekly where progress is not sufficient. We suggest providing a summary as in Figure 10.2 to be shared each week with all stakeholders. We also suggest that the school include all students in all schoolwide assessment.

It is important to show that children in special education are experiencing reduced risk over time. Evaluating these more global improvements can be accomplished by examining several indicators. First, the system can look at the level of performance of children receiving special education versus children not receiving special education services. Systems might anticipate that students receiving special education services would be lower performing (Deno, Fuchs, Marston, & Shin, 2001). Where students receiving special education services are lower performing than their peers, the system might set a goal of accelerating progress of students receiving special education to shrink the gap during the school year. In Figure 10.3, the rate of progress made by students receiving general education is projected for the first semester based on the first 8 weeks of instruction. The progress of students receiving special education

> **It is important to show that children in special education are experiencing reduced risk over time.**

TABLE 10.3. Data Sources for Making Important Special Education Decisions

Decision to be made	Data sources
Identifying a sequence of learning objectives	Begin with screening tasks. The screening tasks should reflect key skills that students are expected to have mastered at that student's grade level. Working backward from the screening task, subskills can be identified and the skill can be arranged in "chunks" of difficulty. This provides a sequence of skills associated with the screening task, and a normative data set from the child's own school/grade is available to compare progress over time. The state standards and common core standards can be used to identify key skills in all content areas; teachers can work backward to specify subskills for each of those standards.
Determining present level of performance	Assess student performance on screening task and sample backward through easier content to identify student's instructional level or stage of learning for expected skills and related subskills in content areas. Curriculum-based measures are ideal for determining present level of performance.
Evaluating instructional strategies to ensure their effectiveness and making instructional changes	Accuracy and fluency on trained skills assessed with tightly controlled materials one to two times per week following standardized assessment procedures and maximizing probability of optimal performance (i.e., use of incentives for improvements, practice items, and more than one trial). Curriculum-based measures are ideal for evaluating student progress and making instructional adjustments.
Evaluating annual progress	Percentage of objectives mastered; reduced risk status as reflected by improved proficiency on year-end assessment, performing above the risk range on universal screening, successfully responding to lower-tier intervention.

can be projected on the same graph based on their first 8 weeks of instruction. On this graph, we can see that a gap exists between the performance of students receiving special education and those who are not receiving special education, but the rate of progress remains the same. The school may set as a goal that the rate of progress for students served in special education will approximate the rate of progress of students in general education in the same grade. Based on the first 8 weeks, this goal is being met. As periodic screenings are administered, the data can be analyzed in this way to ensure that the school's goal of attaining growth for students in special education that is comparable to the rate of growth in general education is met.

HOW TO SHARE RESULTS OF SPECIAL EDUCATION SERVICES WITH SCHOOL PERSONNEL AND PARENTS

As noted in Chapter 8, parents have a right to be provided with transparent indicators of the degree to which their children are benefiting from instruction and reaching proficiency levels

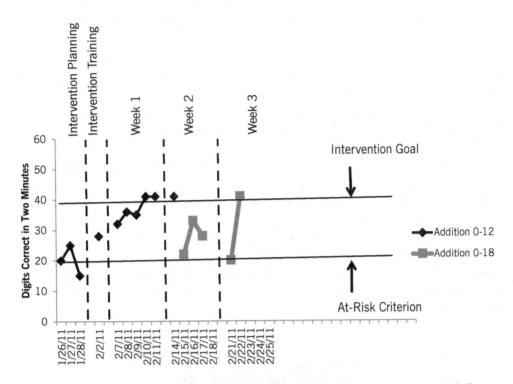

Week 1: Allison showed rapid progress this week and surpassed the goal for mastery for Adding Numbers 0–12. We will continue the intervention for one more day on Monday and if her score remains above the goal, we will increase the difficulty of intervention materials and continue another week.

Week 2: We increased the difficulty this week to Adding Numbers 0–18. Allison only had three days of intervention this week because Friday was a field trip day. We will continue working on this skill in intervention next week.

Week 3: Allison showed rapid progress and reached the intervention goal in two days. We will monitor her progress in the classroom to make sure she remains successful.

FIGURE 10.2. Example of data summary to be shared with stakeholders.

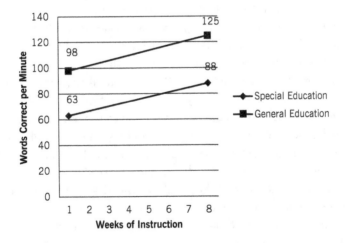

FIGURE 10.3. Graphic depiction of differential progress made by students in general and special education over an 8-week period.

that will help them succeed in school and life. Two types of data are important to characterize the effectiveness of instruction for students. First, data reflecting the occurrence of instructional sessions within the week should be provided. Second, data reflecting student progress including rate of skill mastery, growth on sensitive measures designed to detect short-term growth toward specific skill proficiencies, and generalized learning outcomes over time should be collected frequently. These data are the basis for making instructional adjustments to ensure optimal learning outcomes and, when collected regularly, can simplify the paperwork associated with documenting student progress and conducting reevaluations. Over time and across skill targets, these data become a powerful indicator of the degree to which the student is mastering, retaining, and applying learned skills successfully. Hence, data should be collected on the use of instructional strategies and the effects on student learning, and data teams should consume these data to make midstream changes to instruction when gains are not observed. Student progress data and instructional adjustments made throughout the school year create a record of instruction and student responding that can be the basis for the annual IEP meeting.

HOW TO USE INSTRUCTIONAL DATA DURING THE REEVALUATION TO DETERMINE CONTINUED ELIGIBILITY

Because data are being collected to pinpoint areas of needed improvement, interventions are being implemented to drive those improvements, and data are being collected to verify that the intervention successfully resolves the concern, a data set is generated that can be used to determine continued eligibility for special education. Again, it is important for systems to be sure that all students are included in universal assessments, including children receiving special education services.

Determining continued eligibility is straightforward and should involve harvesting data that already exist, reducing the time involved with triennial reevaluation and the amount of paperwork required. We suggest that teams consider whether the student scores in the risk range on universal screening and below the proficiency criterion on the year-end test, whether the risk status of the child (as indicated by screening and year-end tests) has decreased during the course of special education, and the extent to which short- and long-term learning goals as specified in the student's IEP have been met. Where general risk status is not improved but short-term progress is being made, eligibility should be continued. The special education program of instruction is benefiting the child, but not enough progress is being made to exit the student from special education services. When general risk status is not improved and short-term progress is not being made, eligibility would continue, but troubleshooting must occur to intensify the instruction that is being provided to the student because no discernible benefits can be detected. When the student performs above the risk range and has mastered short-term objectives, special education may be discontinued. Discontinuing special education services can be a low-stakes endeavor because periodic screening can detect whether the student returns to the risk range and can start the chain of intervention activities again without a long delay for the student.

HOW TO USE RESULTS OF SPECIAL EDUCATION SERVICES TO IDENTIFY "RED-FLAG" IMPLEMENTATION PROBLEMS THAT CAN BE ADDRESSED THROUGH SYSTEM REFORM

As noted earlier in this chapter, all children should be included in universal screening and accountability assessment. Systems should track performance gaps on screening tasks for students receiving special education services and for students not receiving special education services. Detected gaps should become a basis for troubleshooting instructional intensity with the goal of closing detected gaps. Routine screening can be used to determine the extent to which gaps are reduced over time and reduced risk status for students receiving special education services. The percentage of students reaching the proficiency criterion on the year-end accountability measure may be smaller in special education, but with intensified instruction across grade levels, improvements should occur. When students in special education do not experience reduced risk over time, systems should take caution and consider the extent to which students receiving special education are deriving the intended benefits. Ensuring improved outcomes for students in special education requires special vigilance because many systems using RTI view special education as the endpoint for students who do not experience intervention success; the interventions provided at Tier 3 are often more intensive than what may be provided through special education. This reality requires systems to adjust their instructional practices to bring new intensity to instruction with special education students and to embrace the priority of all students making progress with instruction. Red flags in RTI implementation that often signal less than ideal special education practices include very high rates of students eligible for special education, high numbers of referrals for evaluation, disproportionate referrals and eligibility decisions (by ethnicity, gender, poverty status), long delays from initial identification to referral decisions (greater than 30 days from screening to beginning intervention, greater than 30 days from intervention start to final intervention decision), high rates of intervention failure (greater than 10% of those receiving Tier 3), and a failure to show incremental gains in proficiency and reductions in risk for special education students over time.

> **Ensuring improved outcomes for students in special education requires special vigilance because many systems using RTI view special education as the end point for students who do not experience intervention success.**

Following the eligibility decision, the focus of the data team shifts to delivering instruction of an intensity level sufficient to produce growth for students served in special education. Ongoing universal screening data, which must include all children (i.e., children receiving special education services for SLD) provides a useful indicator of the extent to which the focus on instructional intensity and progress monitoring produces gains for students receiving special education services in systems. Student data can be used to plan and deliver more intensive instruction, and the progress monitoring data collected during instruction can be used to determine continued eligibility and to set and refine IEP goals.

RTI data provide general education and special education teams opportunities to collaborate and accelerate learning gains for all students in the school. The availability of student data reflecting the performance of all students on key learning outcomes allows teams to identify potential areas of weakness in the instructional program and make adjustments when needed.

CHAPTER 11

Frequently Asked Questions about RTI and SLD

In this chapter we address questions that we have heard since RTI was introduced first as a school reform initiative and later as an alternative procedure for identifying students with SLD under IDEA. Our responses are guided by our understanding of IDEA and its regulations, letters from the federal Office of Special Education and Rehabilitation Services (OSERS), and our own sense of best practices. Our responses are not to be understood as authoritative legal opinions.

When should students be referred for evaluation?

The goal of system reform and RTI integration efforts should be to help all children obtain the support they need to meet important learning benchmarks in the most efficient (i.e., rapid) way possible. With a well-conducted RTI system, students can obtain intervention much more rapidly than has been possible in the past. Because all children are routinely screened, intervention can be initiated often before parents and teachers are convinced that intervention is definitely needed. Stated another way, intervention can be provided prior to the student experiencing a sustained period of academic failure.

Effective intervention delivery is both the linchpin of RTI and its greatest threat. Effective intervention implementation is a formidable and persistent challenge for most school systems. Where the structures of RTI are poorly implemented, the ideals of faster, more effective supports for students will not be realized. The purpose of RTI has never been to delay referral for evaluation for eligibility. However, where RTI is implemented well, the process of RTI carries much greater potential for benefit for the student and the eligibility decision than it does risk of harm in the time required to fully evaluate a student's RTI. In the case of well-implemented RTI, it is prudent to complete the RTI process prior to referral or as part of the comprehensive evaluation. Where RTI is not implemented well, there is risk associated with long delays between a teacher or parent voicing a concern about a student and a referral decision being made. When no intervention is provided in the interim, the delay is a wasted opportunity for intervention and a time interval during which the problem was made known to adults but student failure was allowed to continue. Visionary leaders in RTI recognized early on that RTI implementations belonged primarily in general education and considered their structures consonant with school improvement objectives (Batsche et al., 2005) and amenable to tracking through state and system accountability metrics (i.e., reduced risk of failure on year-end tests). The accuracy of decisions made during RTI about who is at risk and whether the risk persists in the face of increasingly intensive interventions and therefore merits possible special education services depend wholly on the quality with which the RTI structures are implemented and correct decisions are made based on the data.

We recommend that teams track system indicators reflecting the quality of RTI implementation, such as the amount of time between decisions, percentage of students at risk across subsequent screenings, percentage of students successfully responding to Tier 1 instruction and Tiers 2 and 3 intervention, and reduction of performance gaps during instruction (Shapiro & Clemens, 2009). First, the team must consider the quality of RTI implementation and systematically adjust implementation to improve the quality over time. Improving the

> **We recommend that teams track system indicators reflecting the quality of RTI implementation.**

quality of RTI implementation will improve the accuracy of all RTI decisions. We know of one district that struggled to verify that Tier 3 interventions were implemented with integrity. This district decided to create a committee at the district level to review submitted intervention reports and determine whether the intervention had been conducted with sufficient integrity to permit a decision about the student's RTI. Where the committee determined intervention integrity was not adequate, feedback was provided to the school that the student could not proceed for further eligibility consideration until the intervention was completed with integrity. This approach creates a potential for harm because it creates a likely scenario where intervention errors are not "trapped" and repaired, but rather are allowed to continue unchecked. This approach has the real possibility of resulting in high numbers of students for whom RTI decisions are never made and runs the real risk of "watching students fail" (Reynolds & Shaywitz, 2009). Systems must take care to ensure that the policies and structures they create serve the aspiration of faster and more effective services for all students. As a rule, errors in RTI implementation should not cause the referral process to stop altogether. Rather, errors in RTI implementation should result in troubleshooting and reassessment of key indicators to verify that RTI implementation is occurring in a timely way with quality.

In systems using RTI, there is a tipping point. Referring students too soon compromises the referral and eligibility decision accuracies, can waste resources, and can harm the student by qualifying the student with SLD when the student really does not have SLD. Referring students too late can weaken the instructional resources that might have been made available to a student in need. The pragmatic answer here is to conduct RTI with quality, reach decisions at regular timed intervals, repair implementation threats that weaken decision accuracies, and refer students for evaluation when the team suspects that sufficient learning gains are not possible to prevent long-term academic failure without special education services. We further suggest that teams follow special education instructional delivery to verify that the student experiences greater success and reduced risk over time when provided with special education services.

What are the differences between screening assessment and eligibility assessment?

Too often teams decide what assessments to administer without first asking what decision they wish to make with the collected data. As detailed in Chapter 6, we suggest that teams conduct an "assessment inventory" in their school to verify that every assessment has a clear purpose and use, to systematically remove redundant assessments, and to select the strongest available assessment when multiple options are available for a single assessment purpose. In screening, the decision being made is whether a student (or groups of students) is at risk for academic failure. Because all students in a system must participate in the screening assessment, the briefest available assessment option should be used (we have detailed characteristics of adequate screeners in Chapters 2 and 3).

Systems should take care to minimize the cost to instructional time that occurs with screening. Because the purpose of the screening is to rule out students who are not at risk, measures should be selected that are sensitive (i.e., identify a high proportion of students who are really at risk for failure). A sensitive screening criterion is applied, and anyone who surpasses the screening criterion is "ruled out" and considered not to be at risk. This screening process filters the students, leaving a remaining group of students who are at risk for academic failure. Among the filtered sample of students at risk, some students will be incorrectly identified. That is, some students will be identified at risk when in reality they would do fine without intervention. These students are considered false-positive prediction errors (i.e., screening predicts the student will fail, but the student will actually do fine without intervention). Because screening is presumably followed by more assessment with the filtered sample of at-risk students using measures of greater specificity (i.e., correctly predict success for a high proportion of students who will be successful without intervention), false-positive errors are not considered harmful during screening. However, false-positive errors during screening represent potentially wasted or misdirected resources and can create burdens to systems and weaken overall implementation effects. A screening criterion should be selected that does not fail to detect students who are really at risk but does not identify such high numbers of students that the end result is an overburdened system that cannot keep up with intervention demands. Hence, sensitivity is the first priority in screening.

Eligibility assessment is a more final decision, and the goal is to rule in a condition. Importantly, specificity of assessment criteria is the priority when attempting to rule in a condition (like SLD). The specificity of assessments used to determine eligibility is systematically affected by whether proper rule-out filters have been applied. As indicated in Chapter 3 and 4, when a comprehensive evaluation of a student who is being considered for SLD identification incorporates a wide range of assessment procedures, including universal screening, drill-down assessments, and frequent progress monitoring, specificity is enhanced. If serial assessments have ruled out students who perform above a screening criterion, ruled-out students who pass the screening, and ruled-out students who surpass the criterion when provided with short-term intervention delivered with integrity, a filtered sample of at-risk students remains where the probability of "true SLD" is certainly enriched. Under these conditions, low achievement and slow growth are highly specific indicators that may be used to rule in the condition we call SLD.

Teams must have some facility in understanding decision or diagnostic accuracy indicators and the conditions under which decision accuracy is enhanced (or not). Simply providing a child with a comprehensive evaluation that includes a detailed assessment of the student's achievement and profile of strengths and weaknesses is a nonspecific assessment and is not useful for determining eligibility when highly sensitive assessment procedures have not been followed to filter down the sample (i.e., systematically rule out students who are not at risk).

Who has SLD using RTI?

As we described in Chapter 9, when districts use RTI as part of a comprehensive evaluation for a student thought to have SLD, a new definition of the student with SLD emerges. In our view, a student with SLD displays a significant deficiency in level of achievement relative to age-level norms and state standards and demonstrates a significantly deficient response to both core instruction and scientifically supported interventions that were implemented with high degrees of treatment integrity such that the student will not achieve minimal levels of proficiency without an intensive special education program. Furthermore, the student's deficiency in both level and ROI cannot be caused by factors other than SLD, including the rule-out conditions (as described in Chapter 5) or the lack of effective core instruction and robust interventions (as described in Chapter 6). Although there exists no definite test for the existence of SLD, in our view when schools use RTI as part of their comprehensive evaluations of students who are referred for evaluation, those students who are most in need of special education services are identified.

> **A student with SLD displays a significant deficiency in level of achievement and a significantly deficient response to instruction and interventions such that the student will not achieve minimal levels of proficiency without an intensive special education program.**

Are "slow learners" eligible for special education?

One of the frustrations of the ability–achievement discrepancy criterion for determining SLD was that students whose performance was low but consistent with their IQ (also low) were not eligible for special education services, but were highly likely to experience pronounced and sustained academic failure. Under the SLD criteria described in this book, students who demonstrate low achievement in their classrooms relative to same-class peers and national norms and who do not show improvement when provided with effective instruction and increasingly intensive instruction are students who are determined to be in need of more intensive instructional supports such as those that could be provided through special education. These "slow learners" are therefore identifiable as SLD if the district uses RTI, but would not be eligible if the district uses the IQ–achievement discrepancy or another pattern of strengths and weaknesses approach. For many, identifying these students as SLD changes how the construct of SLD is understood, creating the need for a paradigm shift in thinking.

Is the ability (IQ)–achievement discrepancy a valid basis for determining eligibility for SLD?

The ability (IQ)–achievement discrepancy may still legally be used as one of the options under Criterion 2 of the SLD regulation because it is one way to operationalize a student's pattern of strengths and weaknesses. However, as we indicated in Chapter 1, there is little support for continuing to use the ability–achievement approach to identifying students with SLD. This approach has led to the "wait to fail" dilemma in which younger students who may be eligible for special education do not display the discrepancy solely on the basis of the statistical artifact that is involved with assessing young children's ability and achievement. Second, the tests used in the ability–achievement discrepancy approach may well discriminate among students but do not necessarily identify those who are most in need of special education. IQ turns out not to be a valid predictor of which students will or will not readily learn basic skills (especially reading; Fletcher et al., 1994). These tests also fail to inform instruction, which is a key feature needed in any assessment system that is used to prepare the IEP that forms the basis for an effective special education program. Finally, the ability–achievement discrepancy approach leads to the reification of the concept of the slow learner, which operationally creates the exclusion of an entire class of students from receiving special education, based solely on the erroneous and pernicious notion that IQ limits the acquisition of basic skills.

Can a school district use both RTI and an ability–achievement discrepancy (or pattern of strengths and weaknesses) approach to identifying students with SLD?

The IDEA regulations (2006, §300.307) indicate that states must adopt criteria for identifying students with SLD. These criteria must not require that school districts use the ability–achievement discrepancy approach and must permit them to use RTI. As we have noted previously, the definitional criteria for SLD (§300.309) stipulate that, regarding the second criterion for SLD, the school district may use a pattern of strengths and weaknesses (which would include the ability–achievement discrepancy approach) *or* RTI. The "or" in this situation allows for the following possibilities in regard to state policy: (1) a state could mandate that RTI be used for all SLD evaluations, or (2) a state could allow school districts the choice of using a pattern of strengths and weaknesses or RTI. Regarding the latter, the state could require school districts to choose to adopt either the pattern of strengths and weaknesses approach *or* RTI as its agency criterion (for Criterion 2), or it could allow the school district to choose between the pattern of strengths and weaknesses approach or RTI for individual evaluations. It may not prohibit the use of RTI. What is less clear is whether districts may use *both* the pattern of strengths and weaknesses *and* RTI for any evaluations. On the one hand, a questions and answers document disseminated by OSERS (2007b) seems to indicate that the local school district (local education agency) does not have to choose between RTI and a discrepancy model as its standard procedure (for Criterion 2). However, because the regulation clearly indicates *or*, it would appear that a choice between the RTI and a discrepancy model (or a pattern of strengths and weaknesses) must be made at some level. In our estimation, school districts are best advised to use RTI or the pattern of strengths and weaknesses for all of its SLD evaluations (and clearly we prefer RTI). Otherwise, to use the pattern of strengths and weaknesses approach for some referrals and RTI for others would lead to chaotic district policy, incoherent identification procedures, and the appearance that decisions were made arbitrarily or capriciously.

An exception to this recommendation, as indicated in an OSERS letter (2007a), is the situation in which the school district is phasing in the implementation of multi-tier systems of supports across its various schools (e.g., starting at the elementary level and expanding to middle and high schools later). In this scenario, it is prudent (and allowable) to incorporate RTI into the evaluation process for schools that are implementing RTI with a high degree of integrity and use the pattern of strengths and weaknesses in schools that are still building their infrastructure. The OSERS letter did imply the expectation that all schools in the district eventually would use consistent procedures.

In addressing this somewhat knotty question, one thing is clear from OSERS publications: RTI (or any other procedure) may not be used as the sole method of identifying a student as SLD. As we have indicated throughout this book, a student's RTI may be used to address Criterion 2 and to some extent also informs Criterion 4 (as to ruling out lack of instruction). Multiple other assessment procedures are also needed to inform all four criteria, in addition to the required classroom observation. Our perspective is that the majority of these data should be developed as the district provides a program of multi-tier supports.

> **RTI (or any other procedure) may not be used as the sole method of identifying a student as SLD.**

What if my school uses the ability–achievement discrepancy for SLD determination but uses RTI in its multi-tier system of supports?

We have encountered many schools that are making a good-faith effort to implement multi-tier systems of support but have not yet reached a level of integrity to allow for the use of RTI as part of the comprehensive evaluation procedure for SLD. Nonetheless, in many cases they are generating substantial data that are useful in the eligibility decision-making process, such as data about the student's level of performance, and particularly the student's ROI in response to evidence-based interventions. In these situations, where the district or school is still using the pattern of strengths and weaknesses approach, the data collected during the provision of RTI can be used as evidence for Criterion 1 (deficiency in relation to level of performance), Criterion 3 (ruling out other conditions), and especially Criterion 4 (ruling out lack of instruction). However, these data cannot stand as evidence under Criterion 2 because the district has chosen to use the pattern of strengths and weaknesses approach instead of RTI. For example, if a student meets all the criteria for SLD identification (i.e., Criteria 1, 2, and 4), and also has a deficient ROI, but does not display a pattern of strengths and weaknesses (e.g., a discrepancy between ability and achievement), the student would not be identified as having SLD. In this case, the ability–achievement discrepancy data "trumps" the RTI data. However, the RTI data could and should be used to assist in the development of the student's IEP (see Chapter 10).

The reverse is also true in schools that choose to use RTI rather than the pattern of strengths and weaknesses approach. For example, a school has extensive data about the student's level of performance and ROI (Criteria 1 and 2), but for some reason, the school psychologist also administers a test of intelligence (e.g., because an intellectual disability is also suspected and needs to be ruled out). If the results of the intelligence test indicate that the student's IQ is not in the range of intellectual disability and is not discrepant from the assessed academic achievement, this finding has no bearing on the determination of eligibility for SLD because the district is not using the ability–achievement discrepancy approach. In this case, the RTI evidence "trumps" the results of the intelligence testing.

How does the assessment of cognitive processes fit into an RTI approach?

Before and since the passage of IDEA (2004), a number of psychologists have advocated for assessing the child's cognitive processes or neuropsychological functions as a required component of a comprehensive assessment of SLD (Hale, Kaufman, Naglieri, & Kavale, 2006; Hale, Naglieri, Kaufman, & Kavale, 2004). The argument advanced is that the basic definition in IDEA indicates that SLD is "a disorder in one or more of the basic psychological processes" (§620[b][4][A]), and therefore those processes should be thoroughly assessed in the determination of eligibility for this disability category. The presumption is that this type of assessment would constitute the aforementioned "other alternative research-based procedures for determining whether a child has a specific learning disability" (IDEA, 2006, §300.307 [a][3]).

These arguments were raised during the time leading up to the writing of the 2006 IDEA regulations, as reflected by the inclusion of comments to this regard in the preamble to the regulations. In response, the USDOE, which is responsible for promulgating regulations, clearly indicated its disapproval of the cognitive processing position:

> The Department does not believe that an assessment of psychological or cognitive processing should be required in determining whether a child has an SLD. There is no current evidence that such assessments are necessary or sufficient for identifying SLD. Further, in many cases, these assessments have not been used to make appropriate intervention decisions. However, §300.309(a)(2)(ii) permits, but does not require, consideration of a pattern of strengths or weaknesses, or both, relative to intellectual development, if the evaluation group considers that information relevant to an identification of SLD. In many cases, though, assessments of cognitive processes simply add to the testing burden and do not contribute to interventions. As summarized in the research consensus from the OSEP Learning Disability Summit (Bradley, Danielson, & Hallahan, 2002), "Although processing deficits have been linked to some SLD (e.g., phonological processing and reading), direct links with other processes have not been established. Currently, available methods for measuring many processing difficulties are inadequate. Therefore, systematically measuring processing difficulties and their link to treatment is not yet feasible. Processing deficits should be eliminated from the criteria for classification" (p. 797). . . . Cronbach (1957) characterized the search for aptitude by treatment interactions as a "hall of mirrors," a situation that has not improved over the past few years as different approaches to assessment of cognitive processes have emerged.

It is also notable that the regulations published with each reauthorization of IDEA over the years have never stipulated that a formal assessment of cognitive processes should be conducted as part of a comprehensive evaluation of students suspected of having SLD. Rather, the statutory definition has been operationalized as the ability–achievement discrepancy in each iteration of IDEA until the introduction of the RTI provision in 2006. To evaluate the cognitive processing argument, two questions are pertinent: (1) Would an assessment of a student's cognitive processes improve the accuracy of identifying students with SLD? and (2) Would an assessment of a student's cognitive processes lead to robust interventions that would necessarily improve the academic performance of the student with SLD?

As indicated in the USDOE statement in the regulations, the answer to both questions appears to be "no." Regarding the notion of improved identification of students with SLD, there appears to be little evidence to support the hypothesis that assessment of cognitive processes increases accuracy of SLD identification. For example, Fletcher and colleagues (1994) analyzed cognitive profiles of students with reading deficiencies and identified only measures of phonological awareness as robust in distinguishing between readers with and readers without disabilities. No other measures of cognitive processing produced such differentiation. Similarly, meta-analyses that have been conducted on the validity of the IQ–achievement discrepancy model (Hoskyn & Swanson, 2000; Stuebing et al., 2002) have failed to identify particular markers for students with SLD other than those that were associated with IQ (e.g., vocabulary). Rather, all students with deficiencies in reading, regardless of whether they demonstrated an ability–achievement discrepancy, displayed core phonological problems. Pragmatically, these findings and others (Vellutino, Scanlon, & Tanzman, 1998) indicate that reading failure can readily be predicted by direct measures of reading performance and early intervention can prevent reading failure. Cognitive profiles do not enhance diagnostic accuracy and do not improve instructional outcomes. Recently, Stuebing, Fletcher, Branum-Martin, and Francis (2012), using simulation techniques, determined that three popularly advanced procedures incorporating an assessment of cognitive deficiencies in the identification of SLD were not technically adequate and did not improve the diagnosis of SLD.

If RTI can be considered to be a "central inclusionary criterion" (Fletcher & Vaughn, 2009, p. 49), the following troubling scenario emerges when considering the use of the unsupported cognitive processing approach for the identification of students with SLD. Students who display a specific and significant academic deficiency as well as a poor RTI who might therefore be identifiable as having SLD, could be excluded from needed special education services if they did not display a particular pattern of strengths and weaknesses on a battery of tests of cognitive or neuropsychological processes. This scenario would particularly pertain to students who display "flat" profiles, which could be artifacts of the lack of independence of the tests making up the profile (Fletcher, Lyon, Fuchs, & Barnes, 2007; Fletcher, Morris, & Lyon, 2003).

The failure of cognitive processing assessments to lead to useful treatments (including an improved IEP) has a long research history, extending from the early 1970s and the fruitless attempts of special educators to identify aptitude-by-treatment interactions (Kavale & Forness, 1987; Mann, 1979). The notion that specially designed instruction should focus on remedial actions that are aimed at improving cognitive skills to improve the acquisition of basic academic skills has never been empirically supported (Fletcher et al., 2002; Melby-Lervag & Hulme, 2012; Reschly & Tilly, 1999). As summarized by Fletcher, Coulter, Reschly, and Vaughn (2004), "The anecdotal links between cognitive processing and instruction are at best appealing experimental hypotheses that have not been validated despite extensive efforts over the past 30 years" (p. 321). In practice, the result of these attempts has been unsuccessful educational treatments and a distraction from more robust, empirically based strategies.

What happens if a parent requests an evaluation using the ability–achievement discrepancy or the patterns of strengths and weaknesses approach and the district uses RTI as its procedure for assessing Criterion 2?

Parents have the right to request an evaluation at any time if they believe that their child may have a disability and need special education. Although school districts have the prerogative to refuse to conduct a parent-requested evaluation (and provide evidence as to why the child does not display signs of a disability as well as applying parental safeguards), many school districts respond to such requests by providing a comprehensive evaluation. In a district that has made RTI their standard procedure for Criterion 2 (as indicated in its agency evaluation criteria), the district would respond to a parent-initiated request for evaluation by collecting the data needed for the comprehensive evaluation (as described throughout this book), including RTI data. It would not necessarily be compelled to conduct tests of intelligence or other tests associated with a pattern of strengths and weaknesses approach, even if the parent specifically requested them, because these instruments would not serve as the basis for the eligibility decision. The district may agree to conduct any assessment procedure, but the RTI data will not be "trumped" by the results of these assessments. In all likelihood, a student whose parents suspect a disability will probably be receiving Tier 2 or 3 support at the time of the parent's request for evaluation, so the evaluation will consist of formally gathering the existing data that are being developed through the provision of RTI. If a student is not receiving Tier 2 or 3 support, that should signal that the student does not display a deficit in level (Criterion 1), which is required for identification (see Chapter 3). In these cases, more thorough discussions with the parents about the nature of their concern and the federal definition of SLD would be in order.

How should the school deal with "private evaluations" that use an IQ–achievement discrepancy?

The IDEA regulations indicate that local education agencies (e.g., school districts) should have in place criteria for how they conduct comprehensive evaluations. If a school district is using RTI as part of its comprehensive evaluation for students thought to have SLD, the specific procedures for conducting the evaluation, including how both level of performance and ROI are assessed, and how external conditions and the lack of instruction are ruled out, should be articulated in school district policy. All evaluations conducted by the school district should follow these parameters. Furthermore, these parameters become the framework for any independent educational evaluation that the district approves, and should also guide the work of office-based private psychologists who are contracted by the parents and who intend to submit their reports to the school district for consideration. Thus all external evaluators should follow the district evaluation policy guidelines.

One frustration of evolving practices in SLD identification is that many practitioners, particularly those working outside of academic settings and/or outside of school settings, may be unaware of what constitutes contemporary best practices in the identification of SLD. Office-based practitioners may be particularly prone to use single point-in-time batteries of assessment that do not include procedures needed to adequately rule out lack of instruction as a cause of poor academic performance, which is a required part of the SLD identification regardless of whether the school district uses RTI. Importantly, any diagnostic evaluation that does not include adequate procedures to rule out lack of instruction as a cause of poor academic performance will not be useful for determining eligibility for SLD.

Procedures like parent and teacher interviews and rating scales are not an adequate basis for evaluating instructional effects on student learning. However, a great deal of data are available that could be used by an office-based clinician to understand the student's performance relative to his or her classmates and published benchmark criteria that forecast success or failure (i.e., schoolwide screening data). Furthermore, the office-based practitioner could conduct instructional trials following standard functional academic assessment or brief experimental analysis to directly assess the student's RTI that is well matched to the student's need and carried out with integrity. Only by arranging for a period of intervention and assessing the student's ROI, as described in Chapter 4, can a privately conducted evaluation meet the second criterion for SLD eligibility in school districts that have identified RTI as its chosen evaluation procedure for this criterion, as reflected in its agency evaluation guidelines. Without this information, the provided evaluation would be considered as providing evidence for only Criteria 1 and 3.

According to IDEA, school districts must consider all data provided by external evaluators, but the impact of evaluations that fail to meet agency criteria (i.e., consist only of results of ability–achievement discrepancy assessment) may be minimal. It may be helpful for schools to conduct a campaign of information with parents and community stakeholders on contemporary SLD evaluation and caution parents that community-based evaluations that do not include procedures to characterize student performance relative to local standards for learning, local and national norms, and direct assessment of instructional effects cannot be accepted as full and comprehensive evaluations to determine eligibility in the school system.

How can office-based psychologists provide meaningful and valid data to guide eligibility determination for SLD?

We suggest greater collaboration between community and school-based psychological assessment services. If parents wish to obtain private community-based evaluations and pay for those evaluations, it is desirable that those evaluations be as useful as possible. Hence, school systems should identify procedures that can be followed to share local learning standards and periodic student screening data (protecting the anonymity of all but the student for whom the community-based provider is conducting an evaluation with parent consent). All remaining assessments that are recommended and commonly conducted in school settings can be conducted in an office setting as long as the office-based practitioner has (1) appropriate curriculum and assessment materials that are well aligned with instructional sequences used in the school; (2) identified and evidence-supported decision rules for determining risk on serial assessments administered in the office; (3) data sufficient for selecting an intervention from an array of evidence-based interventions that is well aligned with the student's needs; (4) intervention trials that are implemented correctly; and (5) a final judgment about intervention success that forecasts continued risk without an educational placement change.

Applying exclusionary criteria (i.e., sensory deficits) is a rather straightforward endeavor to reach a diagnostic conclusion about SLD. Office-based practitioners could include specific procedures to understand the student's performance in the context of the school environment, which involves access to schoolwide performance data and a working collaboration between providers in both settings. Any diagnostician must consider whether the referred student is learning in a way (performance level and trend) that is consistent with many other students in the student's instructional environment or is lagging behind in an appreciable way. One common risk of community-based assessment involves comparing the student's performance to national normative criteria on norm-referenced assessments and concluding that the student has a learning disability when the student may actually perform comparably to same-grade or same-class peers in his or her school. In this regard, considering that all student problems, including academic deficiencies, exist within an instructional milieu, office-based clinicians would be well advised to conduct an observation of the student in the school situation, in order to obtain a complete picture of the student's functioning.

Can we use RTI for students referred from private schools?

The use of RTI for the determination of Criterion 2 with students who attend private schools is problematic because the public school that is charged with completing a comprehensive evaluation would have little ability to proactively put in place the infrastructure of instruction, interventions, and assessment systems that is required to use and assess RTI properly (as we described in detail in Chapter 2). It would appear that a school district that has adopted RTI as its sole procedure for assessing eligibility under Criterion 2 would have two options. First, it could formally assess the instructional environment of the private school through interviews with teachers and administrators of the private school. One could imagine using an instrument like the Functional Assessment of Academic Behavior (Ysseldyke & Christenson, 2002) to determine how core instruction is provided and how interventions are designed based on student assessment and delivered with fidelity. In some ways, this type of assessment pertains to all such private-school referrals because a lack of instruction needs to be ruled out (Criterion 4), even when RTI is not used. Alternatively, the school district could set in its agency criteria the use of a pattern of strengths and weaknesses as its Criterion 2 procedure for private school referrals, as an exception to its standard use of RTI. However, some effort must still be made to assess the sufficiency of instruction in the private school.

Do we still need school psychologists if we are using RTI instead of the ability–achievement discrepancy approach?

Absolutely! Contemporary school psychology training programs prepare school psychologists for a wide range of activities that support students, teachers, and parents. In fact, testing per se makes up a minority of the courses taken by school psychologists in training. School psychologists typically receive extensive training in the components of multi-tier systems of support including academic interventions, progress monitoring, and collaborative teaming procedures. They are also steeped in interventions that address students' behavior and mental health. This extensive training allows school psychologists to play an important role in all aspects of RTI, including participation on data teams, managing screening and progress monitoring data, developing interventions, interacting with parents, and evaluating overall program effects. School psychologists are also critical in ensuring that the data collected during the provision of RTI are of sufficient quality to enable a valid determination of eligibility.

> **Contemporary school psychology training programs prepare school psychologists for a wide range of activities that support students, teachers, and parents.**

References

Achenbach, T. M., & Rescorla, L. A. (2000). *Child behavior checklist*. Burlington, VT: ASEBA.

Algozzine, B., Ysseldyke, J. E., & Christenson, S. (1983). An analysis of the incidence of special class placement: The masses are burgeoning. *Journal of Special Education, 17*, 141–147.

Alonzo, J., Tindal, G., Ulmer, K., & Glasgow, A. (2006). *easyCBM online progress monitoring assessment system*. Eugene, OR: Center for Educational Assessment Accountability.

American Educational Research Association, American Psychological Association, & National Council on Measurement in Education. (1999). *The standards for educational and psychological testing* (2nd ed.). Washington, DC: American Educational Research Association.

Ardoin, S. P., & Christ, T. J. (2008). Evaluating curriculum-based measurement slope estimates using data from triannual universal screenings. *School Psychology Review, 37*, 109–125.

Ardoin, S. P., Christ, T. J., Morena, L. S., Cormier, D. C., & Klingbeil, D. A. (2013). A systematic review and summarization of the recommendations and research surrounding curriculum-based measurement of oral reading fluency (CBM-R) decision rules. *Journal of School Psychology, 51*, 1–18.

Ardoin, S. P., Williams, J. C., Klubnik, C., & McCall, M. (2009). Three versus six rereadings of practice passages. *Journal of Applied Behavior Analysis, 42*, 375–380.

Artiles, A. J., Kozleski, E. B., Trent, S. C., Osher, D., & Ortiz, A. (2010). Justifying and explaining disproportionality, 1968–2008: A critique of underlying view of culture. *Exceptional Children, 76*, 279–299.

Barnett, D. W., Daly, E. J., Jones, K. M., & Lentz, F. E. (2004). Response to intervention: Empirically based special service decisions from single-case designs of increasing and decreasing intensity. *Journal of Special Education, 38*, 66–79.

Batsche, G., Elliott, J., Graden, J., Grimes, J., Kovaleski, J. F., Prasse, D., et al. (2005). *IDEA 2004 and response to intervention: Policy considerations and implementation*. Alexandria, VA: National Association of State Directors of Special Education.

Begeny, J. C., Laugle, K. M., Krouse, H. E., Lynn, A. E., Tayrose, M. P., & Stage, S. A. (2010). A control-group comparison of two reading fluency programs: The Helping Early Literacy with Practice Strategies (HELPS) Program and the Great Leaps K–2 Reading Program. *School Psychology Review, 39*, 137–155.

Betts, E. A. (1946). *Foundations of reading instruction*. New York: American Book.

Binder, C. (1996). Behavioral fluency: Evolution of a new paradigm. *Behavior Analyst, 19*, 163–197.

Bradley, R., Danielson, L., & Hallahan, D. P. (Eds.). (2002). *Identification of learning disabilities: Research to practice*. Mahwah, NJ: Erlbaum.

Brown-Chidsey, R., & Steege, M. W. (2010). *Response to intervention: Principles and strategies for effective practice* (2nd ed.). New York: Guilford Press.

Brownlee, S. (2007). *Overtreated: Why too much medicine is making us sicker and poorer*. New York: Bloomsbury.

Burney, D. A. (2001). *Adolescent Anger Rating Scale: Professional Manual*. Lutz, FL: Psychological Assessment Resources.

Burns, M. K., & Gibbons, K. (2012). *Response to intervention implementation in elementary and secondary schools: Procedures to assure scientific-based practices* (2nd ed.). New York: Routledge.

Burns, M. K., Riley-Tillman, T. C., & VanDerHeyden, A. (2012). *RTI applications: Vol. 1. Academic and behavioral interventions.* New York: Guilford Press.

Burns, M. K., Zaslofsky, A. F., Kanive, R., & Parker, D. C. (2012). Meta-analysis of incremental rehearsal: Using phi coefficients to compare single-case and group designs. *Journal of Behavioral Education, 21*, 185–202.

Bushell, D., & Baer, D. M. (1994). Measurably superior instruction means close, continual contact with the relevant outcome data: Revolutionary! In R. Gardner III, D. M. Sainato, J. O. Cooper, T. E. Heron, W. L. Heward, J. Eshleman, et al. (Eds.), *Behavior analysis in education: Focus on measurably superior instruction* (pp. 3–10). Pacific Grove, CA: Brooks/Cole.

Chalfant, J. C., Pysh, M. V., & Moultrie, R. (1979). Teacher assistance teams: A model for within-building problem solving. *Learning Disability Quarterly, 2*, 85–96.

Christ, T. J. (2008). Best practices in problem analysis. In J. Grimes & A. Thomas (Eds.), *Best practices in school psychology V* (Vol. 2, pp. 159–176). Bethesda, MD: National Association of School Psychologists.

Christ, T. J., Silberglitt, B., Yeo, S., & Cormier, D. (2010). Curriculum-based measurement of oral reading: An evaluation of growth rates and seasonal effects among students served in general and special education. *School Psychology Review, 39*, 447–462.

Christ, T. J., Zopluoglo, C., Monaghen, B. D., & Van Norman, E. R. (2012). Curriculum-based measurement of oral reading: Quality of progress monitoring outcomes. *Exceptional Children, 78*, 356–373.

Christenson, S. L., & Anderson, A. R. (2002). Commentary: The centrality of the learning context for students' academic enabler skills. *School Psychology Review, 31*, 378–393.

Clemens, N. H., Shapiro, E. S., Hilt-Panahon, A., & Gischlar, K. L. (2011). Student achievement outcomes. In E. S. Shapiro, N. Zigmond, T. Wallace, & D. Marson (Eds.), *Models for implementing response to intervention: Tools, outcomes, and implications* (pp. 77–98). New York: Guilford Press.

Collier, C. (2000). *Acculturation Quick Screen.* Ferndale, WA: CrossCultural Developmental Education Services.

Compton, D. L., Fuchs, D., Fuchs, L. S., & Bryant, J. D. (2006). Selecting at-risk readers in first grade for early intervention: A two-year longitudinal study of decision rules and procedures. *Journal of Educational Psychology, 98*, 394–409.

Consortium on Reading Excellence. (2008). *CORE multiple measures for kindergarten through twelfth grade* (2nd ed.). Novato, CA: Arena Press.

Cortiella, C. (2011). *The state of learning disabilities.* New York: National Center for Learning Disabilities.

Cronbach, L. J. (1957). The two disciplines of scientific psychology. *American Psychologist, 30*, 116–127.

Cummins, J. (1981). Age on arrival and immigrant second language learning in Canada: A reassessment. *Applied Linguistics, 2*, 132–149.

Curriculum Advantage. (1993). *Classworks.* Lawrenceville, GA: Author.

Daly, E. J. I., Martens, B. K., Hamler, K., Dool, E. J., & Eckert, T. L. (1999). A brief experimental analysis for identifying instructional components needed to improve oral reading fluency. *Journal of Applied Behavior Analysis, 32*, 83–94.

Daly, E. J. I., Witt, J. C., Martens, B. K., & Dool, E. J. (1997). A model for conducting a functional analysis of academic performance problems. *School Psychology Review, 26*, 554–574.

Deno, S. L., Fuchs, L. S., Marston, D., & Shin, J. (2001). Using curriculum-based measurement to establish growth standards for students with learning disabilities. *School Psychology Review, 30*, 507–524.

Deno, S. L., Marston, D., & Tindal, G. (1986). Direct and frequent curriculum-based measurement: An alternative for educational decision making. *Special Services in the School, 2*(2–3), 5–27.

Deno, S. L., & Mirkin, P. K. (1977). *Data-based program modification: A manual.* Reston, VA: Council for Exceptional Children.

Dickson, S. V., & Bursuck, W. D. (1999). Implementing a model for preventing reading failure: A report from the field. *Learning Disabilities Research and Practice, 14*, 191–202.

Drummond, T. (1994). *The student risk screening scale (SRSS).* Grants Pass, OR: Josephine County Mental Health Program.

Duncan, G. J., Morris, P. A., & Rodrigues, C. (2011). Does money really matter?: Estimaing impacts of family income on young children's achievement with data from random-assignment experiments. *Developmental Psychology, 47*, 1263–1279.

Duncan, G. J., Yeung, W. J., Brooks-Gunn, J., & Smith, J. R. (1998). How much does childhood poverty affect the life chances of children? *American Sociological Review, 63*, 406–423.

DuPaul, G. J., Jitendra, A. K., Tresco, K. E., Junod, R. E. V., Volpe, R. J., & Lutz, J. G. (2006). Children with attention deficit hyperactivity disorder: Are there gender differences in school functioning? *School Psychology Review, 35*, 292–308.

Education of the Handicapped Act, Public Law No. 94–142 (1975).

Ellis, A. (2001). *Research on educational innovations* (3rd ed.). Larchmont, NY: Eye on Education.

Feinberg, A. B., & Shapiro, E. S. (2003). Accuracy of teacher judgments in predicting oral reading fluency. *School Psychology Quarterly, 18*, 52–65.

Feinberg, A. B., & Shapiro, E. S. (2009). Teacher accuracy: An examination of teacher-based judgments of students' reading with differing achievement levels. *Journal of Educational Research, 102*, 453–462.

Fletcher, J., Shaywitz, S., Shankweiler, D., Katz, L., Lieberman, I., Stuebing, K., et al. (1994). Cognitive profiles of reading disability: Comparisons of discrepancy and low achievement definitions. *Journal of Educational Psychology, 86*, 6–23.

Fletcher, J. M., Coulter, W. A., Reschly, D. J., & Vaughn, S. (2004). Alternative approaches to the definition and identification of learning disabilities: Some questions and answers. *Annals of Dyslexia, 54*, 304–331.

Fletcher, J. M., Lyon, G. R., Fuchs, L. S., & Barnes, M. A. (2007). *Learning disabilities: From identification to intervention.* New York: Guilford Press.

Fletcher, J. M., Lyon, R., Barnes, M. A., Stuebing, K. K., Francis, D. J., Olson, R. K., et al. (2002). Classification of learning disabilities: An evidence-based evaluation. In R. Bradley, L. Danielson, & D. P. Hallahan (Eds.), *Identification of learning disabilities: Research to practice* (pp. 185–286). Mahwah, NJ: Erlbaum.

Fletcher, J. M., Morris, R. D., & Lyon, G. R. (2003). Classification and definition of learning disabilities: An integrative perspective. In H. L. Swanson, K. R. Harris, & S. Graham (Ed.), *Handbook of learning disabilities* (pp. 30–56). New York: Guilford Press.

Fletcher, J. M., & Vaughn, S. (2009). RTI models as alternatives to traditional views of learning disabilities: Response to commentaries. *Child Development Persepectives, 3*, 48–50.

Flugum, K. R., & Reschly, D. J. (1994). Prereferral interventions: Quality indices and outcomes. *Journal of School Psychology, 32*, 1–14.

Franco, J. (1983). An acculturation scale for Mexican-American children. *Journal of General Psychology, 108*, 175–181.

Frostig, M., & Horne, D. (1964). *The Frostig Program for the development of visual perception.* Chicago: Follett Educational Corp.

Fuchs, D., & Fuchs, L. S. (2001). Responsiveness-to-intervention: A blueprint for practitioners, policymakers, and parents. *Teaching Exceptional Children, 38*(1), 57–61.

Fuchs, D., Fuchs, L. S., Mathes, P. G., & Simmons, D. C. (1997). Peer-assisted learning strategies: Making classrooms more responsive to diversity. *American Educational Research Journal, 34*, 174–206.

Fuchs, D., Mock, D., Morgan, P. L., & Young, C. L. (2003). Responsiveness-to-intervention: Definitions, evidence, and implications for the learning disabilities construct. *Learning Disabilities Research and Practice, 18*, 157–171.

Fuchs, L. S. (1986). Monitoring progress among mildly handicapped pupils: Review of current practice and research. *Remedial and Special Education, 7*, 5–12.

Fuchs, L. S. (2003). Assessing intervention responsiveness: Conceptual and technical issues. *Learning Disabilities Research and Practice, 18*, 172–186.

Fuchs, L. S., & Deno, S. L. (1994). Must instructionally useful performance assessment be based in the curriculum? *Exceptional Children, 61*, 15–24.

Fuchs, L. S., Fuchs, D., Hosp, M. K., & Jenkins, J. R. (2001). Oral reading fluency as an indicator of reading competence: A theoretical, empirical, and historical analysis. *Scientific Studies of Reading, 5*, 239–256.

Fuchs, L. S., Fuchs, D., & Speece, D. L. (2002). Treatment validity as a unifying construct for identifying learning disabilities. *Learning Disability Quarterly, 25*, 33–45.

Gansle, K. A., & Noell, G. H. (2007). The fundamental role of intervention implementation in assessing response to intervention. In S. R. Jimerson, M. K. Burns, & A. M. VanDerHeyden (Eds.), *Handbook of response to intervention: The science and practice of assessment and intervention* (pp. 244–251). New York: Springer.

García-Vázquez, E. (1995). Acculturation and academics: Effects of acculturation on reading achievement among Mexican-American students. *Bilingual Research Journal, 19*, 305–315.

Gersten, R., Beckmann, S., Clarke, B., Foegen, A., Marsh, L., Star, J. R., et al. (2009). *Assisting students struggling with mathematics: Response to Intervention (RtI) for elementary and middle schools. A practical guide* (NCEE 2009-4060). Washington, DC: National Center for Education Evaluation and Regional Assistance, Institute of Education Sciences, U.S. Department of Education.

Gersten, R., Compton, D., Connor, C. M., Dimino, J., Santoro, L., Linan-Thompson, S., et al. (2008). *Assisting students struggling with reading: Response to Intervention and multi-tier intervention for reading in the primary grades. A practice guide* (NCEE 2009-4045). Washington, DC: National Center for Education Evaluation and Regional Assistance, Institute of Education Sciences, U.S. Department of Education.

Gickling, E. E. (1994). Foundations of CBA. In *The instructional support team: Pennsylvania's principal training model (PPTM) one-day preparatory training session for use by regional and SSI consultants.* Harrisburg: The Instructional Support System of Pennsylvania.

Gickling, E. E., & Havertape, J. F. (1981). Curriculum-based assessment. In J. A. Tucker (Ed.), *Non-test based assessment*. Minneapolis: National School Psychology Inservice Training Network, University of Minnesota.

Gickling, E. E., & Armstrong, D. L. (1978). Levels of instructional difficulty as related to on-task behavior, task completion, and comprehension. *Journal of Learning Disabilities, 11*, 559–566.

Gickling, E. E., & Rosenfield, S. (1995). Best practices in curriculum-based assessment. In A. Thomas & J. Grimes (Eds.), *Best practices in school psychology III* (pp. 587–595). Bethesda, MD: National Association of School Psychologists.

Gickling, E. E., & Thompson, V. P. (1985). A personal view of curriculum-based assessment. *Exceptional Children, 52*, 205–218.

Gilbertson, D., Witt, J. C., Singletary, L., & VanDer-Heyden, A. M. (2008). Improving teacher use of interventions: Effects of response dependent performance feedback on teacher implementation of a peer tutoring intervention. *Journal of Behavioral Education, 16*, 311–326.

Good, R. H., & Jefferson, G. (1998). Contemporary perspectives on curriculum-based measurement validity. In M. R. Shinn (Ed.), *Advanced applications of curriculum-based measurement* (pp. 61–88). New York: Guilford Press.

Good, R. H., Kaminski, R. A., Cummings, K. D., Dufour-Martel, C., Petersen, K., Powell-Smith, K., et al. (2011). DIBELS Next. Retrieved from *http://dibels.org*.

Good, R. H., & Salvia, J. (1988). Curriculum bias in published, norm-referenced reading tests: Demonstrable effects. *School Psychology Review, 17*, 51–60.

Graden, J. L., Casey, A., & Christenson, S. L. (1985). Implementing a prereferral intervention system: Part I. The model. *Exceptional Children, 51*, 377–384.

Graney, S. B., Missall, K. N., Martínez, R. S., & Bergstrom, M. (2009). A preliminary investigation of within-year growth patterns in reading and mathematics curriculum-based measures. *Journal of School Psychology, 47*, 121–142.

Gravois, T. A., & Gickling, E. E. (2008). Best practices in instructional assessment. In A. Thomas & J. Grimes (Eds.), *Best practices in school psychology V* (Vol. 2, pp. 503–518). Bethesda, MD: National Association of School Psychologists.

Greenwood, C. R., Carta, J. J., Dawson, H., Thompson, T., Felce, D., & Symons, F. J. (Eds.). (2000). *Ecobehavioral Assessment Systems Software (EBASS): A system for observation in education settings*. Baltimore: Brookes.

Greenwood, C. R., Delquadri, J. C., & Hall, R. V. (1984). Opportunity to respond and student academic performance. In U. L. Heward, T. E. Heron, D. S. Hill, & J. Trap-Porter (Eds.), *Focus on behavior analysis in education* (pp. 58–88). Columbus, OH: Merrill.

Greenwood, C. R., Delquadri, J. C., Stanley, S. O., Terry, B., & Hall, R. V. (1985). Assessment of ecobehavioral interaction in school settings. *Behavioral Assessment, 7*, 331–347.

Greenwood, C. R., Dinwiddie, G., Terry, B., Wade, L., Stanley, S. O., Thibabeau, S., et al. (1984). Teacher- versus peer-mediated instruction: An ecobehavioral analysis of achievement outcomes. *Journal of Applied Behavior Analysis, 17*, 521–538.

Greenwood, C. R., Horton, B. T., & Utley, C. A. (2002). Academic engagement: Current perspectives on research and practice. *School Psychology Review, 31*, 328–349.

Grimes, J. P., & Kurns, S. (2003, December). *An intervention-based system for addressing NCLB and IDEA expectations: A multiple tiered model to ensure ever child learns*. Paper presented at the National Research Center on Learning Disabilities Responsiveness-to-Intervention Symposium, Kansas City, MO.

Haager, D., Klingner, J., & Vaughn, S. (2007). *Evidence-based reading practices for response to intervention*. Baltimore: Brookes.

Hale, B., Naglieri, J. A., Kaufman, A. S., & Kavale, K. A. (2004). Specific learning disability classification in the new Individuals with Disabilities Education Act: The danger of good ideas. *The School Psychologist, 58*(1), 6–13.

Hale, J. B., Kaufman, A., Naglieri, J. A., & Kavale, K. A. (2006). Implementation of IDEA: Integrating response to intervention and cognitive assessment methods. *Psychology in the Schools, 43*, 753–770.

Hall, R. V., Delquadri, C. V., Greenwood, C. R., & Thurston, L. (1982). The importance of opportunity to respond to children's academic success. In E. B. Edgar, N. G. Haring, J. R. Jenkins, & C. G. Pious (Eds.), *Mentally handicapped children: Education and training* (pp. 107–140). Baltimore: University Park Press.

Hardman, M. L., McDonnell, J., & Welch, M. (1997). Perspectives on the future of IDEA. *Journal of the Association for Persons with Severe Handicaps, 22*(2), 67–77.

Haring, N. G., & Eaton, M. D. (1978). Systematic instructional procedures: An instructional hierarchy. In N. G. Haring, T. C. Lovitt, M. D. Eaton, & C. L. Hansen (Eds.), *The fourth R: Research in the classroom* (pp. 23–40). Columbus, OH: Merrill.

Harniss, M. K., Stein, M., & Carnine, D. (2002). Promoting mathematics achievement. In M. R. Shinn, H. M. Walker, & G. Stoner (Eds.), *Interventions* for academic and behavior problems II: Preventive and remedial approaches (pp. 571–587). Washington, DC: National Association of School Psychologists.

Hart, B., & Risley, T. R. (1995). *Meaningful differences in the everyday experiences of young American children.* Baltimore: Brookes.

Hartman, W. T., & Fay, T. A. (1996). Cost-effectiveness of instructional support teams in Pennsylvania. *Journal of Educational Finance, 21,* 555–580.

Hasbrouck, J., & Tindal, G. A. (2006). Oral reading fluency norms: An assessment tool for reading teachers. *The Reading Teacher, 59,* 636–644.

Hattie, J. (2009). *Visible learning.* New York: Routledge.

Haughton, E. C. (1980). Practicing practices. *Journal of Precision Teaching, 1,* 3–20.

Haycock, K., Barth, P., Jackson, H., Mora, K., Ruiz, P., Robinson, S., et al. (Eds.). (1999). *Dispelling the myth: High-poverty schools exceeding expectations.* Washington, DC: The Education Trust.

Heartland Area Education Agency 11. (2006). Program manual for special education. Retrieved from *www.aea11.k12.ia.us/spr/HAEAProgManual05. pdf.*

Hintze, J. M., & Shapiro, E. S. (1995). Systematic observation of classroom behavior. In A. Thomas & J. Grimes (Eds.), *Best practices in school psychology III* (pp. 651–660). Washington, DC: National Association of School Psychologists.

Hintze, J. M., Volpe, R. J., & Shapiro, E. S. (2008). Best practices in the systematic direct observation of student behavior. In A. Thomas & J. Grimes (Eds.), *Best practices in school psychology IV* (Vol. 2, pp. 933–1006). Washington, DC: National Association of School Psychologists.

Hoskyn, M., & Swanson, H. L. (2000). Cognitive processing of low achievers and children with reading disabilities: A selective meta-analytic review of the published literature. *School Psychology Review, 29,* 102–119.

Hosp, M. K., Hosp, J. L., & Howell, K. W. (2007). *The ABCs of CBM: A practical guide to curriculum-based measurement.* New York: Guilford Press.

Hosp, M. K., & MacConnell, K. L. (2008). Best practices in curriculum-based evaluation in early reading. In J. Grimes & A. Thomas (Eds.), *Best practices in school psychology V* (Vol. 2, pp. 377–396). Bethesda, MD: National Association of School Psychologists.

Hosterman, S. J., DuPaul, G. J., & Jitendra, A. K. (2008). Teacher ratings of ADHD symptoms in ethnic minority students: Bias or behavioral difference? *School Psychology Quarterly, 23,* 418–435.

Howell, K. W. (2008). Best practices in curriculum-based evaluation and advanced reading. In J.

Grimes & A. Thomas (Eds.), *Best practices in school psychology V* (Vol. 2, pp. 397–418). Bethesda, MD: National Association of School Psychologists.

Howell, K. W., Hosp, J. L., & Kurns, S. (2008). Best practices in curriculum-based evaluation. In J. Grimes & A. Thomas (Eds.), *Best practices in school psychology V* (Vol. 2, pp. 349–362). Bethesda, MD: National Association of School Psychologists.

Howell, K. W., & Nolet, V. (2000). *Curriculum-based evaluation: Teaching and decision making* (3rd ed.). Belmont, CA: Wadsworth.

Hunley, S., & McNamara, K. (2009). *Tier 3 of the RTI model: Problem solving through a case study approach.* Thousand Oaks, CA: Corwin Press.

Ikeda, M. J., Tilly III, W. D., Stumme, J., Volmer, L., & Allison, R. (1996). Agency-wide implementation of problem-solving consultation: Foundations, current implementation, and future directions. *School Psychology Quarterly, 11,* 228–243.

Improving Education Results for Children with Disabilities Act of 2003, House of Representatives No. 108–77. (2003).

Individuals with Disabilities Education Act Amendments (IDEA) of 1997, Public Law No. 105–117. (1997).

Individuals with Disabilities Education Improvement Act of 2004, Public Law No. 108–466. (2004).

Individuals with Disabilities Education Improvement Act of 2004 Regulations, 34 CFR Parts 300 and 301. (2004).

iSTEEP. (2011). *iSTEEP data management system for universal screening, progress monitoring, and reporting.* Miami, FL: Author.

Iwata, B. A., Dorsey, M. F., Slifer, K. J., Bauman, K. E., & Richman, G. S. (1982). Toward a functional analysis of self-injury. *Analysis and Intervention in Developmental Disabilities, 2,* 3–20.

Jenkins, J., & Terjeson, K. J. (2011). Monitoring reading growth: Goal setting, measurement frequency, and methods of evaluation. *Learning Disabilities Research and Practice, 26,* 28–35.

Jenkins, J. R., & Pany, D. (1978). Standardized achievement tests: How useful for special education? *Exceptional Children, 44,* 448–453.

Jimerson, S. R., Burns, M. K., & VanDerHeyden, A. (Eds.). (2007). *Handbook of response to intervention: The science and practice of assessment and intervention.* New York: Springer.

Johnson, K., & Street, E. M. (2013). *Response to intervention and precision teaching: Creating synergy in the classroom.* New York: Guilford Press.

Kamphaus, R. W., & Reynolds, C. R. (2007). *Behavior Assessment System for Children—Second Edition (BASC-2): Behavioral and Emotional Screening System (BESS).* Bloomington, MN: Pearson.

Kavale, K., & Forness, K. (1987). How not to specify learning disability: A rejoinder. *Remedial and Special Education, 8*, 60–62.

Kavale, K., & Mattson, P. D. (1983). "One jumped off the balance beam": Meta-analysis of perceptual-motor training. *Journal of Learning Disabilities, 16*, 165–173.

Kavale, K. A., & Flanagan, D. P. (2007). Ability–achievement discrepancy, response to intervention, and assessment of cognitive abilities/processes in specific learning disability identification: Toward a contemporary operational definition. In S. R. Jimerson, M. K. Burns, & A. VanDerHeyden (Eds.), *Handbook of response to intervention: The science and practice of assessment and intervention.* (pp. 130–147). New York: Springer.

Kavale, K. A., & Forness, S. R. (1999). Effectiveness of special education. In C. R. Reynolds & T. B. Gutkin (Eds.), *The handbook of school psychology* (3rd ed., pp. 984–1024). New York: Wiley.

Kelley, B. (2008). Best practices in curriculum-based evaluation and math. In J. Grimes & A. Thomas (Eds.), *Best practices in school psychology V* (Vol. 2, pp. 419–438). Bethesda, MD: National Association of School Psychologists.

Kelman, M., & Lester, G. (1997). *Jumping the queue: An inquiry into the legal treatment of students with learning disabilities.* Cambridge, MA: Harvard University Press.

Kirk, S. A. (1962). *Educating exceptional children.* Boston: Houghton Mifflin.

Koppitz, E. M. (1963). *The Bender Gestalt Test for Young Children.* New York: Grune & Stratton.

Kovacs, M. (1992). *Children's Depression Inventory.* New York: Multi-Health Systems.

Kovaleski, J. F. (2007). Response to intervention: Considerations for research and systems change. *School Psychology Review, 36*, 638–646.

Kovaleski, J. F., & Black, L. (2010). Multi-tier service delivery: Current status and future directions. In T. A. Glover & S. Vaughn (Eds.), *The promise of response to intervention: Evaluating current science and practice* (pp. 23–56). New York: Guilford Press.

Kovaleski, J. F., & Glew, M. C. (2006). Bringing instructional support teams to scale: Implications of the Pennsylvania experience. *Remedial and Special Education, 27*, 16–25.

Kovaleski, J. F., & Pedersen, J. A. (2008). Best practices in data analysis teaming. In A. Thomas & J. Grimes (Eds.), *Best practices in school psychology V* (Vol. 2, pp. 115–129). Bethesda, MD: National Association of School Psychologists.

Kovaleski, J. F., Tucker, J., & Stevens, L. (1996). Bridging special and regular education: The Pennsylvania Initiative. *Educational Leadership, 53*(7), 44–47.

Lentz, F. E., & Shapiro, E. S. (1986). Functional assessment of the academic environment. *School Psychology Review, 15*, 346–357.

Lyon, G. R. (1996). Learning disabilities. In E. J. Mash & R. A. Barkley (Eds.), *Child psychopathology* (pp. 390–435). New York: Guilford Press.

Lyon, G. R. (1998). *Overview of reading and literacy initiatives.* Testimony before the Committee of Labor and Human Resources, U.S. Senate, 1998. Washington, DC: National Institutes of Child Health and Human Development.

Lyon, G. R. (2002, June 6). *Learning disabilities and early intervention strategies.* Testimony presented at a hearing before the Subcommittee on Education Reform Committee on Education and the Workforce of the United States House of Representatives. Retrieved from *www.reidlyon.com/edpolicy/11-LEARNING-DISABILITIES-AND-EARLY-INTERVENTION-STRATEGIES.pdf.*

Macmann, G., & Barnett, D. (1999). Diagnostic decision making in school psychology: Understanding and copying with uncertainty. In C. R. Reynolds & T. B. Gutkin (Eds.), *Handbook of school psychology* (3rd ed., pp. 519–548). New York: Wiley.

MacMillan, D., Gresham, F. M., & Bocian, K. (1998). Discrepancy between definitions of learning disabilities and what schools use: An empirical investigation. *Journal of Learning Disabilities, 31*, 314–326.

MacMillan, D. L., & Speece, D. L. (1999). Utility of current diagnostic categories for research and practice. In R. Gallimore & L. P. Bernheimer (Eds.), *Developmental perspectives on children with high-incidence disabilities* (pp. 111–133). Mahwah, NJ: Erlbaum.

Mann, L. (1979). *On the trail of process.* New York: Grune & Stratton.

Marston, D., Fuchs, L. S., & Deno, S. L. (1986). Measuring pupil progress: A comparison of standardized achievement tests and curriculum-related measures. *Diagnostique, 11*(2), 77–90.

Marston, D., Lau, M., & Muyskens, P. (2007). Implementation of the problem-solving model in the Minneapolis public schools In S. R. Jimerson, M. K. Burns, & A. VanDerHeyden (Eds.), *Handbook of response to intervention: The science and practice of assessment and intervention* (pp. 279–287). New York: Springer.

Marston, D., Muyskens, P., Lau, M., & Canter, A. (2003). Problem-solving model for decision making with high-incidence disabilities: The Minneapolis experience. *Learning Disabilities Research and Practice, 18*, 187–200.

McConaughy, S. H., & Achenbach, T. M. (2001). *Manual for the Semistructured Clinical Interview for Children and Adolescents* (2nd ed.). Burlington:

University of Vermont, Research Center for Children, Youth, and Families.

McDougal, J. L., Graney, S. B., Wright, J. A., & Ardoin, S. P. (2010). *RTI in practice: A practical guide to implementing effective evidence-based interventions in your school.* Hoboken, NJ: Wiley.

McGraner, K., VanDerHeyden, A. M., & Holdheide, L. (2011). *Preparation of effective teachers in mathematics: A TQ connection issue paper on applying the innovation configuration to mathematics teacher preparation.* Nashville, TN: National Comprehensive Center for Teacher Quality, Vanderbilt University.

McIntyre, L. L., Gresham, F. M., DiGennaro, F. D., & Reed, D. D. (2007). Treatment integrity of school-based interventions with children in the Journal of Applied Behavior Analysis 1991–2005. *Journal of Applied Behavior Analysis, 40*, 659–672.

McMaster, K. L., Fuchs, D., Fuchs, L. S., & Compton, D. L. (2003, December). *Responding to non-responders: An experimental field trial of identification and intervention models.* Paper presented at the Responsiveness to Intervention Symposium, Kansas City, MO.

Melby-Lervag, M., & Hulme, C. (2012). Is working memory training effective?: A meta-analytic review. *Developmental Psychology, 49*, 270–291.

Messick, S. (1995). Validity of psychological assessment: Validation of inferences from persons' responses and performances as scientific inquiry into score meaning. *American Psychologist, 50*, 741–749.

Mortenson, B. P., & Witt, J. C. (1998). The use of weekly performance feedback to increase teacher implementation of a prereferral academic intervention. *School Psychology Review, 27*, 613–627.

Myers, P., & Hammill, D. D. (1976). *Methods for learning disorders* (2nd ed.). New York: Wiley.

National Council on Measurement in Education. (1995). *Code of professional responsibilities in educational measurement.* Madison, WI: Author.

National Council of Teachers of Mathematics. (2006). *Curriculum focal points for prekindergarten through grade 8 mathematics: A quest for coherence.* Reston, VA: Author.

National Governors Association Center for Best Practices & Council of Chief State School Officers. (2010). *Common core state standards.* Washington, DC: Authors.

National Mathematics Advisory Panel. (2008). *Foundations for Success: The final report of the National Mathematics Advisory Panel.* Washington, DC: U.S. Department of Education.

National Reading Panel. (2000). *Report of the national reading panel: Teaching students to read: An evidence-based assessment of the scientific research literature on reading and its implications for reading instructions.* Washington, DC: National Institute of Child Health and Human Development, National Institutes of Health, U.S. Government Printing Office.

Neef, N. A., Iwata, B. A., & Page, T. J. (1977). The effects of known-item interspersal on acquisition and retention of spelling and sightreading words. *Journal of Applied Behavior Analysis, 10*, 738.

No Child Left Behind Act of 2001, Public Law No. 107–110 (2001).

Noell, G. H., Gansle, K. A., Witt, J. C., Whitmarsh, E. L., Freeland, J. T., LaFleur, L. H., et al. (1998). Effects of contingent reward and instruction on oral reading performance at differing levels of passage difficulty. *Journal of Applied Behavior Analysis, 31*, 659–663.

Noell, G. H., Witt, J. C., Slider, N. J., Connell, J. E., Gatti, S. L., Williams, K. L., et al. (2005). Treatment implementation following behavioral consultation in schools: A comparison of three follow-up strategies. *School Psychology Review, 34*, 87–106.

Northwest Evaluation Association. (2004). *Measures of academic progress.* Lake Oswego, OR: Author.

O'Connor, R. (2000). Increasing the intensity of intervention in kindergarten and first grade. *Learning Disabilities Research and Practice, 15*, 43–54.

Office of Special Education and Rehabilitative Services. (2007a). Letter to A. Cernosia.

Office of Special Education and Rehabilitative Services. (2007b). Questions and answers on response to intervention (RTI) and early intervening services (EIS). Retrieved from *http://idea.ed.gov/object/fileDownload/model/QaCorner/field/PdfFile/primary_key/8.*

Office of Special Education and Rehabilitative Services. (July 28, 2008). [Memorandum to State Directors of Special Education.]

Office of Special Education and Rehabilitative Services. (January 21, 2011). [Memorandum to State Directors of Special Education.]

Ortiz, S. O. (2008). Best practices in nondiscriminatory assessment. In J. Grimes & A. Thomas (Eds.), *Best practices in school psychology V* (Vol. 2, pp. 661–678). Bethesda, MD: National Association of School Psychologists.

Pearson Education, Inc. (2011). *AIMSweb.* San Antonio, TX: Author.

President's Commission on Excellence in Special Education. (2002). *A new era: Revitalizing special education for children and their families.* Washington, DC: U.S. Department of Education.

Rashotte, C. A., MacPhee, K., & Torgesen, J. K. (2001). The effectiveness of a group reading instruction program with poor readers. *Learning Disability Quarterly, 24*, 119–134.

Renaissance Learning Inc. (2012a). STAR Early Literacy: Computer-adaptive diagnostic assessment. Wisconsin Rapids, WI: Author.

Renaissance Learning Inc. (2012b). STAR Math: Computer-adaptive math test. Wisconsin Rapids, WI: Author.

Renaissance Learning Inc. (2012c). STAR Reading: Computer-adaptive reading test. Wisconsin Rapids, WI: Author.

Reschly, D. J. (2003, December). *What if LD identification reflected research results?* Paper presented at the National Research Center on Learning Disabilities Responsiveness-to-Intervention Symposium, Kansas City, MO.

Reschly, D. J. (2005, December). *Response to intervention (RtI) in general, remedial, and special education.* Paper presented at the 2005 IDEA and NCLB Collaboration Conference, Arlington, VA.

Reschly, D. J. (2008). School psychology paradigm shift and beyond. In J. Grimes & A. Thomas (Ed.), *Best practices in school psychology V* (Vol. 1, pp. 3–16). Bethesda, MD: National Association of School Psychologists.

Reschly, D. J., & Tilly, W. D. III (1999). Reform trends and system design alternatives. In D. J. Reschly, W. D. Tilly III, & J. P. Grimes (Ed.), *Special education in transition: Functional assessment and noncategorical programming* (pp. 19–48). Longmont, CO: Sopris West.

Reyna, V. F. (2004). Why scientific research?: The importance of evidence in changing educational practice. In P. McCardle & V. Chhabra (Eds.), *The voice of evidence in reading research* (pp. 47–58). Baltimore: Brookes.

Reynolds, C., R., & Kamphaus, R. W. (2004). *Behavior Assessment System for Children* (2nd ed.). Circle Pines, MN: American Guidance Service.

Reynolds, C. R., & Shaywitz, S. E. (2009). Response to intervention: Ready or not? Or, from wait-to-fail to watch-them-fail. *School Psychology Quarterly, 24*, 130–145.

Rosenfield, S. A. (1987). *Instructional consultation.* Hillsdale, NJ: Erlbaum.

Rosenfield, S. A. (2002). *Best practices in instructional consultation* (4th ed.). Bethesda, MD: National Association of School Psychologists.

Rosenfield, S. A., & Gravois, T. (1996). *Instructional consultation teams: Collaborating for change.* New York: Guilford Press.

S. Rep. No. 105-17. (1997). Retrieved from *www.gpo.gov/fdsys/pkg/CRPT-105srpt17/pdf/CRPT-105srpt17.pdf.*

Sanetti, L. M. H., & Kratochwill, T. R. (2009). Toward developing a science of treatment integrity: Introduction to the special series. *School Psychology Review, 38*, 445–459.

Sarason, S., & Doris, J. (1979). *Educational handicap, public policy, and social history.* New York: Free Press.

Saudargas, R. A. (1997). *State–Event Classroom Observation System (SECOS). Observation Manual.* Knoxville: University of Tennessee.

Schmoker, M. (2001). Data driven decisions to improve results. *Video Journal of Education Series X (1040)*: Video Journal of Education (VJE). Available at *http://www.schoolimprovement.com/store/product.php?p=Data_Driven_Decisions_To_Improve_Results_1002.*

Shapiro, E. S. (2011a). *Academic skills problems: Direct assessment and intervention* (4th ed.). New York: Guilford Press.

Shapiro, E. S. (2011b). *Academic skills problems: Fourth edition workbook.* New York: Guilford Press.

Shapiro, E. S., & Clemens, N. H. (2009). A conceptual model for evaluating system effects of response to intervention. *Assessment for Effective Intervention, 35*, 3–16.

Shapiro, E. S., & Derr, T. F. (1987). An examination of overlap between reading curricula and standardized achievement tests. *Journal of Special Education, 21*, 59–67.

Shapiro, E. S., & Kovaleski, J. F. (2008). *Report on the 2007–2008 response-to-intervention pilot districts.* Harrisburg: Pennsylvania Training and Technical Assistance Network.

Shapiro, E. S., & Skinner, C. H. (1990). Best practices in observation and ecological assessment. In A. Thomas & J. Grimes (Eds.), *Best practices in school psychology II* (pp. 507–518). Silver Spring, MD: National Association of School Psychologists.

Shinn, M. R. (2002). Best practices in curriculum-based measurement in a problem-solving model. In A. Thomas & J. Grimes (Eds.), *Best practices in school psychology IV* (Vol. 2, pp. 671–679). Washington, DC: National Association of School Psychologists.

Shinn, M. R. (2008). Best practices in using curriculum-based measurement in a problem-solving model. In A. Thomas & J. Grimes (Eds.), *Best practices in school psychology V* (Vol. 2, pp. 243–262). Bethesda, MD: National Association of School Psychologists.

Shinn, M. R., & Bamonto, S. (1998). Advanced applications of curriculum-based measurement: "Big Ideas" and avoiding confusion. In M. R. Shinn (Ed.), *Advanced applications of curriculum-based measurement* (pp. 1–31). New York: Guilford Press.

Skinner, C. H., Beatty, K. L., Turco, T. L., & Rasavage, C. (1989). Cover, copy, and compare: A method for increasing multiplication performance. *School Psychology Review, 18*, 412–420.

Skinner, C. H., Rhymer, K. N., & McDaniel, E. (2000). Naturalistic direct observation in educational settings. In E. S. Shapiro & T. R. Kratochwill (Eds.), *Conducting school-based assessments of child and adolescent behavior* (pp. 21–54). New York: Guilford Press.

Soukup, J. H., Wehmeyer, M. L., Bashinski, S. M., & Bovaird, J. A. (2007). Classroom variables and acces to the general curriculum for students with disabilities. *Exceptional Children, 74*, 101–120.

Speece, D. L., Case, L. P., & Molloy, D. E. (2003). Responsiveness to general education instruction as the first gate to learning disabilities identification. *Learning Disabilities Research and Practice, 18*, 147–156.

Stanovich, K. E. (1999). The sociopsychometrics of learning disabilities. *Journal of Learning Disabilities, 32*, 350–361.

Stiggins, R. J. (1988). Revitalizing classroom assessment: The highest instructional priority. *Phi Delta Kappan,* 363–368.

Stuebing, K. K., Fletcher, J. M., Branum-Martin, L., & Francis, D. J. (2012). Evaluation of the technical adequacy of three methods for identifying specific learning disabilities based on cognitive discrepancies. *School Psychology Review, 41*, 3–22.

Stuebing, K., Fletcher, J., LeDoux, J., Lyon, G. R., Shaywitz, S., & Shaywitz, B. (2002). Validity of IQ-discrepancy classifications of reading disabilities: A meta-analysis. *American Educational Research Journal, 39*, 469–518.

Sweet, R. W. (2004). The big picture: Where we are nationally on the reading front and how we got here. In P. M. V. Chhabra (Ed.), *The voice of evidence in reading research* (pp. 13–44). Baltimore: Brookes.

Telzrow, C., McNamara, K., & Hollinger, C. (2000). Fidelity of problem-solving implementation and relationship to student performance. *School Psychology Review, 29*, 19.

National Commission on Excellence in Education. (1983). *A nation at risk: The imperative for education reform.* Washington, DC: U.S. Department of Education.

Thomas Beck, C. (2006, February 15–16). *Nine general features of instruction.* Paper presented at the Statewide Coaches' Training, Eugene, OR.

Tilly, D. (2003, December). *How many tiers are needed for successful prevention and early intervention?: Heartland Area Education Agency's evolution from four to three tiers.* Paper presented at the National Research Center on Learning Disabilities Responsiveness-to-Intervention Symposium, Kansas City, MO.

Tindal, G. (1993). A review of curriculum-based procedures on nine assessment components. In J. Kramer (Ed.), *Curriculum-based measurement* (pp. 25–64). Lincoln, NE: Buros Institute of Mental Measurements.

Tindal, G., & Marston, D. (1996). Technical adequacy of alternative reading measures as performance assessments. *Exceptionality, 6*, 201–230.

Torgesen, J. K. (2004). Avoiding the downward spiral: The evidence that early intervention prevents reading failure. *American Educator, 28*, 6–19.

Torgesen, J. K. (2007). Using an RTI model to guide early reading instruction: Effects on identification rates for students with learning disabilities. Retrieved from *http://www.fcrr.org/science/pdf/torgesen/Response_intervention_Florida.pdf.*

Torgesen, J. K., Wagner, R. K., Rashotte, C. A., Rose, E., Lindamood, P., Conway, T., et al. (1999). Preventing reading failure in young children with phonological processing disabilities: Group and individual responses to instruction. *Journal of Educational Psychology, 91*, 579–593.

U.S. Department of Education. (1977). Definition and criteria for defining students as learning disabled. *Federal Register, 42*, 250.

U.S. Department of Education Office of Special Education Programs. (2010, September 13). Children 3 to 21 years old served under Individuals with Disabilities Education Act, Part B, by type of disability: Selected years, 1976–77 through 2008–09. Retrieved from *http://nces.ed.gov/programs/digest/d10/tables/dt10_045.asp.*

VanDerHeyden, A. M. (2005). Intervention-driven assessment practices in early childhood/early intervention: Measuring what is possible instead of what is present. *Journal of Early Intervention, 28*, 28–33.

VanDerHeyden, A. M. (2009). Scientifically-based mathematics instruction at tier 1. Retrieved from *http://www.tqsource.org/publications/RTI%20Evidenced-Based%20Math%20Interventions%205-14-2009.pdf.*

VanDerHeyden, A. M. (2011). Technical adequacy of RtI decisions. *Exceptional Children, 77*, 335–350.

VanDerHeyden, A. M., & Burns, M. K. (2010). *Essentials of response to intervention.* New York: Wiley.

VanDerHeyden, A. M., & Harvey, M. (in press). Using data to advance learning outcomes in schools. *Journal of Positive Behavior Interventions.*

VanDerHeyden, A. M., McLaughlin, T., Algina, J., & Snyder, P. (2012). Randomized evaluation of a supplemental grade-wide mathematics intervention. *American Education Research Journal, 49*, 1251–1284.

VanDerHeyden, A. M., Snyder, P., Smith, A., Sevin, B., & Longwell, J. (2005). Effects of complete learning trials on child engagement. *Topics in Early Childhood Special Education, 25*, 81–94.

VanDerHeyden, A. M., & Tilly III, W. D. (2010). *Keeping RtI on track: How to identify, repair, and prevent mistakes that derail implementation.* Horsham, PA: LRP Publishing.

VanDerHeyden, A. M., & Witt, J. C. (2005). Quantifying the context of assessment: Capturing the effect of base rates on teacher referral and a problem-solving model of identification. *School Psychology Review, 34,* 161–183.

VanDerHeyden, A. M., Witt, J. C., & Gilbertson, D. (2007). A multi-year evaluation of the effects of a Response to Intervention (RTI) model on identification of children for special education. *Journal of School Psychology, 45,* 225–256.

VanDerHeyden, A. M., Witt, J. C., & Naquin, G. (2003). Development and validation of a process for screening referrals to special education. *School Psychology Review, 32,* 204–227.

Vaughn, S., & Fuchs, L. S. (2003). Redefining learning disabilities as inadequate response to instruction: The promise and potential pitfalls. *Learning Disabilities Research and Practice, 18,* 137–146.

Vaughn, S., Linan-Thompson, S., & Hickman, P. (2003). Response to instruction as a means of identifying students with reading/learning disabilities. *Exceptional Children, 69,* 391–409.

Vellutino, F., Scanlon, D., & Lyon, G. R. (2000). Differentiating between difficult-to-remediate and readily remediated poor readers: More evidence against IQ–achievement discrepancy of reading disability. *Journal of Learning Disabilities, 33,* 223–238.

Vellutino, F. R., Scanlon, D. M., & Tanzman, M. S. (1998). The case for early intervention in diagnosing specific reading disability. *Journal of School Psychology, 36,* 367–397.

Vellutino, F. R., Scanlon, D. M., & Zhang, H. (2007). Identifying reading disability based on response to intervention: Evidence from early intervention research. In S. R. Jimerson, M. K. Burns, & A. VanDerHeyden (Eds.), *Handbook of response to intervention: The science and practice of assessment and intervention* (pp. 185–213). New York: Springer.

Vile Junod, R. E., DuPaul, G. J., Jitendra, A. K., Volpe, R. J., & Cleary, K. (2006). Classroom observations of students with and without ADHD: Differences across types of engagement. *Journal of School Psychology, 44,* 87–104.

Volpe, R. J., DiPerna, J. C., Hintze, J. M., & Shapiro, E. S. (2005). Observing students in classroom settings: A review of seven coding schemes. *School Psychology Review, 34,* 454–474.

Vygotsky, L. S. (1978). *Mind in society: Development of higher psychological processes.* Cambridge, MA: Harvard University Press.

Walker, H. M., & Severson, H. (1992). *Systematic screening for behavior disorders (SSBD): Forms and manuals.* Longmont, CO: Sopris West.

Wechsler, D. (2009). *Wechsler Individual Achievement Test* (3rd ed.). San Antonio, TX: Pearson.

White, O. R., & Haring, N. G. (1980). *Exceptional teaching.* Columbus, OH: Merrill.

Wickstrom, K. F., Jones, K. M., LaFleur, L. H., & Witt, J. C. (1998). An analysis of treatment integrity in school-based behavioral consultation. *School Psychology Quarterly, 13,* 141–154.

WIDA Consortium. (2010). *Assessing comprehension and communication in English state to state for English Language Learners: ACCESS for ELLs interpretive guide for score reports.* Madison, WI: Author.

Will, M. C. (1986). Educating children with learning problems: A shared responsibility. *Exceptional Children, 52,* 411–415.

Witt, J. C., VanderHeyden, A. M., & Gilbertson, D. (2004). Troubleshooting behavioral interventions: A systematic process for finding and eliminating problems. *School Psychology Review, 33,* 363–381.

Woodcock, R. W., McGrew, K. S., & Mather, N. (2001). *Woodcock–Johnson III tests of achievement.* Itasca, IL: Riverside.

Ysseldyke, J. E., & Christenson, S. L. (1987). Evaluating students' instructional environments. *Remedial and Special Education, 8,* 17–24.

Ysseldyke, J. E., & Christenson, S. L. (2002). *Functional assessment of academic behavior: A system for assessing individual student's instructional environments.* Longmont, CO: Sopris West.

Ysseldyke, J. E., Thurlow, M., Graden, J., Wesson, C., Algozzine, B., & Deno, S. (1983). Generalizations from five years pf research on assessment and decision making. *Exceptional Education Quarterly, 4,* 75–93.

Ysseldyke, J., Vanderwood, M. L., & Shriner, J. (1997). Changes over the past decade in special education referral to placement probablility: An incredibly reliable practice. *Diagnostique, 23,* 193–201.

Zigmond, N., & Baker, J. M. (1995). Concluding comments: Current and future practices in inclusive schooling. *Journal of Special Education, 29,* 245–250.

Zigmond, N., Kloo, A., & Stanfa, K. (2011). Celebrating achievement gains and cultural shifts. In E. S. Shapiro, N. Zigmond, T. Wallace, & D. Marston (Eds.), *Models for implementing response to intervention: Tools, outcomes, and implications* (pp. 171–198). New York: Guilford Press.

Zirkel, P. A., & Thomas, L. B. (2010). State laws and guidelines for implementing RTI. *Teaching Exceptional Children, 43*(1), 60–73.

Index

Page numbers followed by *f* indicate figure, *t* indicate table